HOW THE CRASH OF 1929 CAUSED THE GREAT DEPRESSION

Volume 1 of

The Great Deleverage Series

The Story of 1929-33

John C. Harvey & Mary Keil

FOUR DIRECTIONS PRESS
RHINEBECK NEW YORK

Published in the United States by Four Directions Press,
P. O. Box 417, Rhinebeck, New York, 12572.

ISBN 979-8-9910734-8-6
Library of Congress Control Number 2024917326

Printed by Ingram Spark
Published April 2026
First Edition

Permissions forthcoming

Book and cover design by Sean McCarthy

Dedicated to Professor Peter Temin

whose book *Did Monetary Forces Cause the Great Depression?*
inspired us to look for the answer.

Acknowledgements:

First and foremost, we acknowledge and express deep gratitude to our spouses for the countless ways they supported us and contributed to our ability to reach this point in *The Great Deleverage Series.*

Our Editor with a capital "E," of both volumes, Sally V. Keil, holds a special position on the list of those to be thankful for as a perceptive, wise and steady presence to both authors over the years. In her unwavering quest for clarity, she edited for ever more verbal precision, hopefully enabling our brave readers to understand clearly our approach, explanations and conclusions.

We are additionally grateful to colleagues Matthew Sambor, Donald Hill, Michael McCormick and Julie Saxton for their help and support; as well as to Sean McCarthy of Four Directions Press, our publisher, for his design expertise, ongoing encouragement and skill in getting us over the finish line.

CONTENTS

Preface i
Introduction. 1
Prologue: Caught Up in the Whirl—The Legacy of the 1920s 22
1: How Do We Account for What Happened in 1929–1933?. 45
2: Herbert Hoover: Liberty Preempts Presidential Action 57
3: The (Keynesian) Income-Expenditure Approach 76
4: The Monetary Approach 101
5: Peter Temin's Invitation and Our R.S.V.P. 121
6: An Evidentiary Treasure Trove in the Attic 136
7: Leverage—The Financial Fuel for Prosperity and Speculation (Through Year-End 1928) 164
8: Furious Speculation Leads to Panic (Through October 23, 1929) 192
9: THE CRASH 221
10: Deleveraging Begins with a Drastic Liquidation of Security Loans (October 24 to November 30, 1929) 243
11: Market Events Reveal Major Over-Indebtedness (October 24 to November 30, 1929) 285
12: A Sudden Reversal of Mood Leads to a Pivot in Behavior (November - December, 1929) 305
Coda: Incipient Conclusions and Looking Ahead 355
References 359
Index 368
Regarding Permissions 383
About the Authors 384

List of Tables and Charts

Tables Title Page Number

Introduction.1 Rates of Change - 1929-1933 8
Prologue.1 Rising Household Indebtedness, 1919-1939 28
Prologue.2 Production of Motor Vehicles, 1920-1929 35
1.1 Gross National Product: Annually, 1929-1934 52
1.2 Relation of Gross National Product, Net National Product, National Income and Personal Income: Annually, 1929-1934 . . 53
1.3 Personal Income and its Disposition: Annually, 1929-1934. . . . 54
1.4 Statistics of Change In Major NIPA Line Items 55
6.1 Aggregate U.S. Corporate Balance Sheet, 1929-1933 140
6.2 Aggregate U.S. Corporate Working Capital 1929-1933. 142
6.3 Rates of Change - 1929-1933 145
6.4 Rates of Change - 1929-1933 148
6.5 Aggregate Balance Sheet, 1929-1932. 153
6.6 Net Earnings Of All Corporations In the United States, 1929-1933 . 161
6.7 Rates of Earnings On Book Value Of Capital 1929-1933 161
6.8 Rates of Earnings of Corporations in The U.S.,1929-1933 . . . 162
7.1 Cars and Trucks Produced Annually. 168
7.2 Call Money Rates on the NYSE 179
7.3 Short-Term Open-Market Rates in New York City 180
7.4 Call Loans by Groups of Lenders 181
7.5 All Member Banks-Classification of Loans On Call Dates . . . 183
7.6 Aggregate U.S. Corporate Balance Sheet, 1927-1929. 188
7.7 Rates of Change - 1929-1930. 190
8.1 Yield Curves: Dec. 1927 - Oct. 1929. 206
8.2 Cars and Trucks Produced 212
8.3 Statistics of U.S. Economic Activity (May-Sept. 1929) 219
9.1 Statistics of U.S. Economic Activity (June-Oct. 1929) 242
10.1 Percent of New York Stock Exchange Loans to Total Market Values of Listed Shares 248

Tables Title Page Number

10.2 Volume of Short-Term Borrowing 249
10.3 Funds Flows That Result from Changes In Call Market Loan Volumes 252
10.4 Investible Funds & Short-Term Open-Market Rates in New York City 257
10.5 Rates Charged on Commercial Loans by Banks in Principal Cities 262
10.6 Average Yields on Short-Term Financial Instruments and Average Bank Borrowing Rates 264
10.7 Yield Curves: Oct. 1929 - June 1930 276
10.8 Statistics of U.S. Economic Activity (July-Nov. 1929) 278
11.1 Statistics of U.S. Economic Activity (July-Nov. 1929) 304
12.1 Automobile Financing (1929 and 1930) 312
12.2 Analysis of Automobile Financing (1928 to 1930) 314
12.3A Monthly Totals of Automobile Installment Credit Changes . . 316
12.3B Monthly Totals of Automobile Installment Credit Changes . . 317
12.4A Expanded Monthly Automobile Installment Credit Changes . . 326
12.4B Expanded Monthly Automobile Installment Credit Changes . . 327
12.5 Monthly Credit Changes of 5 Retailing Groups vs. Autos . . 328
12.6 Statistics of U.S. Economic Activity (July-Dec. 1929) 353

Charts

Chart 4.1 Total Loans and Investments 118
Chart 10.1 Money Stock, Currency, and Commercial Bank Deposits,Monthly 1929 - March 1933 267

Preface to *The Great Deleverage Series*

The two main schools of economic thought—the Keynesians and the Monetarists—have generated much debate over the decades. Asking us to which school we belong, however, would be like asking business executives whether they believe in income statements or balance sheets. Our response might elicit surprise as it is our considered view that the two schools, operating together, as with income statements and balance sheets, provide complementary measures of economic activity. This view requires a deep understanding of each school in order to develop the skills to know how they can work in tandem to achieve a more stable economy and less political friction.

What led us—two private citizens and former economics and history students with broad professional experience but no PhDs after our names—to undertake writing *How the Crash of 1929 Caused the Great Depression*? After years of steady development of a cycling model of the U.S. economy, a welcome dash of serendipity led us to discover focal evidence of a significant economic influence, shown clearly within a major credible statistical archive, that neither historians nor economists appear to have examined closely as factoring tangibly into the causes of the Great Depression. Examining this archive made us realize we wanted to proceed, as economic historians do, to explore this intriguing and compelling historical evidence and its context. As we became increasingly fascinated, we followed threads and clues offered in that data, as well as in substantial additional research, that brought us to where we are now: having determined a new, even predominant, data-based causal factor for the development, duration and severity of the Great Depression.

Our explorations have resulted, so far, in two volumes, with a third in the works, of what we call *The Great Deleverage Series. How the Crash of 1929 Caused the Great Depression* takes us from the boom years of the 1920s to the Crash of 1929 and its aftermath, when a cascade of money movement, virtually all of it discontinued leverage, led to the repayment of nearly $2.8 billion to U.S. banks alone, with even more repaid to finance companies, retail stores and other credit-granting entities, in the first month following the Crash—November 1929. This quantity exceeded the entire growth of the money supply in 1927 and 1928. In the final chapter of this first volume, we offer statistically incontrovertible evidence of a direct linkage between the Great Crash and the beginning of the Great Depression. Our research also indicates that by May 1930, the dynamic of the Great Depression was fully underway.

In the pages ahead and in our second volume, *The Deflation of 1930*, we explore in depth the development of the familiar downward spiral of the Great Depression with falling economic activity and revenues and growing unemployment, and we feature our estimates that indebted U.S. individuals repaid $4+ billion dollars to U.S. banks and other U.S. corporations in 1930 alone. Indebted individuals—consumers who had embraced borrowing during the 1920s to acquire automobiles, houses and household goods—reduced consumption expenditures in order to accumulate the funds they needed to make the repayments. We further estimate that debtors repaid $7+ billion in 1931, crushing consumption even more.

In our second volume, *The Deflation of 1930*, we focus intently on the effects of deflation and, providing substantial contributions of well-known economists of the time and later, we describe an increasingly urgent shift toward repaying loans and getting out of debt as individuals came to recognize their increasingly grave realities. Under the direct effects of deflation, they had to work harder and longer to earn the cash necessary to repay their loans at a time when work opportunities were receding. Growing deflation and debtors' expectations of yet worsening deflation to come made the economic situation increasingly dire—a great deflation brought on by a great deleverage.

We hope our readers find *How the Crash of 1929 Caused the Great Depression,* as well as our entire *The Great Deleverage Series,* informative, thought-provoking and also enjoyable to read. We invite responses. Please send questions and observations to comments@tidemillgroup.com.

Introduction

How the Crash of 1929 Caused the Great Depression reveals how the Great Depression had *two* major causes.

One arose in the business sector and constitutes the core of the traditional explanation of the events of 1929-1933 given by many economists and historians. According to this narrative, the Great Depression was principally caused by a precipitous drop in fixed investment by American businesses which did, indeed, take place. Fixed investment fell 26.8% in 1930 from 1929 and 79.5% over the four-year period 1930-1933 from 1929.

How the Crash of 1929 Caused the Great Depression—which we will hereafter shorten to *How the Crash Caused*—posits that there was a critical, even predominant, second cause: the aggregate behavior of consumers in the wake of the Crash. According to analyses we conducted, Americans in debt—including household consumers, many business owners and ex-speculators devastated in the Crash—realized that they were much deeper in debt than was prudent, autonomously cut their spending and began using the resulting funds to repay that debt as fast as possible.

Using Aggregate U.S. Corporate Balance Sheet statistics for each year of 1929-33 that we found in 2018 deep within the archives of a division of the U.S. Treasury Department, we determined that each year from 1930-33 American consumers, broadly speaking, repaid their lenders *more than the drop in fixed business investment for the year*—at least 3.0% more in 1930, 80.0% more in 1931, 80.6% more in 1932. In 1933, fixed investment had again dropped—it could hardly fall further—but American consumers repaid their lenders more than 100.0% of this drop in fixed investment by business. American consumers did this *by reducing their personal consumption expenditures*—in other words, by tightening their belts. As an expression of the era intoned, they "used it up, fixed it up, made it do, wore it out or went without."

Thus, in order to repay their debts to U.S. corporations, including banks and merchants, American consumers, who during the Roaring Twenties routinely made many purchases using credit—including speculating in the stock market—reduced their consumption expenditures by -9.5% in 1930 alone and by -40.7% from 1929 to 1933.

Did anyone foresee a Great Crash as a result of speculation or a Great Depression as a natural outcome of that Crash? In March of 1929, Paul M. Warburg, the eminent financier, long-time Federal Reserve Governor and its Vice Chairman in 1916-1918, foresaw and predicted both. As Alexander Dana Noyes, respected long-time financial editor of *The New York Times,* described Warburg's prediction:

> Unless what [Warburg] bluntly called "the orgy of unrestrained speculation" could be stopped, not only would ultimate collapse cause personal disaster to the speculators, "but it would also bring about a general depression involving the entire country."[1]

But Warburg was alone among his peers in voicing this prediction publicly in the lead-up to the Crash, and the reputational costs to him for doing so were considerable. Even today Warburg's view is not the generally accepted position of economists and historians. In his Pulitzer Prize winning history, *Freedom from Fear; The American People in Depression and War 1929-1945,* David M. Kennedy wrote:

> The disagreeable truth, however, is that the most respon-

1 Alexander Dana Noyes, *The Market Place: Reminiscences of a Financial Editor*, Little, Brown and Company, 1938, p.324.

sible students of the events of 1929 have been unable to demonstrate an appreciable cause-and-effect linkage between the crash and the depression.[2]

There were indeed lessons to learn from exploring the nexus Warburg had in mind when warning of an ultimate collapse followed by a general depression. In this first volume of *The Great Deleverage Series* we demonstrate, using empirical evidence in Chapter 12, the actual cause-and-effect linkage between the Crash of 1929 (the cause) whose seeming suddenness and overwhelming magnitude shocked every attentive American. From there, we track the linkage in dramatically falling monthly statistics of installment credit *sought and agreed to* by purchasers of automobiles (labeled *"credit granted"* in the statistics), of which the speed of decline accelerated as time passed. After seven months of initiating linkage, we observe the result (the effect) as being the commencement at full-scale of the Great Depression in May 1930.

Stock Market Call Loans Fuel "Jubilant" Speculation

The evidence published by the Federal Reserve in *Banking and Monetary Statistics 1914-1941* (*BMS*) showed that the total volume of call market lending that fueled stock speculation rose 92.4% in the twenty-one months from December 31, 1927, to October 4, 1929. Critically, in the same period, the volume of call market lending from sources *other than banks* soared 362.8%, from comprising 41% of total call market lending to a whopping 78% of call market lending.[3] According to Noyes:

> The result was jubilant insistence by the speculators—one heard it on every side—that speculation, however far it might be carried, could not this time be checkmated, as in former great speculations it had in the long run usually been, by a

2 David M. Kennedy, *Oxford History of the United States*, Volume IX, Oxford University Press, 1999, p. 39.

3 Board of Governors of the Federal Reserve System(U.S.), *Banking and Monetary Statistics 1914-1941, 1943,* p. 494.

"money squeeze."[4]

Although Noyes commented on breaks in the market, he observed that they actually reinforced speculators' confidence:

> For when, as happened in December 1928 and in March of 1929, a sudden break in stocks was quickly followed by a tempestuous recovery to heights previously unattained, belief in an indefinitely continued rise seemed to be irresistible.[5]

Later in 1929, for example, in August through October, when call money rates began to decline as the volume of call market lending continued to rise aggressively, speculators saw this as yet another positive sign that the spectacle would go on. [6]

No Credible Real Warning Signal Preceded the Crash of 1929.

Reflecting on one significant difference between the Crash of 1929 and prior experience, Noyes observed:

> The end of the great speculation came at the moment when the whole community seemed to have convinced itself that the end would never come, but it did not come exactly as the others came. It had been the tradition of our older panics that, under the tightening strain on credit, breakdown of some over-expanded business enterprise would give the signal. In the early summer of 1907, the Western Electric suspended payments; in March 1893, the Reading railway went into receivers' hands; there were large bank and commercial failures in the summer or spring of 1873.

4 Noyes (1938), p. 321.

5 Ibid., p. 324.

6 *BMS*, pp. 456 and 498.

Those failures occurred, in each of the three earlier panic years, four to six months before the Stock Exchange crisis. They stopped the fury of speculation instantly; the effort of speculators thenceforward was to extricate themselves, but the resultant fright of banking lenders over the insolvencies, and the progressive disorder of the credit market, made the effort vain. Usually, when the entire community had taken alarm and the stock market was already falling, another wholly unexpected company disaster—Jay Cooke's suspension in September 1873, the Erie railway receivership in July 1893, the Knickerbocker Trust Company's bankruptcy in October 1907—precipitated Stock Exchange panic. All holders of stocks would endeavor to sell at once and at any price on the unexpected news; the credit mechanism broke down in the face of the general distrust and money was not procurable at any rate.

In 1929 there was no such preliminary warning. No banking institution, no industrial company, closed its doors. On the contrary, incorporation of new investment trusts with large capital, formed for no purpose but to trade stocks, proceeded without diminution of enthusiasm.... In eight months, total company issues had exceeded [$6 billion], nearly [$2 billion] being sold to the public by investment trusts. In the face of this enormous outpour of new securities for public subscription, Stock Exchange prices rose in August to the highest ever reached.... A long list of favorite railway and industrial prices rose 20 to 50 points during August 1929.... Speculative enthusiasm, both among professional operators and among the outside public, seemed to have reached its maximum.

Ringleaders of the professional speculation, whose original purpose had presumably been to "unload" at a propitious moment on the public, but who now had themselves yielded

> unreservedly to the mania, came personally into the limelight, giving out interviews and radio broadcasts which the newspapers printed, declaring that Stock Exchange prices were too low, rather than too high. They denounced volubly the Federal Reserve's unsuccessful efforts to inspire some sense of caution.[7]

Noyes's account of what led up to the Crash offered no evident exogenous shock. Thus, given the absence of any early warning signal and given that the stock market crisis was unlike earlier ones, speculators became trapped by the cascade of margin calls that occurred during the Crash, leading so many speculators—amateur and professional alike—to be "wiped out."

In *The Great Crash 1929*, John Kenneth Galbraith also portrayed the Crash as the product of an endogenous process:

> As already so often emphasized, the collapse in the stock market in the autumn of 1929 was implicit in the speculation that went before. The only question concerning that speculation was how long it would last. Sometime, sooner or later, confidence in the short-run reality of increasing common stock values would weaken. When this happened, some people would sell, and this would destroy the reality of increasing values. Holding for an increase would now become meaningless; the new reality would be falling prices. There would be a rush, pellmell, to unload. This was the way past speculative orgies had ended. It was the way the end came in 1929. It is the way speculation will end in the future.[8]

The chapters to come explain how slowly developing contractionary forces led from early Spring 1929 onwards to the beginnings

7 Noyes (1938), p. 325-7.

8 John Kenneth Galbraith, *The Great Crash 1929*, Houghton Mifflin Harcourt Publishing Company, 1954, p. 169.

of recession in the Fall. We do not consider the Crash to have precipitated recession, but we do consider the Crash to have greatly accelerated the contractionary process and to have converted what might have been a modest recession into the worst depression our country has ever experienced. We regard the speculation leading to the Crash and the Crash leading to the Great Depression to constitute an endogenous—and, indeed, *predictable*—process which we will portray.

In *The Great Crash 1929*, Galbraith questioned the relationship between the Crash and the Great Depression:

> On the whole, the great stock market crash can be much more readily explained than the depression that followed it. Among the problems involved in assessing the causes of depression none is more intractable than the responsibility to be assigned to the stock market crash. Economics still does not allow final answers on these matters. But, as usual, something can be said.[9]

In fact, Galbraith devoted his last chapter, entitled "Cause and Consequence," principally to the causes of the Great Depression. We find the chapter to be an excellent survey of the state of economic thinking on this subject as it stood in the 1950s and as updated in a later edition, and we urge readers to read Galbraith's lively and fascinating book. We note, however, that he did not address whether *anyone*—let alone consumers—began tightening their belts and reducing expenditures in order to repay debt obligations in the immediate wake of the Crash. To make such an assertion, Galbraith would have needed the statistical support that we have found. As it turns out, although much of what we have uncovered was available by the end of the 1930s, we found no other researchers who have connected the various strands of data—"the dots"—with the historical context as clearly as we do in *How the Crash Caused.*

9 Ibid., pp. 168-9.

Vital Statistics of Repayment of Indebtedness —A Brief Statistical Synopsis

Also ahead, we systematically lead the reader to a new understanding of the causes and protracted duration of the Great Depression. We present both recognizable and startling new facts

Table Introduction.1

Rates of Change - 1929-1933

(Assumes **100%** of corporate payables are owed to corporations)
($ million in current dollars)

1929	1930	1931	1932	1933	% Change from 1929
Fall in GNP[1]					
103,420	90,700				-12.3
		76,073			-26.4
			58,280		-43.6
				55,818	-46.0
Fall in personal consumption expenditures[1]					
77,251	69,916				-9.5
		60,482			-21.7
			48,591		-37.1
				45,811	-40.7
Fall in fixed Investment[1]					
14,483	10,601				-26.8
		6,768			-53.3
			3,445		-76.2
				2,970	-79.5
Decline from prior year					
	-3,882	-3,833	-3,323	-475	
Fall in notes and accounts receivable **held** by U.S Corporations[2]					
66,810	59,675				-10.7
		48,667			-27.2
			39,564		-40.8
				35,835	-46.4
Fall in notes and accounts payable **owed** by U.S. Corporations[2]					
29,453	26,870				-8.8
		23,251			-21.1
			20,562		-30.2
				19,362	-34.3
Fall in debt — due and payable within one year — owed by non-corporations to U.S. Corporations[2]					
37,358	32,805				-12.2
		25,416			-32.0
			19,002		-49.1
				16,473	-55.9
Decline from prior year					
	-4,553	-7,389	-6,414	-2,529	

Sources:

[1]Dept. of Commerce, Bureau of Economic Analysis, *National Income and Product Accounts of the United States, 1929-76 Statistical Tables*, Sept. 1981, p. 1.

[2]Dept. of Treasury, Internal Revenue Service, *Statistics of Income* 1929-1933.

gleaned through careful and deep analysis of historical and statistical research combined with broad-based research of familiar—and unfamiliar—authorities. At its core, however, *How the Crash Caused* plumbs a rich and largely unused archival data source for the insights waiting to be revealed. From the earliest days of the Great Depression, professional and academic economists, and especially economists of what has become known as the Keynesian school, attributed the depression to a precipitous drop in fixed investment. Table Introduction.1 confirms our earlier statement that fixed investment did, indeed, drop -26.8% in 1930 alone and -79.5% from 1929 to 1933.

Alternatively, monetarists Milton Friedman and Anna Schwartz took the position in their *Monetary History* that while the Great Depression started due to non-monetary forces, the monetary character of the economic situation changed dramatically in November 1930 when a series of bank crises began and grew in severity until Franklin Roosevelt declared a nationwide Bank Holiday the day after his inauguration in 1933. It was the view of Friedman and Schwartz that the bank crises were caused by flawed Federal Reserve policy that led to monetary collapse and the brutal severity and length of the Great Depression.

In 2018, we found in the archives of a well-known division of the Treasury Department the potent statistics that comprise the foundation of the top down analyses we will put forth. (We tell the story of finding the archive and its statistics in Chapter 6, and we call it a top down analysis because it reveals an overall picture regarding the aggregate corporate sector.) In those archives, we located publicly available statistics containing fully tabulated aggregate balance sheets of nearly all operating business corporations in the U.S. from 1927 through 1933 and onwards. Using a sources and uses analysis, a familiar tool of financial analysis, we examined how U.S. corporations, in aggregate, funded themselves over the course of the Depression.

Analysis of these statistics revealed a gargantuan repayment of debt by individual Americans to U.S. corporations, which included banks and retail merchants. As a point of reference, the Gross National Product (GNP) of the U.S. was $103.4 billion in 1929.[10] (To be true to the time, we have chosen to use current dollars throughout.) Table Introduction.1 presents year-end 1929 Notes and accounts receivable owed to U.S. corporations as totaling $66.8 billion, and Aggregate corporate notes and accounts payable equaling $29.5 billion. Making the assumption that all corporate payables were owed to other corporations, then non-corporate parties—most importantly and largely American consumers—owed $37.4 billion to U.S. corporations, the net of the two amounts. Four years later, by the end of 1933, Aggregate corporate notes and accounts receivable had declined -46.4%. We estimate that notes and accounts owed to U.S. corporations by non-corporate parties had fallen -55.9%—a drop of -$20.9 billion, considerably larger than the drop in fixed investment. Indeed, this first volume of *The Great Deleverage Series* explains what happened when U.S. consumers, who by November 1929 had become *major debtors*, proceeded at a growing rate to *repay their debts*. To do so, they reduced their consumption, thereby making the Depression increasingly worse.

Table Introduction.1 presents the most important statistics upon which we base this work. Given that we scrutinize these statistics closely and repeatedly year-by-year throughout our account, we simply introduce them here. Of the six categories, the statistics in the first three—Falls in GNP, in Personal consumption expenditures, and in Fixed investment—are from the National Income and Product Accounts (NIPA) as compiled by the U.S. Commerce Department (and reviewed in our Chapter 1). GNP fell -46.0%. Personal consumption expenditures—74.7% of GNP in 1929—fell from 1929-1933 by -40.7%, as mentioned earlier. Fixed investment in property, plant and equipment, despite comprising a far less material 14.0% of GNP in 1929, fell -79.5% from 1929-1933, a precipitous drop that was unquestionably a major cause of the Great Depression.

We base the final three categories on data from reports called *Statistics of Income* submitted annually to the President by the Treasury

10 In 1991, the U.S. changed the measurement designation from Gross National Product or GNP to Gross Domestic Product or GDP.

Department. Each annual report included an Aggregate Corporate Balance Sheet for U.S. corporations from which we drew the fourth category. Aggregate corporate notes and accounts receivable fell -46.4% over 1929-1933, very close to the -46.0% rate at which GNP fell. The fifth category, Notes and accounts payable owed by U.S. corporations, also fell significantly, -34.3%. The crucial sixth and final category is the result, broadly speaking, of subtracting Notes and accounts payable by U.S. corporations from aggregate Notes and accounts receivable held by U.S. corporations. This net amount notably shows the aggregate debts due within one year owed to U.S. corporations by parties that were not U.S. corporations.

Who, in point of fact, were these parties that were not U.S. corporations? The great majority were individuals, and virtually all of them were consumers, specifically indebted consumers. (The category of "individuals" also included sole proprietors who, besides being consumers, operated businesses.) As described in Chapter 5 in *The Deflation of 1930*, we estimated that in 1930 "individuals" repaid to corporations (including banks, merchants, etc.) debts that amounted to $4+ billion in 1930 dollars.

Even if few indebted consumers kept books of account or employed accountants, they likely shared with many of their fellow Americans at that time a personal moral imperative to repay their debts in a timely fashion, and our sources regarding consumer finance repayments confirm that consumers reliably repaid their debts. In fact, their debt obligations fell from 1929 to 1933 by -55.9%, indicating how motivated these non-corporate parties were, in aggregate, to get out of debt as fast as they could.[11] In 1929, the due and payable debt of non-corporations was 26.8% *greater than* the Notes and accounts payable of corporations. By 1933, the due and

11 Government entities were included in the designation "non-corporate." Events generally forced all levels of government to *increase* their borrowings in 1930-1933 due to reduced revenue from taxation, meaning that consumers' repayments necessarily had to fall faster than the increase in government rates of borrowings in order for the average fall in debt repayments for the non-corporate category to be 55.9%.

payable debt was -14.9% *less than* the Notes and accounts payable of corporations. Clearly, this operative debt repayment by strongly motivated "individuals and others" was also a major cause of the Great Depression.

But, between these two major causes—drop in fixed investment (3rd category) and debt repayment by individuals (6th category)—which was the stronger force?

Comparing the "Decline from prior year" figures in fixed investment with the "Decline from prior year" figures in debt repayment by non-corporations (mostly individuals) reveals how much larger personal consumption expenditures were than fixed investment expenditures. In addition, the dollar amounts in debt repayment by individuals as measured in the last category were also larger each year than the declines in fixed investment. The -55.9% decline (-$20,885 million) in the last category from $37,358 million in 1929 to $16,473 million in 1933 far exceeds, in dollar amounts, the -79.5% decline (-$11,513 million) in fixed investment from $14,483 million in 1929 to $2,970 million in 1933. In our view, of the two major forces, the debt repayment by "non-corporations"—most particularly by consumers—was the more consequential force. The implications of this finding form the backbone of *The Great Deleverage* volumes.

To lay out the full story, we employ a cast of characters such as Repentant Ex-Speculators (post-Crash), Debtors (in general), Corporate Financial Officers, Wall Street Professionals and others to show how the thinking and consumption orientation of an economically significant part of the population changed overnight in late October and early November 1929, when people went from borrowing freely, including for stock speculation, to repaying debt at a rapidly growing rate, thus stifling consumption. As bank loans were paid back, deflation developed and worsened, short-term interest rates fell and bank income and finance-sector performance suffered greatly, which resulted in the bank crises that began in late 1930 and worsened significantly thereafter. Meanwhile, fixed investment fell precipitously for reasons familiar to economists and business executives at the time. Thus, the economy's downward spiral, well known to history, began and intensified. *How the Crash Caused* tells the story from this new perspective, backed by ample empirical data.

The Pivot from Growing Borrowing to Increasing Repayment

In the Prologue and Chapters 7 and 8 we discuss in greater detail that by the time of the Crash, U.S. consumers had become major debtors. Strikingly, for example, call market loans to speculators on Wall Street grew 92.4% in the twenty-one months from December 31, 1927, to October 4, 1929, according to the Fed's *BMS*. As for many individuals who had borrowed money for other purposes, the growth statistics for 1927-1929 (Table 7.7) show that the Notes and accounts payable owed by individuals and non-corporate others to U.S. corporations (including banks, automobile manufacturers, retailers and other entities) grew 31.8% in 1928 alone and a further 5.6% by year end 1929, despite the dampening effect of the Crash late that year.

Clearly, the volume of borrowing by individuals grew very rapidly before the Crash. Then, loan repayment occurred from late 1929 onwards in sufficient volume that the amount that individuals repaid in 1930 (which we estimated as $4+ billion) exceeded the fall of fixed investment in 1930 of -$3,882 million. Repayment increased strongly thereafter, while fixed investment fell slightly in 1931 then declined significantly in size.

When did individuals pivot from growing borrowing to increasing repayment and why?

Again, the repayment of loans was considered a normal and routine function—even a moral imperative in American culture—but, it was not until the end of 1931 that the Fed sounded an outright alarm as to what was happening to bank loans—they were shrinking. The narrative account from the Fed in the *Annual Report of the Board of Governors 1931* reported:

> The decline in bank loans which had *begun in the autumn of 1929* continued throughout 1930 and 1931.... After the middle of 1930, however, the reduction became pronounced and continuous, and after the middle of 1931 extremely rapid.[12] (emphasis ours)

To tell our story of the Great Depression, highly credible data from a non-governmental source will show that a major shift in the demand for borrowed money for consumer goods and other needs or desires began in the immediate wake of the Crash. November 1929 was pivotal. The demand for borrowed money fell, and -$2.7 billion in bank loans were repaid. In Chapters 10-12, we will focus on statistics that clearly show this turnabout and the resulting repayment. As time passed, demand began to fall faster and faster, indicating a shift in what we call the "demand curve for borrowed money to spend" (to distinguish it from any demand curve for borrowed money to hold on deposit at banks). No longer did borrowers want to borrow more and more to spend. Instead, they *came to want to repay* more and more. This shift was ultimately massive and had major implications.

Even by the summer of 1929 statistics show industrial activity beginning to slow, suggesting that cautionary signs had begun to appear. High call market interest rates were attracting some businesses to lend funds in the call market that they probably would have invested in property, plant and equipment in more normal times. Owners of stock who had developed stock market profit-taking disciplines over time (i.e., investors as opposed to speculators), began to reduce their exposures to risk. Some even exited the stock market entirely. Yet, it is hard to imagine that investors who reduced their exposure to stock market risk spent much of the money they took out of the market on personal consumption. It is much easier to imagine that they, too, lent it in the call money market. Whatever the case, as we will see in Chapter 10, in the autumn of 1929 the sums lent in

---

12 *Annual Report of the Board of Governors of the Federal Reserve System 1931*, p. 4.

the call market surged and call market rates fell.

In the prior financial crisis of 1920-21, no stock market crash occurred to propel the nation into major depression. Instead, by 1922 the economy was recovering and entering a period of considerable prosperity. Had the speculative frenzy of 1928-29 subsided in a manageable fashion (as Paul Warburg appeared strongly, perhaps even desperately, to urge) and the Crash of 1929 not taken place, it is imaginable that the economic contraction that began in 1929 *might* have ended relatively quickly in a similar fashion to the Depression of 1920-2 and that the 1930s might have enjoyed a measure of prosperity.

But the speculative frenzy of the late 1920s did not end in a manageable fashion. It ended—and only temporarily—with a huge, almost week-long shock in late October. As we will recount in Chapters 9 and 10, a period of seeming madness took place as great numbers of speculators strove mightily to meet margin calls. By the time calls for margin paused in mid-November, $10-20 billion of wealth had simply evaporated. Even more painful was the fact that, for many, significantly heightened debt obligations had replaced that vanished wealth.

According to Alexander Dana Noyes, "the panic of 1929 brought sudden recognition of the economic realities. It punctured, almost overnight, the ill-fated Stock Exchange illusions."[13] This profound change brought Americans—not only speculators but also observant consumers who were not speculators—to their senses very fast. Realizing they were deeply in debt, Americans immediately and to a significant extent *ceased purchasing more on credit and began repaying those debts.*

In this volume's final chapter, we look closely at how others including Galbraith, historian Frederick Lewis Allen and by 1932, economist Irving Fisher, also witnessed a dramatic change in mood in this period leading to the exercise by consumers of strong financial caution post-Crash—what Noyes called the "downward readjustment." Their behavior rapidly impacted key American business ac-

13 Noyes (1938), p. 337.

tivity. We introduce a 1940 National Bureau of Economic Research (NBER) study which will enable us to examine installment sales statistics, especially the crucial category of automobile financing, for the months of 1928 through 1933. As we will see, installment credit granted by dealers to automobile buyers in August 1929 was $240.9 million, and total automobile installment credit outstanding peaked at the end of August at $1,456.2 million. Following that peak month, contraction in the amount of car sales on credit developed and quickly began to worsen.

When Did the Great Depression Begin?

Statistics in the bellwether automotive industry show that monthly net credit change statistics for automobile installment sales—monthly credit granted minus monthly preexisting required debt repayments—became negative immediately following the August 1929 peak. In other words, the amount of credit that new borrowers obtained from dealers to acquire new and used cars fell below the amount that earlier credit agreements required buyers to repay. In fact, the net credit change statistics showed a gap between new installment agreements taken out and the amounts owed on existing agreements in September and October of a total of -$9.7 million. (See Table 12.3). We regard this negative number, though seemingly small, as a significant harbinger of the Crash and add it to our list of other hints, forewarnings and cautionary signs of serious trouble ahead.

Then the Crash took place.

Reflecting on the immediate impact once the Crash week had passed in late October 1929, a host of American historians have observed that stock market illusions were punctured, and reality suddenly began breaking through, even to those who had not speculated. Indeed, as the prime example, the statistics found in the illuminating NBER study certainly show that reality quickly broke through to automobile buyers. In November and December 1929, the net credit change statistics fell sharply, a total of -$129.0 million.

From the end of October to the end of December, total credit sought by automobile purchasers and granted to them by automobile dealers declined a concerning -8.9%, indicating that, in the immediate wake of the Crash, fewer Americans bought automobiles on credit, while automobile debt repayments began to exceed automobile credit granted. In fact, in the four months from the end of October 1929 through February 1930, the decline in total automobile credit outstanding accelerated -20.8%, or -$298.5 million. By the end of February 1930, these drops establish that *the nation's path of descent was not just into a recession, but into the Great Depression.*

Chapter 12 presents automobile and other installment sales statistics that point to *May 1930 as the month the Great Depression was fully operative in the United States.* This data indicate that it took the nation little more than half a year to go from the Crash to when we assert the Great Depression— though that label was not used then—had begun in earnest.

Looking at the Effects of the Crash from the Bottom Up

Earlier we touched on the value of top down statistics and analyses. But we also emphasize the importance of bottom up statistics—for instance, the behavior of automobile and other retail customers that reveals the processes of debt repayment and the falling consumption that accompanied it. (See Table 12.4 that includes data for Five Types of Retail Establishments Combined) Table Introduction.1 gives compelling evidence of the significance of falling personal consumption expenditures with the large and growing volume of loan repayment by non-corporations, especially by individuals and consumers, to U.S. corporations—core elements of the Great Depression.

As a result of the shock and magnitude of the Crash, the "virtuous circle" of prosperity reversed and became a "vicious circle," and it got worse quickly thereafter in a process that started with margin calls at the beginning of the Crash or just before it. No longer did the sums that consumers spent on personal consumption grow. Business worsened as demand fell. Following the enormous repayment of bank borrowings that underwrote call loan lending to speculating borrowers, new borrowing at banks slowed and repayment of bank loans grew. To meet their already existing debt repayment obligations, consumers tightened their belts more and more and spent less and less. All of these phenomena are described in detail in the chapters to come.

As the income-expenditure approach predicted, business investment dropped dramatically with the worsening of the insidious downward spiral. But equally important or more so, from the Crash on into (and beyond) 1930, debt repayment kept increasing, while spending by consumers on consumption kept falling. Incomes declined, unemployment developed and grew, the money supply started noticeably to fall, prices declined and deflation developed and accelerated. The Great Depression had begun and entered history.

Our Particular Data-oriented Approach

How the Crash Caused takes readers down a varied path from that of pure history, sociology or certainly economics. Our intention has been to present the story as revealed in actual data for the period. Doing this required considerable use of our educational and professional skills, particularly in accounting, business and history.

Entry level accounting courses introduce students to at least two basic ways businesses account for and evaluate their activities: the income statement and the balance sheet. Financial managers also use a third technique, sources and uses of funds analysis. In reality, whether or not someone ever takes an accounting course, very few make it through their professional lives without some rudimentary accounting—even among Depression Era farmers, as we will see in *The Deflation of 1930*. Ultimately, principles of accounting apply to everyone who uses money in life. Accounting principles have certainly helped us translate data from a dry category to clear real-world implications that everyone, we hope, can relate to.

Examining historical economic events through the lens of financial management tools and accounting principles opens up the potential for a richer perception of both micro and macro events. In tackling the complex elements of what happened from 1929 to 1933, we combined our grounding in those tools and principles to present material, already well-covered by many respected scholars, from the perspective of credible—and eye-opening—statistics, some of which have been hidden in plain sight for decades. Originating in the industrious back offices of statistical units, the data we have explored and carefully examined offer important insights that have, to a large degree, remained unnoticed, or at least, we might suggest, untranslated.

As it turns out, data have had volumes to tell us about our period of focus. What was happening industry-wide? What was happening with the suppliers and customers of that industry? Were conditions the same nationwide or were certain regions harder hit? Then, adding in historical evidence, we could reasonably speculate about the individual constituents of, say, an industry group. American individuals of the Crash and Depression period came specifically into view.

Some Words on How We Tell the Story

We set the stage for our period of focus in the Prologue about the 1920s focusing on many innovative trends, including the spread of credit. Many excellent and more thorough works, of course, have been written about this groundbreaking decade. We consider Frederick Lewis Allen's *Only Yesterday*, published in 1931, to be among the finest examples. That said, these years extend over some of the most studied, analyzed and pondered events in American history and have inspired exceptionally fine accounts by economists, historians and others that could never be surpassed. With great appreciation and respect, we incorporate (with proper attribution, of course) their own words to enrich our narrative of these events.

Of note is that we have chosen to focus this book on the United States during the Crash and Depression period and address international considerations only when necessary to offer relevant explanations of the American experience. For instance, we will focus on gold and the gold standard only when they are important to our story about the United States.

As we stated earlier, we have chosen to keep dollar amounts in current dollars. Compared to the amounts that are pertinent now, the scale of the U.S. economy was, of course, much smaller. For a U.S. population in 1929 of 121.8 million (vs. over 347 million as of June 2025), the GNP in 1929, as stated earlier, was $103.4 billion (vs. GDP of above $30 trillion now). We rely, in terms of our analysis, on comparison and directionality more than on the gross numbers; percentage change in cardinal measurements is a key interpreter of the data, regardless of size.

Finally, several chapters include "Endnotes" that cover information that augments the chapter with more detail.

The narrative we tell in *How the Crash Caused* interweaves familiar information about the Crash and the dramatic period that followed with extensive, carefully gathered data—some fresh discoveries, some newly-interpreted or reinterpreted—that may be unfamiliar to readers. Our goal is to share the insights we have gained from our diligent research so that readers may gain an enriched understanding about the causes and duration of the Great Depression and apply that understanding to the challenging economic conditions of today.

Prologue

Caught Up in the Whirl: The Legacy of the 1920s

In his 1960 memoir *The Public Years*, respected financier and governmental advisor Bernard Baruch recalled the decade of the 1920s:

> The 1920s was, among other things, the era of the New Economics, which could best be described as a system in which everything on the charts of business activity was supposed to go up and nothing was supposed to come down. Experience, as well as common sense, showed that this could not be. Yet, in the overheated atmosphere of the great boom, few questioned it seriously. Indeed, it was difficult not to be caught up in the whirl.[1]

Millions of Americans certainly got caught up in the whirl of which Baruch wrote, and their daily lives changed immeasurably as a result. Because the focus of this book is on what happened at the culmination of such a pivotal decade, a look at the decade itself offers invaluable context and, indeed, sets the stage for what took place as the 1920s made their historic ending. The October 1929 Crash and the Great Depression were not exogenous events that sprang out of nowhere, like a flood, drought or the cotton boll weevil. The decade

---

1 Bernard Baruch, *The Public Years*, Holt, Rinehart and Winston,1960, p. 217.

consisted of endogenous events that emerged from the uniquely peculiar American culture, its modes of enterprise and its philosophy of governance, with one element building upon another. This Prologue attempts to present some of these crucial factors, particularly those relating to the financial lives of Americans whose autonomous spending behavior characterized the 1920s and, when aggregated, culminated in the Crash that toppled the country into a cavernous depression.

The word autonomous conveys the sense that individuals made up their own minds about their behavior. But do individuals really behave completely autonomously? The 1920s are instructive in this regard. Americans were making many personal choices and decisions in their economic lives. They were presented with an increasing number of new products and services on which to spend their money. But the 1920s also exposed individuals to powerful intangible influences, ideas and forces exerting pressure on them at many levels. "It was our national philosophy that each individual American could go as far as his ability and determination would take him,"[2] Lorena Hickok, journalist and intimate friend of Eleanor Roosevelt, later wrote after traveling throughout America to report to FDR's Secretary of Commerce Harry Hopkins on conditions in American lives. Many individuals held firmly to this national philosophy, without any awareness of just how deeply it manipulated their behavior and how taxed their personal and financial resources would become.

The aptly labeled Roaring Twenties generated a kind of loudness. In acoustics, loudness is the subjective perception of sound pressure.[3] That ambient sound pressure was as deafening as an assembly line operating at 100% capacity, and the unrelenting noise exerted aspirational pressures on Americans at every level in society.

---

2 Lorena Hickok, *One Third of a Nation: Lorena Hickok Reports on The Great Depression,* edited by Richard Lowitt and Maurine Beasley, 1981, University of Chicago Press, p. xxv. (from her unfinished autobiography.)

3 Wikipedia entry for "loudness."

One of the loudest voices of the period clamored for more economic participation—also known as consumption.

In reality, U.S. enterprise already had a long history of stimulating consumption—i.e., demand—in highly persuasive and inventive ways, including one particularly influential method—the offering of credit. Credit plans by retailers and merchants date back to the early 19th century. Informal credit given to neighbors by local shop owners throughout the country was commonplace. At least one New York retailer was offering installment credit by 1807. Recognizing that the cost of a sewing machine was beyond the means of most, Singer sold them on time by 1856. Similarly, there were installment sales of pianos by 1875. Then came encyclopedias, lightning rods, radios and reapers and other agricultural implements for farmers whose land was often already mortgaged. Banks and others offering mortgages also made homeownership—a societal "good" loudly promoted as an almost patriotic duty—more attainable nationwide.[4]

"If you can't enlist, invest!"[5]

By the 1920s, the U.S. government had already introduced millions of Americans to installment buying, as well as to the concept, and practice, of investing. It took an actual war—World War I— for the federal government to launch a new kind of strategic campaign—the advertising campaign. The "sound finance" concepts prevalent in Washington made anything but a balanced budget highly unpopular, so to pay for the necessary mobilization for war, the federal government supplemented tax revenue by issuing war bonds, called, rousingly, Liberty or Victory Bonds. The goal of the nationwide war bond campaign was to sell them as broadly and deeply as possible into the population, encouraging citizen participa-

4 U.S. Department of Commerce, Census Bureau, *Sixteenth Census of the United States: 1940*, "Sales-Finance Companies and Banks' Holdings of Retail Installment Paper," p. 25.

5 Slogan from Liberty Bonds marketing poster, 1918.

tion to build national pride and morale. Under the surface was the additional goal of diverting funds from inflationary consumption. Wartime marketing efforts exposed many ordinary citizens, even school children, to investing in the country's future as a patriotic gesture, a notion with enduring appeal. War bonds introduced many Americans, especially at the lower income levels, to installment buying as they purchased bonds over time for a small amount weekly. The bonds also introduced many to the concept of investing in a financial instrument, in this case with the government as borrower and the average citizen, assured of repayment and earning interest for his or her patriotism, as lender.

The advertising and marketing campaign for war bonds was by all measures highly successful, with long-lasting effects on public economic behavior. Since Federal Reserve member banks sold the bonds, Americans who had previously not been part of the banking system walked through the doors to make their purchase and thereby began a more sophisticated financial life. For bankers and buyers alike, the success of war bonds paved the way for installment purchasing of all manner of consumer goods and services, from automobiles to life insurance and, more portentously, stocks.

The notion of combining good citizenship with economic participation took hold in the 1920s. According to economic historian Julia Ott, wartime bonds, stamps and other programs "invited Americans to imagine the nation as a financial market, one in which an investment both made and manifested citizenship."[6] By 1929, Ott estimated:

- at least 20 million Americans had purchased a war bond
- roughly 10 million owned shares in publicly traded corporations
- nearly 2 million employees had acquired employers' stock
- 1.5 million utility customers had purchased shares

6 Julia Ott, "When Wall Street Met Main Street: The Quest for an Investors' Democracy and the Emergence of the Retail Investor in the United States, 1890-1930," *Enterprise & Society*, Dec. 2008, Vol. 9, No. 4, p. 623.

in a utility
- 4.5 million Americans had acquired shares of investment trusts and
- roughly 1.5 million held a brokerage account.[7]

In addition, Ott's calculations arrived at a figure of 10 million Americans (8.1 percent of the population, or 33 percent of households) who were participating in the stock market.[8] The perceived safety of purchasing government bonds translated smoothly into acquiring stocks, especially in a booming stock market. Pride in property ownership, not just in homes, but also shares in American industry, gave Americans a sense that they had what Ott called a "stake" in the American political and economic system.[9]

From Citizen to Consumer

In his book *Financing the Consumer* published in 1930 under the auspices of the Twentieth Century Fund, writer Evans Clark, a director of the Fund as well as a government advisor, observed, "Less than two generations ago America discovered mass production. Scarcely one generation ago America discovered mass distribution. In the present generation America is discovering mass finance."[10]

The 1920s was when the moniker "consumer" came to describe an individual citizen's primary contribution to society. Individuals' consumption, as much as their productivity, now measured their value to the economy, and business led the way as ingenuity and technological innovations in manufacturing processes—financed by capital raised by enthusiastically marketed new stock issues—gave rise to an appealing assortment of goods from radios and phonographs to washing machines, refrigerators and vacuum cleaners. The assembly line, developed by corporations that invested in mechanization, made mass production of these desirable, time saving electrical products

7 Ibid., p. 620.

8 Ibid.

9 Ibid., p. 622.

10 Evans Clark, *Financing the Consumer*, Harper & Brothers, 1930, p.1.

possible. It was, of course, in the best interests of these businesses to enable as many buyers as possible to consume as much as possible on an ongoing basis. Just as in nature, a symbiosis formed between manufacturer (or service provider, such as insurers) and consumer. This strong symbiosis simply needed the right mechanism, and that turned out to be credit—the ability to buy now and pay over time.

Automobile manufacturers led the way in the 'teens. But it was during the 1920s when credit availability exploded. By then, Americans purchased homes, automobiles and a broad range of manufactured items such as appliances and home furnishings and even life insurance on credit.

The data presented in the table on the next page (Olney's Table 1 on Rising Household Indebtedness, 1919-39)—the first of many in our data-focused work and pertinent to the origin narrative of our indebted consumerist economy and culture—tells the convincing story of nonmortgage household debt growth from 1919-1939. Because statistics for the period were scarce, UC Berkeley economist Martha Olney combed various independent sources to create this table showing that borrowing was clearly becoming the new normal. As Olney stated, "Contemporaries noted that in the 1920s it first became common for merchants to assume that a customer was buying on credit rather than with cash."[11]

In *Financing the Consumer* of 1930, Evans Clark observed that as the 1920s came to a close, American individuals had come to be thought of as businesses in themselves, and like all business ventures, they required and used credit. He offered an intriguing

11 Martha L. Olney, "Avoiding Default: The Role of Credit in the Consumption Collapse of 1930," *Quarterly Journal of Economics*, February 1999, pp. 320-321. Professor Olney's works, including *Buy Now, Pay Later: Advertising, Credit, and Consumer Durables in the 1920s* from 1991, came to our attention quite early in our research, and her contributions to the topic of early consumer indebtedness remain seminal.

Table Prologue.1			
Rising Household Indebtedness, 1919-1939			
	Consumer nonmortgage debt as a percentage of income (% Percent)	Nominal consumer nonmortgage debt ($ Thousands)	Nominal installment debt ($ Thousands)
Year	(1)	(2)	(3)
1919	4.6	$2,918	$1,867
1920	4.7	3,304	2,114
1921	5.5	3,249	2,079
1922	5.9	3,469	2,220
1923	5.6	3,860	2,469
1924	5.9	4,159	2,648
1925	6.9	4,928	3,139
1926	7.2	5,510	3,531
1927	7.5	5,714	3,571
1928	8.7	6,567	4,129
1929	9.3	7,628	4,906
1930	9.3	6,821	4,299
1931	8.8	5,518	3,585
1932	8.5	4,085	2,632
1933	8.7	3,912	2,668
1934	8.5	4,389	3,062
1935	9.4	5,434	3,914
1936	10.3	6,788	4,937
1937	10.6	7,480	5,419
1938	10.9	7,047	5,081
1939	11.4	7,969	5,967

Sources:

Column (1): Martha L. Olney, *Buy Now Pay Later*, The North Carolina University Press, 1991, Table 4.1, pp. 88-90.

Column (2): Raymond William Goldsmith, Dorothy S. Brady and Horst Mendershausen, *A Study of Saving in the United States*, Volume III, Princeton University Press, 1956, p. 79.

Column (3): Goldsmith [1956, Table D-4, sum of columns (2) through (9)].

comparison between how the "average man" manages his household finances and business management practices:

> In this campaign for markets the average man has undergone a metamorphosis. He is revealed as a sort of business concern in himself. Collectively he has become an economic institution—"The buying public."
>
> Today it is admitted, even in the most conventional circles, that the individual in the business of running a family must and should borrow on occasions, just like the manager of any other business: to consolidate his debts, to meet some unexpected emergency, or to finance some improvement that will establish him on firmer financial footing.
>
> It has long been a commonplace of traditional economics that production must be financed through suitable credit facilities; but only in recent years has it been recognized that consumption must also be financed by the extension of reasonable credits.[12]

This linkage between business and individual household management practices led to an exponential expansion in another type of business—finance companies that supplied personal installment loans. These loans were especially for automobiles and home furnishings, but were equally used, significantly, for the liquidation of other debts.

Credit Creates the Indebted Consumer

Purchasing on time certainly led to a rise in the standard of living for the average American household, and for many it instilled a discipline in household financial management. The proverbial

12 Clark (1930), pp. 3-4.

cookie jar of simpler times where payments went for the rent and the coal dealer now went for the refrigerator, dining room furniture or life insurance policy, and the jar would get filled no matter what. Households had multiple cookie jars going, and many had generational conflicts about this new reality. As the old-fashioned grandmother in journalist Josephine Lawrence's best-selling 1935 cautionary novel *If I Have Four Apples* comments about the younger generations' reckless attitudes towards money, "Nobody teaches them how to spend. They cry always for more to spend, when what they need is to learn how to buy.... Dreams feed no hungry mouths."[13]

In his 1930 article about the 1920s, Charles E. Persons, Harvard Ph.D. economist and the briefly tenured Census Bureau Expert in Unemployment, noted presciently, "The past decade has witnessed a great volume of credit inflation. Our period of prosperity in part was based on nothing more substantial than debt expansion."[14] Journalist Samuel Strauss lamented the manufacturer-consumer symbiosis as early at 1924. In his weekly publication *The Villager*, he wrote:

> It is becoming a matter of general remark that the economic emphasis is changing; it is shifting from how to make things to how to dispose of the things that are made so that the machine can be kept in constant operations. The problem before us today is not how to produce the goods, but how to produce the customers. Consumptionism is the science of compelling men to use more and more things. Consumptionism is bringing it about that the American citizen's first importance to his country is no longer that of citizen but that of consumer.[15]

Today we take credit availability almost for granted whether in the form of a mortgage or home equity loan, other personal loans

13 Josephine Lawrence, *If I Have Four Apples*, Grosset & Dunlap Publishers, 1935, p. 264.

14 Charles E. Persons, "Credit Expansion, 1920 to 1929, and its Lessons," *Quarterly Journal of Economics*, Vol. 45, No. 1 (November 1930), p. 116.

15 Samuel Strauss, *The Villager*, 1924.

such as for a car or an education, as well as the nearly ubiquitous credit card. We accept having our debt levels monitored and carefully watch our "report card" of creditworthiness, our "credit score," which carries with it the peculiar implication that the higher our score the more debt creditors are willing to extend. Most of us are accustomed to this system, if not always comfortable with its implications (or with experiences of its pitfalls). We may think of this system as being relatively recent and don't realize that the origins of massive society-wide consumer debt go back to the 1920s, when in order to keep the factories humming, the forces promoting, supporting and advocating for consumption coalesced with an explosion in the use of indebtedness in order to achieve or maintain a desirable lifestyle. Commerce provided both the products and the means of acquiring them. Americans provided the desire.

Entering the Psychological Age

The hows and whys this all happened are interwoven with dynamics in the realm of the psychological, a concept barely grasped by many people at the time. Sigmund Freud (1856-1939), arguably the first Westerner to gain a following by those interested in exploring the human psyche, led the way. It isn't Dr. Freud, however, but rather his nephew Edward Bernays (1891-1995) who is regarded as the father of public relations and the man, or at least one of the principal figures, who guided the shift in Americans' self-awareness and, indeed, their primary economic function, as that of consumers. "The concentration of American business genius on the problem of markets now rivals that which was formerly lavished on the problem of methods," Evans Clark observed about the rise of the public relations field in the 1920s. "Executives, efficiency experts, and business scientists have turned upon sales the same sort of passionate research that used to be lavished on production."[16]

Edward Bernays made use of psychological principles to identify and then assist business clients in marketing to Americans' deepest

16 Clark (1930), pp. 2-3.

wants and desires. As he counseled clients, "Any person or organization depends ultimately on public approval, and is therefore faced with the problem of engineering the public's consent to a program or goal."[17] His influence has been described in biographies, in general histories and in documentary films, such as "The Century of the Self." In a special edition of *Life* magazine published by Time, Inc. in 1990, Bernays was included on *Life's* list of the 100 most important people of the 20th Century.[18] For some, he is a hero; for others, his concept of "engineering consent" made him quite the opposite.

The Call of Modernity

The 1920s are unique due to the confluence of a particular set of socio-economic forces. Three "M" words—modernity, mobility and more—offer useful motifs to explore dominant and groundbreaking themes of the period. They also provide insight into Americans' motivations for making the economic decisions they made that coalesced into the distinctly American economy, culture and psyche we have to this day.

We begin with the idea of what a modern society even is. Though in a country as diverse are ours, where tradition necessarily clashes with and resists the changes implied by modernity, the 1920s inspired those who saw opportunity and potential in the new to embrace modernity. Technological inventions and innovations in the early 20th century were already radically altering the everyday life of Americans. Experts might argue about the order or priority of these changes, but the list would undoubtedly include the same leading forces: electricity and electrification, the assembly line and the automobile, the radio and, critical to the growth of these and other commercial sectors, consumer credit.

During the 1920s there was a rowdy rush to modernity, and the pressures came from different directions almost simultaneously.

---

17 Edward L. Bernays, *Public Relations,* 1945. Book available at forgottenbooks.com.

18 www.nku.edu/turney/prclass/readings/bernays.html

It is well worth a brief review of some significant developments and innovations that gained a full head of steam during the 1920s and brought with them far-reaching changes to the American way of life up to that point:

Electricity and electrification: Electrification made virtually all of the modernity that followed possible. Electricity enabled the assembly line to put Americans to work producing multiple quantities of the same item, not only consumer durables like refrigerators but also consumer nondurables like beauty products. Electrification lit homes and city streets. Lighting alone was transformational, but much else in life became possible—and, more importantly, desirable—with electricity. As optimistic modern-thinking entrepreneurs embraced the opportunities electric power made available, innovations in manufacturing fostered a remarkable explosion in new product development. Productivity grew and output expanded. Further, stable factory employment created a new working class living well above the poverty level and able to participate in the economy not just as producers but also as consumers.

The automobile: Edison-trained engineer Henry Ford saw into the future and designed the Model T and the assembly line to make it in order to offer an automobile, initially just a novelty for the wealthy, affordable for everyone. In the 1920s the automobile became an American obsession, transforming lives, the landscape and the cityscape as roads and the suburbs proliferated.

The radio: The radio played a titanic role in connecting, informing and entertaining Americans, and its ability to stimulate product demand via commercials and sponsorship was part of that enormous influence. The radio is another key American industry that scholars and others have written about extensively. Here we can but touch upon the broad strokes. At first, the cost of a radio was a deterrent. According to an article by writer and editor Alex Aronson in *Country Living*, "At the beginning of the 1920s, a new radio cost over $200 (over $2,577.00 today). But by the end of the decade, prices dropped to a more affordable $35 ($451.14 today)."[19]

---

19 Alex Aronson, "Here's What Things Cost 100 Years Ago," *Country Living*, July 30, 2020.

Since early radios were expensive and well beyond the reach of most households, installment credit supplied the means to get more radios into more homes.

Americans avidly embraced the radio, as they had the automobile, and those large and growing audiences created demand for improved transmission power and, of course, programming. In lockstep, manufacturers and sellers of the many new products and services entering the marketplace, who had formerly been limited to advertising via print or billboards, quickly saw opportunity and potential in the new medium. They seized on the ability of radio programming to reach large audiences and create product recognition, loyalty and demand via commercials and programming sponsorship. The A&P Gypsies, The Chase and Sanborn Hour, The Standard (Oil) Symphony Hour and The Voice of Firestone are a few of the many radio programs that aired in the 1920s, accomplishing the goals of providing entertainment and creating nationwide brand recognition and demand.

Consumer credit: All three of the above tectonic developments propelling modernity relied on growing credit availability. American enterprise, ever on the lookout for the next sure thing, stepped in once again with various new credit instruments and plans to enable consumers to fulfill the demand created by advertising for all the alluring new products. If demand was limited only by means, then give people the means! "Buy now, pay later" installment debt options, gave people the ability to own that automobile, radio or just about anything else, via so-called "easy" credit. Henry Ford's Model T may have begun America's love affair with the automobile, but it was General Motors—under the leadership of William C. Durant, a risk-taking businessman and co-founder of GM, as well as Frigidaire—that took the new ability to create products and linked it with making them more widely available and into people's hands via credit. Unlike Ford, Durant embraced credit early and established an auto finance subsidiary, General Motors Acceptance Corporation. Though a pioneering engineer, Henry Ford strongly disapproved of incurring debt in order to enjoy an automobile before it was actually paid for. Instead, he offered his employees an opportunity to own a Model T through what was actually a savings plan. Title didn't transfer until the employee had fully paid for the car. While Ford's conservative stand may have been costly to him in terms of the growth of Ford Motor, Americans eagerly embraced both the automobile and the debt that likely came with it as the following table shows.

Auto and Truck production statistics in 1920s

Table Prologue.2

Production of Motor Vehicles, 1920-1929

(in Thousands)

Year	# Cars	# Trucks	Total	% Change
1920	1,906	322	2,228	
1921	1,529	153	1,682	-24.5
1922	2,398	248	2,646	57.3
1923	3,780	400	4,180	58.0
1924	3,328	410	3,758	-10.1
1925	3,905	523	4,428	17.8
1926	3,984	522	4,506	1.8
1927	3,093	487	3,580	-20.6
1928	4,025	577	4,602	28.5
1929	5,651	805	6,456	40.3

(Data differs from Table 8.2 due to source difference).

Source: Based on Persons, "Credit Expansion, 1920 to 1929," *Quarterly Journal of Economics,* Nov. 1930, p. 123.

Mobility Matters

The rapid increase in the number of vehicles on the road leads us to the second "M" word, mobility, another key aspect of the American ethos. Mobility in the form of ships brought first a few and then many British and Europeans to the North American continent. Mobility in the form of slave ships forcibly brought Africans to plantations to raise crops such as cotton, which then was transported north to factories making finished goods, and rice and tobacco that were exported all over the world. Mobility drove national expansion into new territory via horseback, wagons and, eventually, railroads. We may have been called settlers, and some did settle down in one place, but we were a nation of wanderers, adventure-seekers, opportunists and explorers, as people took to the road to see "the territory ahead," as Mark Twain described it in 1884 in *The Adventures of Huckleberry Finn*, even if just for a Sunday drive.

In the 19th Century, the railroad made travel possible for more than just the adventurous or wealthy. But that was only the beginning. With the passionate embrace of the automobile in the early 20th Century—usually bought on credit as Durant established—cars became the means to explore. Those wanting mobility discovered through an automobile loan that they didn't have to wait; they could gain the freedom of mobility now. Highways soon followed—the pioneering Bronx River Parkway was completed in 1925—and filled with eager travelers. Americans quickly saw how travel enriched their lives, expanded personal horizons and offered new experiences. Having a car represented not just freedom, but aspiration. When people travelled, perhaps their accommodations matched their income level, but everyone saw the same inspiring sights along the way. Inspiration in and of itself was aspirational.

The entry of the U.S. into World War I brought mobility to millions of American men—and women—many of whom had never left their county, much less crossed the Atlantic Ocean. Soldiers returning from the Great War had seen "Paree" as the 1919 song "How Ya Gonna Keep 'Em Down on the Farm?" attested. Many, in fact, were no longer inclined to stay on the farm. Peacetime brought an affordable automobile within reach to anyone who could come up with a down payment and the job to justify a loan and unleashed the wanderlust to see and experience more, qualities that inhabit many of us to this day.

Mobility also became more important, even critical, as people moved from cities to the newly developed suburbs, away from shops and other urban conveniences once available by foot or trolley. Road construction exploded with all the ancillary commerce to attract locals and passersby. The vehicle production statistics above show how important the automobile had become to the movement of people, and trucks played a huge role in the movement of goods to get to those people.

The desire for physical mobility as an inherent aspect within the American character included another form of mobility—upward mobility. The ready availability of installment credit encouraged aspiration, as credit gave more people at more income levels the means to share opportunities similar to those of their wealthier neighbors who lived on the hill or right side of the tracks. Seeing new places, observing the lifestyles of those more affluent, even just meeting new people outside of one's community, all encouraged and expanded the vision of what was possible in life. That growing aspirational aspect implied by car ownership played out in Josephine Lawrence's novel *If I Had Four Apples* in which one character affirmed, "Everyone who was anybody at all had a car. Intolerable, not to be anybody at all."[20] Status had become inextricably linked to car ownership.

Mobility had its costs. In his 2012 book *Borrow: The American Way of Debt*, Cornell-based economic historian Louis Hyman referenced a *Yale Review* article by Yale economist C. Reinhold Noyes from 1927, in which Noyes issued a warning, citing especially "the motor industry to be the storm centre of the next period of depression, and it will be entirely to blame" for infusing installment credit so thoroughly into the economy. As Hyman offered,

20 Lawrence (1935), p. 47.

> The Depression, which [Noyes] correctly predicted in 1927 to be "two or three years" away, would be "automatic and inevitable" as it was the result of "retribution for economic sin." The "various bubbles" of cars and houses would burst and drag down the economy. Noyes, like all bellyachers, was blissfully ignored.[21]

... And More, When Man's Desires Overshadow His Needs

The third "M" is the idea of the desire for more. America has always been where "more" became possible for more people. As they arrived on the continent, each group of immigrants (at least those who had not been forced here) had its own list of what "more" they wanted for their lives—more religious freedom, more autonomy, more opportunity for them and certainly for their children, more space and more land than they could ever have imagined. As the nascent nation grew and expanded, "more" became built into the individual and collective psyche.

In the late 1920s, Paul Mazur, a senior partner at Lehman Brothers, wrote:

> Any community that lives on staples has relatively few wants. The community that can be trained to desire change, to want new things even before the old have been entirely consumed, yields a market to be measured more by desires than by needs. And man's desires can be developed so that they will greatly overshadow his needs.[22]

This quote captures the enormity of the entire shift that had taken place in America and in American business practices in the

---

21 Louis Hyman, *Borrow: The American Way of Debt, Vintage Books,* 2012, pp. 58-9.

22 Paul Mazur, *American Prosperity: Its Causes & Consequences,* 1928, Viking Press, pp. 24-5.

late 19th and early 20th centuries. In full bloom by the late 1920s, persuasive forces came to shape man's desires for "more," as Mazur and Edward Bernays espoused, but more also described American enterprise in general.[23] Technology, of course, enabled the production of identical products more quickly, but it also required more complex business management practices as distribution and sales and marketing became more essential to profitability. These trends brought a sea change in the business world as it transitioned from the simpler structures of sole proprietorships, partnerships and closely held and controlled companies to more corporations, more management, more consolidations and more stock offerings.

Credit was available every step of the way to having more. The car loan had put thousands behind the wheel, but nowhere was the expansion of credit more societally influential than in homeownership. Homeownership fit in perfectly with the yearning for more, and mortgage lenders eagerly stepped in to meet the demand for ownership as the supply of housing grew. The growth in housing stock was staggering as the suburbs proliferated: 2.6 million new units (single-family houses and apartment units) were constructed in the 1920s alone. For scale, in the 2000s the country added exactly half that number: 1.3 million units, for a population 2.7 times larger than the population in 1920 (282.2 million v. 106.5 million)[24] Clearly, this huge growth in housing stock demanded occupants. For that to take place, American heads of household (mostly men at the time) needed to value the idea of homeownership. Psychological pressures, as society's consent was engineered, were, and still are, influential. Penter Hoe, the misguided, debt-strapped head of household in

23 Corporations (other than spirits-makers) supported Prohibition because of the perception that men who drank didn't buy.

24 Eugene N. White, Kenneth Snowden and Price Fishback, *The Housing and Mortgage Markets in Historical Perspective,* University of Chicago Press, 2014, p. 118.

Josephine Lawrence's novel *If I Have Four Apples*, expressed the prejudice he had been convinced was valid:

> Show me a renter and I'll show you a shiftless cuss.... You see, I don't believe in renting. A man with a family ought to own his own home, not be paying his good money to landlords. Young folks ought to be putting their money into something solid, they ought to remember there was no gilt-edged investment to equal house and lot.... [T]hat was what made the grind endurable, for a man to feel that he slept under his own roof.[25]

Mortgages made homeownership—once a fantasy to most—possible, even though many mortgages available at the time were relatively short-term (3 to 5 years) with either a balloon payment at the end or the necessity to rollover the remaining debt into a new mortgage. On top of that, installment debt enabled this new crop of homeowners to furnish their homes. But filled with home furnishings and with a car parked outside, a home became the hub from which Americans expressed their urge to be mobile—to commute to work, run errands, go out on Saturday nights, take Sunday drives after church and even go away on vacations.

Stock Ownership as Means to More

As the 20th Century proceeded, increasingly complex businesses raised capital by issuing—and vigorously marketing—stock to the public. According to the research of New School history professor Julia C. Ott, before World War I no more than 500,000 Americans owned stock—about 3% of U.S. households—but by 1929 approximately 8 million households, or 25% of households

25 Lawrence (1935), p. 12

owned shares.[26] The powerful, independent (and unincorporated) member-controlled New York Stock Exchange. was a major player in this development. Bernays' rival in the fledgling public relations field, Ivy Lee, effectively employed new public relations techniques to promote stock ownership for the NYSE by focusing on educating a broader public. According to Ott:

> After 1921, the NYSE's new Committee on Publicity transformed defensive publicity into pro-active public relations, adding visits and hosting speaking tours, movies, and academic programs. From 1913 to the Crash of 1929, publicists defined the NYSE as the "free and open" "people's market" first to build a community of political sympathizers, then to expand NYSE members' retail markets.[27]

The NYSE Committee on Publicity widely promoted gallery visits to watch Exchange activity—by 1929, the gallery attracted several thousand "casual visitors" per month, Ott reported—and the Committee "greatly increased the volume of 'facts' it published." Ott continued:

> It forwarded its publications, its speeches, and favorable articles to an ever-widening distribution list, culled from the rolls of visitors and speakers' audiences, libraries, politicians, NYSE branch offices, Better Business Bureaus newspapers, listed corporations, educational institutes, granges, trade groups, civic and professional associations, and banks.[28]

---

26 Julia C. Ott, "The Free and Open People's Market," *The Journal of American History,* June, 2009, p. 45. A Gallop poll in April 2022 indicated that 58% of American households own stock.

27 Julia C. Ott, "The Free and Open People's Market: Public Relations at the New York Stock Exchange, 1913-1929," Business and Economic History on Line, thebhc.org, vol. 2, 2004, p.1.

28 Ibid., p. 27.

As a direct result, more and more Americans became stockholders of the growing supply of available shares. NYSE member brokerages helped accomplish this by offering credit—purchasing stock on margin. Stock, once owned by a thin sliver of affluent Americans, became attainable by just about anyone via buying on margin.

Speculation, The American Way to More

The term speculation had precedent earlier in the country's history in such enticing if unpredictable events as the Gold Rush, but also for monetizing inventions like the internal combustion engine and the construction of canals and railroads, but it took on special meaning—and velocity—during the 1920s. Speculation during the Florida real estate boom and then on Wall Street grabbed headlines.[29] But speculating was also going on in a more everyday form. It wasn't called speculation when someone made a down payment on a car and then made monthly payments until the car was paid for. Yes, there was the risk of losing that car and all prior payments if payments weren't made. But as the purchaser drove off the lot, probably believing he'd gotten a good deal, and started enjoying the car immediately, he (or she) had no thought that the purchase was a form of speculation, though the car's future value was uncertain. Its value was unlikely to go up. It could break down or be involved in an accident, requiring expensive repairs. Besides there was no guarantee that there would be the future income to make loan payments. The implications of this kind of speculation would take on greater meaning.

Unlike with a radio, car or other consumer good, stock ownership had a potentially large economic upside. In a rising market, such as the one that prevailed throughout much of the 1920s, margin

29 From a letter sent by a nephew of co-author Mary Keil's grandfather, "I tried to convey the story of how uncle lost a lot of money on a Florida real estate venture. He had to borrow money to finance it, but then could not keep up the payments – went broke. He had the foresight, though, because it was land around Orlando...Shucks."

buyers anticipated a rise in that stock price for a quick gain (as well as the pleasing sensation of having gotten a good deal.) The risks of leverage seemed worth it. However, distinct from buying a car via installments, if a stock price went down, and the broker made a margin call, the owner had to come up with cold hard cash then and there to meet the shortfall or, depending on the decline, a great deal more than the "down payment" on the stock. The purchase, then, wasn't such a good deal after all. "Buy now, pay later" perversely became "Sell now, pay now." In the saga of the Crash period and its aftermath told in the chapters ahead, we will reveal the dramatic economic realities in concrete data.

A Confluence of Forces Set the Stage

In order to enjoy a better life, Americans throughout the 1920s became more and more accustomed to being in debt. More of everything usually meant more debt. Debt became the means to many ends. With the lure of modernity, mobility and more, the decade of the 1920s was a perfect confluence of forces—innovations using electricity designed to make home life easier, the methods to produce multiple quantities of the same item, louder and more manipulative marketing techniques to stimulate wants, the radio to convey carefully focused messages and a credit industry to enable acquisition now rather than later. This remarkable confluence of forces created the veneer of a rise in the nation's standard of living, but veneers can be vulnerable and delicate, prone to scratches and dents, and sometimes the veneer separates entirely exposing the weaknesses just below the surface.

There would be unintended consequences of bringing human wants and desires out of the recesses of purchasers' mostly unexamined psyches and into the tangible world of the many desirable products that had become part of everyday life. Stock ownership, purchased on margin, became one of those products, with a potentially life-altering upside—and downside. As historian Lendol Calder wrote about the decade to follow, "For an unknown but certainly large number of Americans, the scramble to keep ahead of the bill collector was the main business of life in the 1930s."[30]

We close this Prologue with words from economist John Maynard Keynes, whose ideas we will be featuring ahead:

> It seems an extraordinary imbecility that this wonderful outburst of productive energy should be the prelude to impoverishment and depression.[31]

By touching on factors that led to events that shook the country to its foundations, this look at the whirl of the 1920s reveals that along with its "wonderful outburst of productive energy," one particular component, or "prelude," of that outburst stood out: debt. In the chapters ahead, we explore how borrowing and indebtedness in all its forms proved to be the force that would plunge the country into the tragedy of "impoverishment and depression."

---

30 Lendol Calder, *Financing the American Dream*, Princeton University Press, 1999, p. 267 and 269.

31 John Maynard Keynes, *Collected Writings of John Maynard Keynes; Vol. XIII; The General Theory and After, Part I Preparation,* Cambridge University Press, 1973, p. 349.

CHAPTER 1

How Do We Account for What Happened in 1929-33?

TODAY OLD IDEAS are constantly being challenged by new data. We are accustomed to seeing both current and historical data of all sorts, and from many different sources. This was not always the case. In order to look back on the Great Depression with an eye towards understanding what happened, we, of course, have had to rely on historical data. Data collection has evolved considerably over the decades as the country's economy has grown and technology has enabled researchers and others to gain deeper understanding of what data tell us and, just as important, of what data we still need in order to make sound policy decisions. Data is neutral except in the eyes of researchers who look for patterns and seek explanations.

When we began this project, we knew what we didn't know and what we wanted to know; we just didn't know where to get the evidence to support our hypotheses. In fact, supporting evidence and proof seemed to be missing altogether. The evolution of this work has included making ample use of credible and respected data sources, then recognizing that these sources didn't supply key data we needed. Then, quite serendipitously, we tapped into a federal government archive within the Treasury Department, seldom used by economists or historians, whose principal function is well familiar to virtually all Americans. That archive has provided more than enough data for us to draw entirely credible conclusions. In the chapters to follow, we will present our findings based on careful examination of that archive as well as drawing on other credible data sources.

To be sure, even before 1929, our governmental institutions collected and used statistics and reports to assess and describe economic conditions, but these efforts too often lacked overall focus and coordination. The Federal Reserve System, for example, inaugurated only sixteen years before the Crash, maintained a variety of indices including its Index of Factory Employment and its Index of Industrial Production. But the arrival of the Great Depression illuminated the many inadequacies in the collection of economic data at that time and stressed the need for the federal government, as small as it was relative to now, to step up to the challenge of collecting data. However, data is only as accurate as the definitions used to categorize and the means to collect those statistics. The intrepid, mostly unsung statisticians whose integrity in identifying what it was important to know and then determining how to gather that information remain under-appreciated by most. But those of us who make use of the results of their labors recognize the enormity of the task they undertook, unaware, as they were, of how future generations of researchers might endeavor to gain worthwhile new insights from those efforts.

A bright light shines on the challenges of working with the revisions in data the various sources have made over the years due in part to definitional changes. A prime example, and one that is of central importance to our period of focus, is unemployment—what exactly unemployment means and how it is measured. Most of us have an idea of what the term means, and we understand its regard as a key indicator of economic health. We know unemployment figures come out monthly with great fanfare. But we also are aware that, more often than not, unemployment statistics are revised the following month. The question of what statistics to use when working with unemployment data is an ongoing dilemma. We must rely on the statistics-gathering guidelines of established sources. In the U.S., those guidelines mainly remain the purview of the federal government.

Besides our as yet unnamed archive, one important source of the statistics we will be examining is the U.S. Commerce Department's Bureau of Economic Analysis (BEA), reorganized in 1972, long after our period of focus, to consolidate the scattered governmental statistics-gathering entities under one roof. The BEA *Survey of Current Business* produced a supplement entitled *The National Income & Product Accounts of the United States, 1929-76 Statistical Tables,* which came out in September 1981. These statistics—called "NIPA"—while key to understanding the economic realities of 1929-33, do have limitations since they have been subject to revision, as the *Supplement's* Introduction states:

> This Supplement to the Survey of Current Business is one of a series of reports that presents the revised national income account (NIPA) estimates that resulted from the comprehensive revision completed in December 1980. This report presents estimates for the periods before 1977.[1]

It was in part due to the realization that working with statistics subject to change over time has inherent challenges that we began searching for a more permanent and, for historical purposes, reliable source of data, despite our being uncertain such a source even existed. We, indeed, found such a source. Nevertheless, we have also found, among other governmental and private sources, the BEA's NIPA supplement, the Federal Reserve's *Banking and Monetary Statistics* and the National Bureau of Economic Research's little known *Bulletin 55*, which came out in 1935, to be troves of important and detailed statistical information about the Depression period and refer to them throughout the book both as supporting evidence and, in some cases, to be wrestled with and questioned.

---

1 DoC/BEA (1981) p. vii. Only one annual table—Table 1.2, p. 72—includes data before 1929.

Measuring Unemployment

It is useful to note how even the most fundamental—and familiar—economic indicators have evolved since 1929. Unemployment is a pertinent example. This measurement of slack in our economy with regards to employment is a statistic watched closely by all levels in and out of government, including the Federal Reserve. While there are proponents of redefining unemployment in a way that includes more categories of those out of work, the current definition, with what some consider inherent limitations, is widely accepted.[2] In the Depression period, unemployment was an urgent and obvious problem, but it was then an ill-defined concept. We knew how many were employed in various parts of our economy, but we had no idea how many were actually unemployed involuntarily. No one focused on the societal implications of having a large number of workers unable to find work until unemployment became a critical and glaring society-wide issue.

Assuming there was what 18th century Scottish economist Adam Smith described as an invisible hand that guided a market economy to perfect competition, American economists and politicians held to the belief that everyone who wanted a job could find one. Indeed, the prosperity experienced in the 1920s included ample opportunities for employment. But as the Depression worsened, unemployment rose in all its complex realities, and by 1932 one quarter of our workforce was out of work, symbolized by images of former family breadwinners standing on street corners selling apples in plain sight of dismayed passersby.

It took the Depression to reveal that we had no official concept of "involuntary unemployment," and long years were required to define its meaning for statistical purposes and to begin gathering the relevant data necessary to compile meaningful statistics. The

2 See, for instance, *The Vanishing American Dream*, edited by Gene Ludwig from a symposium at Yale Law School in April 2019. Ludwig advocates for what he calls TRU, a true rate of unemployment. For further information see LISEP.org.

task of developing these statistics on unemployment fell to the Bureau of Labor Statistics (BLS) of the U.S. Department of Labor, which didn't fully settle the definitional issue until the late 1950s. After considering many alternate ways of defining unemployment, conducting statistical sampling and developing different means of measurement statistics, the BLS finally settled on the simple but clear definition of an unemployed person as someone who is actively seeking a job but is unable to find one.

Beginning in 1959, what we know as "the unemployment rate" began to be released to the public as a focal element of the Labor Department's monthly jobs report.[3] (Recent labor statistics are based on samples and surveys of approximately 144,000 businesses and 60,000 households.) However, statistics are regularly adjusted by the various data gathering entities, and this presents researchers with the dilemma of determining which data version to use.

Measuring the Economy: National Income and Product Accounts Today

As any beginning student of economics learns, there is economics at a macro or overall level, such as a nation, and at a micro, or single unit level, such as a firm or even an individual. In the course of the dire events of 1929-33, it became apparent that although there had been a national census since 1790, reflecting the responses of individuals, there was a good deal we didn't know about our nation at a macro level. In fact, at the onset of the Depression, the idea of there being a national economy was nascent. Despite the Fed's efforts at indexing following World War I, we had a limited understanding of our economy's aggregates in general. According to Zachary Karabell in his 2014 book *The Leading Indicators: A Short*

3 Zachary Karabell, *The Leading Indicators*, Simon & Schuster, 2014, pp. 43-4.

History of the Numbers That Rule Our World:

> Before there were metrics and indicators, [what we now know as] "the economy" didn't exist. No, economic activity wasn't invented in the middle of the twentieth century. But this thing called "the economy" was. Until the 1940s, there was no "the economy." People did not use the term and they had only just begun to think of the material affairs of a nation as a coherent and cohesive subject that could be defined, measured, and tracked over time.[4]

The most macro-level statistic conceived of to measure the overall size of the U.S. economy was originally called the Gross National Product, intended to present the aggregate size of U.S. output. According to Karabell:

> [I]n 1942, to solve the central question of whether the United States could devote the vast majority of its government spending and its private industry to the war without upending society, economists and statisticians finally unveiled what had been years in the making: gross national product. GNP provided a way to calculate precisely how much the government could spend and how much it could increase taxes to pay for defense. GNP wasn't a weapon, but it helped win the war.[5]

In 1991, an important definitional change was made.[6] In Karabell's words:

> Nothing matters [to economists today] more than GDP. Even that is new. In 1991, after years of debate and study,

---

4 Ibid., p. 78.

5 Ibid., p. 69.

6 Not shown in our recreation of NIPA Tables 1.1, 1.2 and 1.3 because we made use of statistics from before 1991.

> the Bureau of Economic Analysis shifted from gross national product to gross domestic product instead.... The difference between GDP and GNP is that GDP measures only goods and services produced within the United States, whereas GNP includes all goods and services produced by US nationals regardless of where in the world production occurs.[7]

As Karabell makes clear, effective use of statistics requires careful examination not just of the sources, but also of definitions, revisions, how items are categorized and even whether the dollar values were current, inflation-adjusted or time-adjusted.

Looking Back at the Depression Years

Despite their limitations, statistics collected and published later can still reveal much about the Depression era, at least at a macro level. For example, Tables 1.1, 1.2, and 1.3 following present a valuable overview offering progressively more detailed data employing the definitional account structure used by the National Income and Product Accounts (NIPA) as published in 1981, a decade before GNP morphed into GDP. We gained important insights from these data—including about their shortcomings—that then prompted us to dig further.

Table 1.1, on opposite page, (a reproduction of NIPA Table 1.1) presents Gross National Product in millions of dollars annually for the years 1929-1934. (The entries are in "current" dollars, the actual dollar values recorded in the years in question, not in "real" dollars adjusted in any way to reflect deflation or inflation.) The table breaks down GNP into a series of major line items (in bold above): Personal consumption expenditures, Gross private domestic investment, Net exports of goods and services and Government purchases of goods and services.[8] Each of these line items told its own Depression era

7 Ibid., p.158.

8 Further information about the NIPA definitions today can be found at www.bea.gov/resources/methodologies/nipa-handbook/pdf/glossary.pdf.

Table 1.1 Gross National Product: Annually, 1929-1934 ($ million)						
	1929	1930	1931	1932	1933	1934
Gross national product	**103,420**	**90,700**	**76,073**	**58,280**	**55,818**	**65,291**
Personal consumption expenditures	**77,251**	**69,916**	**60,482**	**48,591**	**45,811**	**51,344**
Durable goods	9,243	7,166	5,483	3,641	3,464	4,219
Nondurable goods	37,686	34,022	28,956	22,741	22,257	26,691
Services	30,322	28,728	26,043	22,209	20,090	20,434
Gross private domestic investment	**16,197**	**10,249**	**5,620**	**965**	**1,406**	**3,328**
Fixed investment	14,483	10,601	6,768	3,445	2,970	4,063
Non residential	10,610	8,325	5,031	2,705	2,390	3,177
Structures	5,118	4,145	2,388	1,245	954	1,079
Producers' durable equipment	5,492	4,180	2,643	1,460	1,436	2,098
Residential	3,873	2,276	1,737	740	580	886
Nonfarm structures	3,620	2,078	1,602	667	497	783
Farm structures	175	131	78	38	43	52
Producers' durable equipment	78	67	57	35	40	51
Change in business inventories	1,714	-352	-1,148	-2,480	-1,564	-735
Nonfarm	1,836	-83	-1,608	-2,590	-1,370	195
Farm	-122	-269	460	110	-194	-930
Net exports of goods and services	**1,149**	**1,032**	**516**	**407**	**358**	**601**
Exports	7,035	5,448	3,641	2,474	2,402	2,975
Imports	5,886	4,416	3,125	2,067	2,044	2,374
Government purchase of goods and services	**8,823**	**9,503**	**9,455**	**8,317**	**8,243**	**10,018**
Federal	1,441	1,552	1,613	1,578	2,122	3,123
National defense	----------	----------	----------	----------	----------	----------
Nondefense	----------	----------	----------	----------	----------	----------
State and local	7,382	7,951	7,842	6,739	6,121	6,895

Source: *The National Income & Product Accounts of the United States 1929-76; Table 1.1*, p.1.

story about what went on in our particular years of study, at least as seen from 50,000 feet.

Of note, for instance, is the small size of the federal government relative to the total expenses of state and local governments. Even with the advent of the Roosevelt administration in March 1933, and as late as 1940, state and local government expenditures dwarfed federal expenditures. Only with the start of full-scale, active U.S. participation in World War II in 1942 did federal expenditures balloon at a breathtaking speed.

Continuing this overview perspective, Table 1.2 (NIPA Table 1.7) presents, again in millions of current dollars, Gross National

Product, then refines those aggregate figures by deducting certain key items to yield Net National Product, National Income and Personal Income. From our vantage point, it is in those refining deductions, which include depreciation (such as of plant and equipment), corporate profits and personal interest and dividend income, that a more detailed view emerges of the deteriorating conditions taking place, although that view is still an overview.

With Table 1.3, on next page, (NIPA Table 2.1), we drop down one level further in terms of specificity to learn more about individuals, in aggregate, during our years. Surprisingly, personal savings in 1930 and 1931 were not far below the amount saved in

Table 1.2

Relation of Gross National Product, Net National Product, National Income and Personal Income: Annually, 1929-1934

($ million)

	1929	1930	1931	1932	1933	1934
Gross national product	**103,420**	**90,700**	**76,073**	**58,280**	**55,818**	**65,291**
Less: Capital consumption allowances with capital consumption adjustment	9,731	9,564	8,913	7,788	7,442	7,774
Capital consumption allowances without capital consumption adjustment	7,308	7,496	7,528	7,147	6,786	6,587
Less: Capital consumption adjustment	-2,423	-2,068	-1,385	-641	-656	-1,187
Equals: Net national product	**93,689**	**81,136**	**67,160**	**50,492**	**48,376**	**57,517**
Less: Indirect business tax and nontax liability	7,051	7,202	6,900	6,803	7,082	7,842
Business transfer payments	587	534	649	737	659	641
Statistical discrepancy	1,104	-512	897	457	704	629
Plus: Subsidies less current surplus of government enterprises	-152	-129	-56	-67	-32	217
Equals: National income	**84,795**	**73,783**	**58,658**	**42,428**	**39,899**	**48,622**
Less: Corporate profits with inventory valuation and capital consumption adjustments	9,049	5,795	1,221	-1,820	-1,748	874
Net interest	4,705	4,921	4,953	4,618	4,068	4,126
Contributions for social insurance	243	253	262	278	285	304
Wage accruals less disbursements	0	0	0	0	0	0
Plus: Government transfer payments to persons	919	1,009	2,075	1,443	1,466	1,562
Personal interest income	6,889	6,448	6,465	6,071	5,547	5,661
Personal dividend income	5,801	5,468	4,066	2,544	2,038	2,567
Business transfer payments	587	534	649	737	659	641
Equals: Personal income	**84,994**	**76,273**	**65,477**	**50,147**	**47,004**	**53,749**

Source: *The National Income & Product Accounts of the United States 1929-76*, p.23.

1929. The data also reveal that in 1932, at the bottom of the Depression, individuals, at least in aggregate, were living off their savings (a phenomenon of concern that economists call "dissaving".)

1929-33: Crucial Economic Indicators Drop

The NIPA supplement provided important information on the downward economic changes that have come to define the Depression years. For instance, as Table 1.1 clearly shows, there was a dramatic

Table 1.3

Personal Income and its Disposition: Annually, 1929-1934

($ million)

	1929	1930	1931	1932	1933	1934
Personal income	**84,994**	**76,273**	**65,477**	**50,147**	**47,004**	**53,749**
Wage and salary disbursements	**50,460**	**46,214**	**39,157**	**30,514**	**29,027**	**33,734**
Commodity-producing industries	21,505	18,548	14,297	9,936	9,815	12,064
Manufacturing	16,092	13,850	10,810	7,678	7,827	9,643
Distributive industries	15,558	14,491	12,523	9,758	8,804	9,918
Service industries	8,436	7,996	7,053	5,828	5,245	5,655
Government and government enterprises	4,961	5,179	5,284	4,992	5,163	6,097
Other labor income	**527**	**515**	**473**	**414**	**378**	**412**
Proprietors' income with inventory valuation and capital consumption adjustments	**15,043**	**11,865**	**9,179**	**5,696**	**5,857**	**7,583**
Farm	6,144	4,343	3,430	2,086	2,522	2,894
Nonfarm	8,899	7,522	5,749	3,610	3,335	4,689
Rental income of persons with capital consumption adjustment	**4,910**	**4,367**	**3,564**	**2,880**	**2,184**	**1,746**
Personal dividend income	**5,801**	**5,468**	**4,066**	**2,544**	**2,038**	**2,567**
Personal interest income	**6,889**	**6,448**	**6,465**	**6,071**	**5,547**	**5,661**
Transfer payments	**1,506**	**1,543**	**2,724**	**2,180**	**2,125**	**2,203**
Old-age, survivors, disability and health insurance benefits	-------------	-------------	-------------	-------------	-------------	---------
Government unemployment insurance benefits	-------------	-------------	-------------	-------------	-------------	--------
Veterans benefits	558	599	1,576	782	555	444
Government employees retirement benefits	128	140	154	169	192	215
Other transfer payments	820	804	994	1,229	1,378	1,544
Aid to families with dependent children	-------------	-------------	-------------	-------------	-------------	---------
Other	-------------	-------------	-------------	-------------	-------------	--------
Less: Personal contributions for social insurance	**142**	**147**	**151**	**152**	**152**	**157**
Less: Personal tax and nontax payments	**2,595**	**2,460**	**1,817**	**1,420**	**1,437**	**1,568**
Equals: Disposable personal income	**82,399**	**73,813**	**63,660**	**48,727**	**45,567**	**52,181**
Less: Personal outlays	**79,126**	**71,097**	**61,425**	**49,332**	**46,466**	**51,988**
Personal consumption expenditures	77,251	69,916	60,482	48,591	45,811	51,344
Interest paid by consumers to business	1,532	875	664	524	464	482
Personal transfer payments to foreigners (net)	343	306	279	217	191	162
Equals: Personal saving	3,273	2,716	2,235	-605	-899	193
Addenda:						
Disposable personal income:						
Total, billions of 1972 dollars	229.5	210.6	201.9	174.4	169.6	179.8
Per capita:						
Current dollars	676	599	513	390	363	413
1972 dollars	1,883	1,710	1,626	1,395	1,349	1,421
Population (mid-period, thousands)	121,878	123,188	124,149	124,949	125,690	126,485
Personal saving as percentage of disposable personal income	**4.0**	**3.7**	**3.5**	**-1.2**	**-2.0**	**0.4**

Source: *The National Income & Product Accounts of the United States 1929-76*, p.34.

year-by-year fall in key indicators: GNP, Personal Consumption Expenditures and Fixed Investment.

To highlight these noteworthy declines, Table 1.4 shows the year-to-year drop in these three categories both in current dollars and as percentages. We can readily see from the table, regarding the aggregate U.S. economy, GNP fell 46.0% from 1929 to 1933 alone, from $103.4 billion to $55.8 billion, an almost unimaginable three-year contraction of aggregate economic activity.

As to individuals, Personal Consumption fell 9.5% from $77,251 million in 1929 to $69,916 million in 1930, but in 1933, Personal Consumption had fallen relentlessly to $45,811 million, a 40.7% decline from year-end 1929.

Businesses fared even worse. During 1930, Fixed Investment fell 26.8% from year-end 1929, from $14,483 million to $10,601 million. But that was only the beginning. By year-end 1933, Fixed Investment had dropped to $2,970 million, a whopping 79.5% fall

Table 1.4

Statistics of Change In Major NIPA Line Items

($ million)

1929	1930	1931	1932	1933	Cummulative % change	Annual $ change
Fall in GNP (Line Item 1 in table 1.1)						
103,420	90,700				-12.3	-12,720
		76,073			-26.4	-14,627
			58,280		-43.6	-17,793
				55,818	-46.0	-2,462
Fall in personal consumption (Line Item 2)						
77,251	69,916				-9.5	-7,335
		60,482			-21.7	-9,434
			46,591		-39.7	-13,891
				45,811	-40.7	-780
Fall in fixed investment (Line Item 7)						
14,483	10,601				-26.8	-3,882
		6,768			-53.3	-3,833
			3,445		-76.2	-3,323
				2,970	-79.5	-475

Source: *The National Income & Product Accounts of the United States 1929-76*, p.1.

from 1929, indicating that businesses basically stopped investing in their futures.

As statistics gathering evolved following the Crash and the Depression period, later researchers, such as Raymond W. Goldsmith, endeavored to compile accurate data critical to estimating the evolution of the U.S. national balance sheet and the amounts of saving in America. We have found Professor Goldsmith's efforts invaluable in helping us understand what happened as the Depression deepened. NBER's *Bulletin 55,* which came out in 1935, also performed a critical function in its attempts to show that the economy had turned a corner by 1935 and informing readers that, "fears of the end of the profits system must, in light of the figures, be modified." (Further discussion of Goldsmith's work and NBER's *Bulletin 55* is presented in Chapter 6.) The 1981 NIPA report has provided researchers with the most comprehensive information thought to be available of the general overall picture. However, as will unfold in future chapters, these existing and widely consulted statistics had limitations that only became apparent to us when another, more comprehensive data source came to the fore.

Of course, all U.S. economic activity has existed under the leadership of our duly elected officials. From the most macro of levels of declining GNP to the micro level of the unemployed factory worker trying to feed his family, the government during the 1929-33 era had to respond to what was going on. At the helm throughout most of this entire period was one man, a man with an impressive track record and a demonstrable respect for fact gathering and statistics, but with one particular blind spot. We now take a look at this key figure in the federal government's response, or lack of it, at the time of the Crash and during the crucial early years the Great Depression. His name, unfortunately associated for many with failed governmental action in the national crisis, was Herbert Hoover.

CHAPTER 2

Herbert Hoover: Liberty Preempts Presidential Action

EVERY TRULY GREAT STORY needs a hero with a flaw. The classic example is Achilles, Homer's hero from the *Iliad,* who was the Trojan War's best fighter on the side of the Greeks. When his mother, the goddess Thetis, baptized him in the protective waters of the sacred River Styx, she held him by his heel, which, as a consequence, did not touch the waters and become invulnerable. Achilles's heel was his vulnerability, in his case fatal, and it became a poignant metaphor for almost-heroes throughout the centuries. In President Herbert Hoover, we have such a flawed protagonist in the onset of the war against the Great Depression.

A Hero for the Dynamic 1920s

The 1920s in America was a remarkable decade of changes: societal, technological and industrial. The decade began with the enactment of two key Constitutional amendments — Prohibition and voting rights for women. It was a decade of electrification and expanded ways to use electricity, including movies and the wide availability of the radio with its increasingly influential programming and, inevitably, commercials. As we described in the Prologue, it was the decade when a higher standard of living became attainable to more people, as buying on time proliferated enabling acquisition of homes, automobiles, other possessions and newly invented laborsaving devices, and the U.S. population became valued by industry as consumers.

It was also a decade of heroic personalities, both real and created: of Babe Ruth, Charlie Chaplin, Charles Lindberg, Amelia Earhart, Duke Ellington; of F. Scott Fitzgerald and *The Great Gatsby*, Margery Williams and *The Velveteen Rabbit*; of jazz, blues, swing, big band and ragtime; of the advent of talkies and sun glasses, car radios, Art Deco; of Prohibition with its shady offshoots like bootleggers, speakeasies, flappers and the unfortunate and lasting offspring of crime syndicates, highlighted by Al Capone. Mother Nature also played a key role as debilitating floods destroyed vast areas, and a drought accelerated the onset of the Dust Bowl portending the potent economic events of the 1930s — rising unemployment, price deflation, bank panics and failures and shantytowns.

All of this was happening against the backdrop of a government dominated to a significant extent by someone many Americans considered to be truly heroic: Herbert Clark Hoover. In her 2007 book on the Depression era *The Forgotten Man*, economic historian Amity Shlaes described Hoover in action during the devastating Mississippi flood of 1927:

> When the waters of the Mississippi broke through banks and levees that spring, the disaster was enormous. A wall of water pushed down the river, covering the area where nearly a million lived. Commerce Secretary Herbert Hoover raced to Memphis and took command. Hoover talked railroads into transporting the displaced for free and carrying freight at a discount. He commandeered private outboard motors and built motorboats of plywood. He urged the people who were not yet flooded out, such as the population around the Bayou des Glaises levee, to evacuate early, then rescued with the trains those tens of thousands who had ignored his warning. He helped the Red Cross launch a fund drive; within a month the charity had already collected promises of more than $8 million, an enormous figure for the time.

> Several hundred thousand ended up in new refugee camps, many planned, right down to the latrines, by Hoover and his team. Hoover asked governors of each state to name a dictator of resources — he used the word "dictator" — and the governors complied. The dictators then managed the dysentery and the hunts for the missing along the floodwaters in their states hour by hour. He and the Red Cross sent the refugees to...camps at Vicksburg, Delta, and Natchez. One hundred thousand blankets from army warehouses were shipped to warm the refugees.... Switchboard operators were still working — albeit from new posts, high up above the waters, on scaffolding.[1]

Among the many authors who have written about Herbert Hoover, Wesleyan University economic historian William J. Barber in his 1985 book *From New Era to New Deal; Herbert Hoover, the Economists, and American Economic Policy, 1921-1933*, described the promise seen in the future president:

> As a candidate for the leadership in the development of [the proper ordering of a "new era" for the American economy], one figure — Herbert Hoover — towered above all others. He was the example, par excellence, of the practical idealist. As a professional engineer, he had demonstrated outstanding talents as an efficiency expert and, by the age of thirty-five, had acquired a financial independence that would permit him thereafter to serve public causes with indifference to his compensation. As a relief administrator in war-torn Europe and as the director of the War Food Administration under President Wilson, he had displayed both his humanitarian concerns and his administrative skills. Nor could there be any doubt of his conviction that America should reject the way of the Old World and should blaze a fresh trail toward

1 Amity Shlaes, *The Forgotten Man*, Harper Perennial, 2007, pp. 15-6.

social betterment. This conviction had been sharpened by his experience at the Peace Conference of 1918 and 1919. With few kindred spirits other than John Maynard Keynes, Hoover had sensed the undercurrent of vindictiveness in the Versailles settlement and the unfortunate consequences it was likely to generate. By 1920 no American in public life was regarded more highly for a capacity to form judgments on the basis of facts and without regard for partisan or personal advantage. Hoover's name was mentioned prominently as a presidential candidate by both major parties, and in the opinion of Franklin D. Roosevelt, then assistant secretary of the navy, no one was better qualified for the nation's highest post.[2]

An Influential Secretary of Commerce

As far back as the election of 1920, Hoover was a presidential candidate in the making. In his *Memoirs* published in 1952, he described how "politically amateur friends" of his began to work for his nomination for President. Because of his nonpartisan behavior in both word and deed during World War I, Hoover might have had standing in either political party. But when he gave thought to which political party he felt most sympathetic, Hoover found that his attitudes were closest to those of the rank and file membership of the Republicans, especially in the north and western parts of the country where he'd spent his later childhood. Out of his own personal experiences, Hoover came to believe that the primary role of government was to support the American ideals of individual liberty, initiative and opportunity. Born in West Branch, Iowa in 1874, orphaned by 11 and eventually living with an uncle in Oregon, Hoover set his sights on attending the new Leland Stanford Junior University, named after a railroad magnate's son who had died of typhoid, and Hoover was, in fact, in its inaugural class entering in

---

2 William J. Barber, *Ftom New Era to New Deal*, Cambridge University Press, 1985, p. 5.

1891. At Stanford, he majored in geology and became a successful mining engineer spending some years in China, Australia, England and elsewhere where he earned financial independence. The end of World War I provided Hoover with an opportunity to shine and gain respect, even renown, as he led food relief efforts in Europe.

Hoover allowed his friends to talk him into running in the 1920 California Republican presidential primary, and though he did not win, he made a strong showing. The Republican Presidential nomination went to Ohio Senator Warren G. Harding, and following the election, Harding asked Hoover to join his Cabinet, as either Secretary of the Interior or of Commerce. Hoover chose Commerce, making some significant conditions.[3] In his biography of Hoover, presidential historian and biographer Richard Norton Smith observed:

> Late in February 1921, after securing the president-elect's promise that he would have a hand in all economic policy-making, and that other departments must yield to this remarkable power grab, Hoover accepted the job. The strongest figure in the new administration, he was assigned the most obscure department in government. Hoover saw it otherwise. Commerce, he reasoned, would provide the perfect training ground in which to perfect his vision of a society always advancing, through individual genius and warmhearted cooperation.[4]

Crisis Calls for an Economic Stabilization Strategy

Hoover's vision was immediately tested as the country fell into a recession, bringing unemployment and deflation with it. Central to Hoover's efforts then, and, after Harding died suddenly in 1923,

3 Herbert Hoover, *Memoirs of Herbert Hoover, Vol. 2,* Macmillan Publishers, 1951, pp. 33-6.

4 Richard Norton Smith, *An Uncommon Man: The Triumph of Herbert Hoover*, Simon & Schuster, 1984, pp. 97-8.

as a member of the Coolidge Administration, was developing techniques for efficiently smoothing the business cycle, and, also of importance to him, without employing relief programs. He did so by enthusiastically forming committees and calling conferences, gathering together experts, business leaders and people of influence in their fields to analyze issues and come up with solutions, thus revealing his fundamental belief in the government's role as encouraging cooperation, coordination and proposals, as opposed to Federal legislation, regulation or aid programs. According to Barber, Hoover's enthusiasm for convening was his "technique" for proper governance:

> The importance of a technique for taming the business cycle was driven home forcefully early in Hoover's career as secretary of commerce. The year 1921 witnessed a sharp downturn in economic activity, which was accompanied by a disturbing increase in unemployment. Hoover's reaction to this situation was to convene a gathering of business and labor leaders in Washington to consider remedies for the recession. Though officially styled the President's Conference on Unemployment, it was organized on Hoover's initiative and he chaired the proceedings. Crucial to the deliberations of the conference was the groundwork laid by an economic advisory committee appointed by the secretary of commerce.[5]

About this economic advisory committee and his penchant in general for convocations, Hoover wrote in his *Memoirs:*

> Fifteen days after taking office (March 19) I invited twenty-five leaders in business, labor, and agriculture to serve as an advisory committee on policies and undertakings of the Department. At our meeting we determined upon the broad direction [the Department] should follow. We also decided

5 Barber (1985), p. 16.

> that we would at a later date summon an extensive national conference on reconstruction and development problems, but that before doing so we should grant subcommittees some months to prepare a program for the larger meeting, which was set for September.[6]

A committee appointed by Hoover almost simultaneously was called the Advisory Committee on Statistics.[7] This committee would prove to be one of Hoover's major, if perhaps unsung, contributions influencing future generations of economists. In fact, the field of economic statistical research increased exponentially under Hoover's efficiency-based concept of government. As Barber wrote:

> This was a formidable assemblage of talents which embraced some of the most respected names in American academic economics.... [T]his group presented "urgent recommendations" in June 1921, that the statistical services of the government should be strengthened, that they be consolidated under the jurisdiction of the Department of Commerce, and that timely data on the activities of the economy's key sectors should be published regularly.[8]

Evidencing this new emphasis on gathering economic facts and analysis to aid policy and business decision-making, one of the members appointed to Hoover's newly formed Advisory Committee on Statistics was Wesley Clair Mitchell, a professor at Columbia University and a leading expert on what some then called "economic fluctuations," now called business cycles. According to Barber, Mitchell had served as head of the Price Statistics Section

6 Hoover, (1951), p. 41.

7 Barber, (1985), p. 199. In footnote #2, page 199, Barber says, "Formal invitations to the members of the advisory committee were dispatched on March 16, 1921."

8 Ibid., p. 8.

of the War Industry Board during World War I and became President of the American Statistical Association in 1918. Mitchell was one of the founders of the National Bureau of Economic Research (NBER) formed by an act of Congress in 1920 and served as its inaugural director of research from 1920 through 1945. In 1924, he also became president of the American Economic Association. Mitchell and Hoover were closely aligned in their belief in science, research and data.

In 1921, the Department of Commerce's new economic advisory committee recommended something that broke new ground as to federal government involvement in response to economic crises: government spending on public works projects. Continuing his commentary, Barber wrote:

> The primary conclusion of the economic advisers was that spending on public works, if properly timed, could smooth much of the fluctuation in business activity and employment.
>
> A novel concept was central to an understanding of the argument supporting this finding. The impact on the economy of an accelerated public works program in times of depression, it was maintained, would be much greater than the direct stimulation would give to incomes and jobs in the construction industry. Indirect effects would also be felt throughout the system when this added purchasing power augmented the demand for consumer goods. Nor would the expansionary effects end there. Still more jobs and more income would be created when the producers of consumer goods began to spend their enlarged incomes.[9]

The advisory committee went on to stress the prevailing view of the Harding-Coolidge-Hoover era that "a sound public works

9 Ibid., p. 16.

program would be required to satisfy the usual tests of efficiency and its purpose was to provide jobs, not handouts."[10]

The President's Conference on Unemployment

Early in the autumn of 1921, Secretary Hoover addressed the worsening economic conditions and the resulting unemployment by organizing the proposed Presidential conference under his leadership. Describing this conference in his *Memoirs*, Hoover, ever advocating efficiency, argued that the booms and slumps of the business cycle and especially the unemployment the slumps brought about were a "waste" of an economy's strength and resources:

> In cooperation with the Departmental Advisory Committee, we assembled the general Economic Conference in September 1921. We had selected some three hundred leaders from production, distribution, banking, construction, labor, and agriculture. In the meantime the post-war slump had deepened, and unemployment had seriously increased. The original purpose of the Conference to deal with the long-view reconstruction and development was overshadowed by the need to deal with the immediate crisis.
>
> Our advisory committees presented ideas upon: (1) the alleviation of the unemployment situation over the winter 1921-1922; (2) the development of industrial efficiency and elimination of waste; (3) the stimulation of foreign trade, including the provision of credits to foreigners; (4) the long view study of the business cycle of booms and slumps and their alleviation.
>
> In view of the increased unemployment, I emphasized this immediate problem in opening the Conference....

10 Ibid.

> The unemployment had increased over the summer to more than 5,000,000. Under the committee on unemployment we set up a vigorous organization with headquarters in the Department. I gave it personal direction.... Our other committees now expanded, undertook exhaustive research in two broad policies of reconstruction and development. Their reports over the years became landmarks in the progress of economic thought.
>
> These measures were singularly helpful and aided the natural recuperative power of the country. By the spring of 1922 economic forces had begun to recover, and we were soon over the unemployment hump.[11]

With Hoover's robust sponsorship as Secretary of Commerce, a new economic approach was formulated throughout the 1920s under the aegis of the President's Conference on Unemployment with staff support supplied by NBER researchers. In his *Memoirs*, Hoover observed:

> I determined the practical approach to the elimination of waste problem [meaning principally the "reduction of the great waste of booms and slumps of the 'business cycle' with their intermittent waves of unemployment and bankruptcy"[12]] by the Department of Commerce was to take up some area where progress was manifestly possible, thoroughly investigate its technology, and then to convene a preliminary meeting of representatives of that particular segment of the industry, business and labor. If the preliminary meeting developed a program, a committee was appointed to cooperate with us in its advancement. There was no dictation or force of law. During my term as Secretary of Commerce more than 3000 such conferences or committees were brought into action.[13]

11 Hoover (1951), pp. 44-6.

12 Ibid., p. 63.

13 Ibid., pp. 61-62.

In 1929, the Commerce Department issued its "Report from the Committee on Recent Economic Changes of the President's Conference on Unemployment" for the years 1922-1929. Entitled *Recent Economic Changes*, the document began:

> As an outgrowth of the President's Conference on Unemployment of 1921, three national surveys [were] set up to enlarge general understanding of our economic system and to stimulate the continuing reduction of unemployment. The first of these surveys was a study of Business Cycles and Unemployment made in 1922-23.... The second was a study of Seasonal Operation in the Construction Industries made in 1923-24.... [The third was a] survey of Recent Economic Changes begun in January 1928 and completed in February, 1929, [as] an analysis of post-war developments in American economic life, particularly since the recovery from the depression of 1920-21.[14]

Recent Economic Changes was based on surveys made under the auspices of the NBER with "the assistance of an unprecedented number of governmental and private agencies." The report emphasized, however, that "[w]hile the National Bureau is solely responsible for the basic survey, the committee is solely responsible for the interpretation of the facts set up in the following brief report."[15] At over 900 pages, the report was hardly brief.

Columbia University Professor Wesley Clair Mitchell, who was director of research for NBER, personally authored a 69-page "Review" that began on page 841 and ended the main body of the report. In the final text of his Review, Mitchell addressed "How Matters Stand in the Spring of 1929," where he gave a less than sanguine reading of the statistics compiled by NBER that was both eloquent and full of portent. Since Hoover's third economic advisory

---

14 NBER, *Recent Economic Changes in the United States*, 1929, p. v.

15 Ibid., p. v.

committee was "solely responsible for the interpretation," committee members presumably agreed with Mitchell, whose worrisome final statement was:

> Forecasting the future is no part of the present task. But we should not close the record without noting that recent developments may appear less satisfactory in retrospect than they appear at present.
>
> Even on the face of affairs, all is not well. Americans have seen more uniformly fortunate times: for example, in 1906, the Secretary of the Treasury was praying that the country might be delivered from more prosperity. The condition of agriculture, the volume of unemployment, the textile trades, coal mining, the leather industries, present grave problems not only to the people immediately concerned, but also to their fellow citizens. How rapidly these conditions will mend, we do not know. Some may grow worse.
>
> Nor can we be sure that the industries now prosperous will prolong indefinitely their recent record of stability. That we have not had a serious crisis since 1920 or a severe depression since 1921 is no guarantee that we shall be equally prudent, skillful and fortunate in the years to come. If we had to maintain business prosperity, we must continue to earn it month after month and year after year by intelligent effort. The incomes disbursed to consumers, and to wage earners in particular, must be increased on a scale sufficient to pay for the swelling volume of consumers' goods sent to market. The credit structure must be kept in adjustment to the earnings of business enterprises. Security prices must not outrun prospective profits capitalized at the going rate of interest. Commodity stocks must be held in line with current

> sales. Over-commitments of all sorts must be avoided. The building of new industrial equipment must not be over-rapid. These and the similar matters which might be mentioned present delicate problems of management which will find their practical solutions in the daily decisions of business executives. Perhaps errors are being kept within the limits of tolerance. Perhaps no serious setback will occur for years to come. But we are leaving 1921 well behind us, and there are signs that the caution inspired by that disastrous year is wearing thin.
>
> Whether the recent rate of progress in the arts of industry and business can be maintained is another uncertainty. Past experience, as summed up in the introductory chapter, suggests that the pace will slacken presently, and that years may pass before we see such another well-maintained advance. But that is a matter in which experience is not a trustworthy guide. Scientific research, industrial invention and business pioneering all lead into the unknown. They are fascinating ventures which energetic minds will ever be trying, whether the tangible rewards prove great or small. All that is certain is that whatever progress in efficiency we continue to make must be won by the same type of bold and intelligent work that has earned our recent successes.[16]

As spring bloomed in 1929, Herbert Hoover could not have said it better himself.

Heroic Strengths and Limitations

Herbert Clark Hoover was elected the 31st President of the United States in November 1928 by a landslide and was inaugurated

16 Ibid., pp. 909-10.

on March 4, 1929. Of his reputation, Hoover biographer Richard Norton Smith wrote:

> It was hard for thoughtful Americans in 1928 to conjure up anyone more ideally suited to be President. Hoover appeared more realistic than Wilson, more committed to excellence than Harding, more innovative than Coolidge, and more purely American than Al Smith. Dazzled by his achievements, few of his countrymen paused to investigate the price of success or calculate the odds on hero worship without hubris.[17]

Hoover combined the head of a brilliant mining engineer, international consultant, efficiency expert and highly experienced war and flood relief administrator with the heart of a true humanitarian. Mining a trove of presidential archives released in the 1970s, Hoover's biographers have revised and expanded the traditional view of him to describe a man of great breadth of vision together with an astonishing grasp of detail, who could see clearly opportunities that others missed. Under his leadership, broad-scale, workable plans were put together by some of the best and the brightest in his circle that were later mined and selectively implemented by a different-minded administration. As for his grasp of economics, according to Barber:

> As president, Herbert Hoover understood one of the basic insights of a theoretical system later to be identified as Keynesianism: that the behavior of the macroeconomic system is determined by the aggregate volume of spending. Indeed, he grasped this point as well as anyone did of his time — and better than did most of the economists in that period. This was the basis for his initial effort in depression fighting when he called for accelerated construction spending by public authorities and for increased capital outlays by the

17 Smith (1984), p. 102.

> major private investors. Similarly, his appeals to employers to resist wage cutting was a plank from what later would be regarded as a Keynesian platform.
>
> Nor did he lose sight of the importance of demand management when he made tactical adjustments to his programs in late 1931 and 1932.... In the circumstances of the time, the ultimate objective would be beyond reach unless an instrumental one, solvency in the banking system, could be secured first.[18]

Yet, despite all his qualities, qualifications and energy, Hoover's efforts during a multi-faceted national crisis were severely inhibited by an impediment—a flaw, to continue our Achilles heel analogy—having to do with his view of the proper role of the federal government. While we cede overall assessment of Hoover's psychology to experts, we offer a few revealing observations from the comprehensive 2004 study *Personality, Character, and Leadership in the White House* by psychologists Steven J. Rubenzer and Thomas R. Faschingbauer. To conduct their study, the authors asked 120 historians, biographers, presidential advisors and other experts to fill out standardized personality tests as well as the authors' own extensive questionnaire regarding the personal qualities of U.S. presidents. According to Rubenzer's and Faschingbauer's findings, Herbert Hoover was viewed an introvert; in tests rating the personality quality of extraversion, Hoover scored 3rd lowest (Coolidge was lowest). According to a Hoover anecdote the authors cited: "When political backers wanted to publicize his rescue of a child in China, he tore up the article and told them, 'You can't make a Teddy Roosevelt out of me.'"[19] Hoover scored high in the categories of Order (neat, tidy,

---

18 Ibid., p. 189.

19 Steven Rubenzer and Thomas R. Faschingbauer, *Personality, Character, and Leadership in the White House*, Potomac Books, Inc., 2004, p. 63.

well-organized; thorough)[20] and Conscientiousness,[21] but he scored low on Agreeableness and "Readiness to reexamine (or reject) social, political and religious values; unconventional."[22] Overall, the authors concluded that for Hoover, along with John Quincy Adams, "[t]he presidency was the least successful facet of his career."[23]

Barber's account offered further insights into Hoover's personality strengths and weaknesses and his skills, particularly as Hoover confronted economic conditions that tested his nature and beliefs and revealed, again, his Achilles heel:

> Hoover's actions — though not his words — suggest that he had an intuitive comprehension of the mechanisms of income determination which was in advance of the thinking of most professional economists. Why then did his management of a depression economy fail so disastrously? A conceptualization that specifies the dimensions of the fundamental problem is a crucial step in the formulation of effective policies. But this alone is not sufficient. Results depend on the successful implementation of programs that the analysis suggests are required. The Achilles heel of the Hoover administration was its inability to follow through with the second step. In part this shortcoming may be attributed to the political and cultural environment of the times. It was also, in part, a reflection of constraints on action which were self-imposed. The latter were the more important. A leader can try to change society's perceptions of the proper way things should be done. But he can only do so when he himself is prepared to break from the conventional mold. This was something that Hoover was hesitant to do publicly. Behind the scenes, he could be highly innovative

20 Ibid., p. 14.
21 Ibid., p. 28.
22 Ibid., p. 12.
23 Ibid., p. 125.

> in packaging programs to widen his freedom of maneuver. But there were still limits beyond which this exercise could not be pressed. The end product had to be presentable in a way that kept it within the bounds of Hoover's conception of the legitimate scope of federal authority.
>
> This was the root of a fundamental tension in the mindset of the Hoover administration. The diagnosis of the ills of the economy was reasonably well in hand. But the president's willingness to prescribe remedies was bounded by the premises of his political philosophy. Foremost was the importance he attached to the principals of constitutionalism which defined the division of jurisdictions between various governmental units and limited the scope of federal intervention in the private economy. [24]

In summation, in Hoover's mind his reservations regarding the role of the federal government "limited the scope of federal intervention in the private economy." They allowed presidential diagnoses of the problems and even prescriptions for return to health, but they prevented presidential action in terms of doing whatever was necessary to put the needed remedies into effect.

Is it fair to characterize Hoover's principles as flawed, when he was so capable and masterful in overseeing the development of analyses and plans for getting America out of the Great Depression? Perhaps. To Hoover, who wrote the aptly titled *American Individualism*, the belief in America's uniqueness in allowing and facilitating individual enterprise and initiative was real and important to him (and to many others at the time), but it inhibited his presidential actions at a personal, fundamental level. After he left office in 1933, he wrote *The Challenge to Liberty* in which he explained his objectives in governance as preserving and providing opportunities to citizens and avoiding regimentation and acts that some might consider dictatorial. American citizens were at liberty to benefit financially, as

24 Ibid, p. 190.

entrepreneurs do, by putting presidential prescriptions into effect. In Hoover's mind the federal government had neither the right nor the liberty to deprive citizens of the opportunities to get well *on their own.*

Is there a statement by Hoover as President explaining his unwillingness to act? Yes, there is. Hoover's convictions were very clearly stated in his veto of the controversial Muscle Shoals Bill authorizing the construction of a dam on the Tennessee River at government expense and the sale of the electricity produced. In the veto statement he delivered to Congress on March 3, 1931, he described the proposed purpose of the legislation:

> This bill proposes the transformation of the war plant at Muscle Shoals, together with important expansions, into a permanently operated government institution for the production and distribution of [electrical] power and the manufacture of fertilizers.
>
> I am firmly opposed to the government entering into any business the major purpose of which is competition with our citizens. There are national emergencies which require that the government should temporarily enter the field of business, but they must be...matters where the cost of the project is secondary to much higher considerations.... But for the federal government deliberately to go out and build up and expand such an occasion to the major purpose of a power and manufacturing business is to break down the initiative and enterprise of the American people; it is the negation of the ideals upon which our civilization has been based.
>
> I hesitate to contemplate the future of our institutions, of our government, and of our country if the preoccupation of its officials is to be no longer the promotion of justice and equal opportunity but is to be devoted to barter in the

markets....

This bill...would invade and weaken the authority of local government.... The real development of the resources in the industries of the Tennessee Valley can only be accomplished by the people in the valley themselves.... Any other course deprives them of liberty.[25]

The carefully researched and analyzed results of Hoover's many committees and conferences were available and ready for action when in March 1933 the Roosevelt administration began with a new philosophy of government. In his first 100 days in office, for instance, Franklin Roosevelt and the Congress chartered the Tennessee Valley Authority to pursue the very enterprise that Hoover had vetoed in 1931.

Hoover was certainly comfortable with the federal government, and with its agencies such as the Federal Reserve acting as "lender of last resort." His farm aid program and the Reconstruction Finance Corporation, enacted in 1932, became a backbone of the New Deal. But in his profound personal belief in protecting and providing for individual liberty, he considered it unprincipled and improper for the federal government to act as "entrepreneur of last resort." Unfortunately, the Great Depression needed more than lending. It needed action at the federal level and the attendant funding to act.

Given the drastic countrywide circumstances, Hoover's unwillingness to reexamine and adjust his principles to the reality of the times became the flaws that delayed desperately needed federal action and cost him the presidency. The engineer and efficiency expert in him, however, made substantial contributions to the field of economic research that have been incalculably valuable for future generations, including the authors of this book.

---

25 *Herbert Hoover, The Annals of America, Volume 15*, Encyclopedia Britannica, 1968, pp. 79-82.

CHAPTER 3

The (Keynesian) Income-Expenditure Approach

MANY ECONOMISTS HAVE POINTED to a vertiginous drop in business investment as perhaps the pivotal cause of the Great Depression. As we saw in Chapter 1, NIPA statistics for 1929-33 showed fixed investment by businesses plummeting nearly 80%. In fact, prior to the publication in 1963 of *A Monetary History of the United States, 1867-1960*, (hereafter referred to as *Monetary History*) by monetarists Milton Friedman and Anna J. Schwartz, most economists explained what happened in 1929-33 using the income-expenditure approach, according to which, among a number of influences and factors, "a collapse in investment" was preeminent.

The income-expenditure approach to analyzing economic conditions is now associated with economist John Maynard Keynes, but, because Keynes's pivotal book, *The General Theory of Employment, Interest, and Money,* was not published until 1936, we chose to place Keynesian, a term not used until well after Hoover left office, in parenthesis in the title of this chapter. We now offer a review of American economic thinking at the time of the Depression, including Keynes's own developing theories, as well as economic policy decisions President Hoover made during his term in office which ended March 4, 1933.

Economic Policy Thinking in America in 1929-1933

While economics was relatively new as a distinct academic field and subject taught at colleges and universities at the beginning of the 1930s — it was only newly released from the study of "political economics" to stand on its own — the country had many economists inclining toward an incipient income-expenditure approach for addressing the worsening economic situation. According to economics professor J. Ronnie Davis in *The New Economics and the Old Economists*, published in 1971:

> [American] economists representing the classical tradition were more Keynesian in their policy prescriptions [in 1930-36] than they are commonly credited (or blamed) for being. Leading economists did not favor what has come to be understood as the typical classical prescription — reduction of money wages — but instead took the typically Keynesian position that aggregate demand had to be increased and that the best way to do this was through public expenditures financed by bond issues.... [1] Keynes cannot claim to have converted leading members of the economics profession to his views on policy, for the reason that the profession already held his views (in some cases, before he did).[2]

In Chapter 2, we learned how President Hoover initiated the development of an economic stabilization strategy within weeks of becoming Secretary of Commerce in 1921, and while his implementation efforts may have been hampered by his "flawed" political philosophy that held it improper for government to compete in the business realm with private citizens and corporations and prevented the government from acting as "entrepreneur of last resort," he pursued his strategy's elaboration, publicization and dissemination throughout the 1920s. In the process, professional economists throughout America could hardly avoid becoming familiar with at

1 L. Ronnie Davis, *The New Economics and the Old Economists,* The Iowa State University Press, 1971, p. xv. For "American" see p. ix and for "1930-36" see the last sentence on p. 153.

2 Ibid., p. 7.

least the concept of government spending on public works timed to smooth fluctuations in business activity and employment as well as with deficit financing as necessitated by various Hoover programs, ultimately including the Reconstruction Finance Corporation.

Keynes Gets the First Word

In *The Keynesian Revolution*, University of Pennsylvania's Nobel-laureate and Keynesian economist Lawrence R. Klein positioned Keynes's thinking as of the outset of the Depression:

> A period of swift intellectual growth was concluded with the appearance in 1930 of the famous *Treatise on Money.* Economists eagerly awaited this long-publicized work, which Keynes had been writing over many years. We are told in the preface that many of the author's ideas underwent great change during the process of writing this *Treatise*; and one reviewer has characterized the book as a transitory phase of rapid development. The most striking characteristic of the *Treatise* is its loosely knit theory with many lines of thought incomplete. But we can accept this book as the summation of all the lines of thought covered in the several debates of the 1920s…with the possible exception of the question of public works schemes brought up in the elections of 1929 [sic].[3]

According to MIT economist and economic historian Peter Temin, "Keynes gave what may be the first expression of the spending approach as it applied in the Great Depression in the *Treatise on*

3 Lawrence R. Klein, *The Keynesian Revolution*, McMillan Publishers, 1966, p. 15. We believe the elections Klein referenced were in 1928 not 1929.

Money."[4] Temin went on to quote Keynes:

> The boom of 1928-9 and the slump of 1929-30 in the United States correspond respectively to an excess and to a deficiency of investment.[5].... I attribute the slump of 1930 primarily to the deterrent effects on investment of the long period of dear money which preceded the stock-market collapse, and only secondarily to the collapse itself. But the collapse having occurred, it greatly aggravated matters, especially in the United States, by causing a disinvestment in working capital.[6]

Professor Klein, from his vantage point more than three decades later, explained Keynes's thinking in 1930 within the context of traditional economic thought as it stood at the start of the Great Depression:

> We can describe the *Treatise* as a book in classical economics based on two important and well-known theories. These two theories are the business-cycle theory which makes investment fluctuations the prime mover of the capitalist system...and the theory that the rate of interest is determined in equilibrium by the equality of savings and investment....
>
> Briefly, the argument of the *Treatise* ran as follows: The business cycle is caused by fluctuations in the rate of investment relative to the rate of savings. This notion is based on the theories of Tougan Baranovski, Spiethoff, Schumpeter, and Robertson. In fact, Schumpeter's theory of innovations was unreservedly accepted by Keynes as the moving force of

4 Temin (1976), p. 31.

5 Keynes, *The Treatise on Money*, Vol. 2, 1930, p. 194. (In The Royal Economic Society 1971 edition this is p. 174.)

6 Ibid., p. 196. (In The Royal Economic Society 1971 edition this is p. 176.)

> the capitalist fluctuations. According, however, to the interest theory, fluctuations in the market rate of interest about the natural rate (the rate which would equate savings and investment) are uniquely related to the fluctuations in the discrepancy between savings and investment which in turn are related to fluctuations in the price level. Then Keynes argued that investment is the really dynamic factor which fluctuates when the market and natural rates of interest diverge, and that the fluctuations in prices are a result of the discrepancies generated between savings and investment.[7]

Monocausal Theories — A Warning

It is important to recognize that many factors influence the business cycle. According to Harvard professor Gottfried Haberler writing in the late fifties:

> Such a complex phenomenon as the business cycle, which embraces almost all parts of the economic system, does not easily lend itself to explanation by any one factor. Even if we assume from the beginning that the same explanation of the business cycle holds good in the highly industrialized countries of Western Europe and America as well as in the industrially less developed countries such as New Zealand or Romania, and in the twentieth century as well as at the beginning of the nineteenth—neither of which assumptions is by any means self-evident—it is not easy to speak of *the* cause of a business cycle. Few writers have ventured to proclaim just one single factor as the cause of the business cycle or of depression in particular. In fact, explanations which run in terms of one single cause have been more and more discredited and should be regarded with suspicion. The majority of modern writers on the subject are careful to point

7 L. Klein (1966), pp. 15-6.

> out that a whole set of factors, and perhaps not always the same combination of factors, contribute toward producing an alternation of prosperity and depression. [8]

In the chapters ahead, we will offer insights into how economic theories of all stripes are supported or counter-indicated by the factual evidence in data.

April 1931 — Professor Wesley C. Mitchell on the Causes of Depressions

On April 24, 1931, the venerable Academy of Political Science (founded in 1880) held a conference on Depressions and Revival at New York's Astor Hotel at which Columbia professor Wesley C. Mitchell, the aforementioned leading expert in business cycles who was also then serving as chief of research at the NBER, led a discussion on the causes of depression. His concluding talk, published in the proceedings of the conference in June, gave an excellent overview of how economists of the time were trying to understand the complexity of factors in the situation they faced. Mitchell's own words summarized the discussion and also revealed an important aspect of his own particular orientation:

> This morning's discussion illustrates admirably the complexity of the problem with which we are wrestling. Many economists speak of "the cause" of cyclical fluctuations in business, as if some single antecedent explains the multiform results. Our program committee revealed a different conception when they chose as the title for this session "Causes

8 Gottfried Haberler, *Prosperity and Depression,* The League of Nations, 1937, pp. 5-6.

of Depression."[9]

After summarizing briefly each presentation made during the morning meeting, Mitchell continued, placing emphasis on cyclical factors:

> Each of our speakers in his turn has been persuasive. Nor, in attempting to sum up the whole discussion, do I see reason for rejecting as wrong or unimportant any line of analysis suggested. Emotional errors in business judgment, monetary and banking policies, political unrest, tariff changes, the plight of agriculture, and other factors not mentioned, have all contributed to make the business depression of 1930-31 exceptionally severe and exceptionally wide in its geographic sweep.
>
> If our interest lay solely in seeking to understand this one depression, we might rest content with the listing of the factors involved and an attempt to make up their relative importance. [I]f we seek to gain such an understanding of economic processes as will help us to avoid future misfortunes of the sort we now suffer, then we must ask how far the depression of 1930-31 is due to cyclical factors proper and how far it is due to influences which are unlikely to recur in their present combination.
>
> Study of the many business cycles is the safest guide in an effort to disengage the recurrent from the non-recurrent causes of depression. On the basis of such study I venture the following opinions. Political stability both affects and is affected by business conditions; but there is no regular conformity between political upsets and cyclical depressions. A

9 Wesley Mitchell, *Business Cycles and Their Cause*, University of California Press, 1931, p. 82.

similar remark applies to tariff changes. Also the fortunes of farmers run a course which is very far from parallel with the course of business cycles. Thus I would classify [these three] influences … as random factors. By this I do not mean that future business cycles will be uninfluenced by politics, tariffs and farming. But I see no reason to expect that the political, tariff and agricultural factors will be regularly favorable to business during prosperity and regularly unfavorable to business during depression.

[P]ast experience does justify us in saying that business sentiment, industrial output, monetary and banking conditions fluctuate with the activity of trade….

When economic life is organized predominantly on the basis of making and spending money incomes, all economic activities become mutually interdependent. This mutual interdependence gives rise to business cycles. Prosperity in any part of the system tends to spread to other parts, and to become more intense. But prosperity carried beyond certain limits creates difficulties, which spread from their points of origin, become grave, and bring on recessions in activity. Contraction then spreads and cumulates in its turn; but it ultimately works out conditions which start a revival of activity. Thus, our economic organization develops within itself rhythmical alternations of expansion and contraction.

Besides this mutual interdependence among different processes which leads to business cycles, our economic organization is a second characteristic which causes endless complications in the cyclical movements.

Business is sensitive to almost everything which affects

human life. It is notably sensitive to the effects produced by weather, by inventions, by fashions, by politics—to name but a few factors. All the time, finance, trade and industry are feeling the influence of a host of changes which arise outside the business realm and have no organic connection with its rhythm. Some of these random factors are favorable to business activity; some are unfavorable. The favorable and unfavorable random factors may offset each other at a given time, or one set may preponderate over the other. What course in any given business cycle follows depends in large measure upon the particular constellation of the random influences which it encounters. Indeed, the cyclical movements make use of these influences from outside the realm of business; they cumulate and enhance effects of all the favorable or unfavorable influences which bear on the markets. Were it not for continual changes in these random circumstances, business cycles would be far more regular than they are in duration and intensity.

To apply this analysis to the depression of 1930-31 is not difficult. The general rhythm of business made a recession probable in 1929. That recession took a catastrophic form in the stock market, because of the follies committed during the proceeding speculation. The depression which followed was bound to be characterized by severe financial liquidation. It was rendered still more severe by the depression of agriculture, by the raising of tariff barriers in the way of commerce, by political unrest and fears. The constellation of random factors—of which I have mentioned only a few—was exceptionally unfavorable in its cast, and influenced most of the great commercial nations in the same way. Hence depression in the United States was aggravated by depression in Europe, and depression in Europe was aggravated by depression in United States.

> On some such lines as these, I think, we can incorporate all the contributions made this morning in a consistent explanation of the present depression. All that is needed to complete the explanation is treatment of several other random factors in addition to those here discussed, and an analysis of the way in which *cyclical fluctuations originate in the business realm.*[10] (emphasis ours)

With this definitive conclusion about the origins of cyclical fluctuations, written in the midst of a tumultuous global downturn, Mitchell reflected on the prevailing assumption among his fellow economists limited their focus to functions that originated in the business realm to explain broader cycling economic experience . The limitations of this assumption are at the heart of the explorations we undertake within these pages. We also emphasize that Mitchell commented on neither deflation nor on the sizable repayment of bank loans *by consumers,* both taking place in accelerating volume in 1930 and 1931.

We now turn to John Maynard Keynes himself, who in 1931 visited the United States and witnessed first-hand depression conditions that had set in.

June 1931 — Keynes Gives Three Lectures in Chicago

In 1973, a team of respectful and thorough editors began publishing *The Collected Writings of John Maynard Keynes,* the mammoth twenty-nine volume series that included Keynes's prodigious scholarly output in addition to his extensive correspondence with many notable people of the times. According to the editors' introduction to Keynes's Chicago trip:

> In June 1931, Keynes contributed to the Harris Foundation lecture series in Chicago three lectures entitled 'An

10 Ibid., pp. 398-400.

> Economic Analysis of Unemployment' which although they were not couched in *Treatise* terms, gave some indications of further development [toward the writing of *The General Theory*] with their greater emphasis on movements in output... and their hints of equilibrium at less than full employment.[11]

In his first lecture, entitled, "The Originating Causes of World-Unemployment," Keynes gave a brief history of the later years of the 1920s in order to identify the originating causes of the slump and then devoted himself to analyzing and explaining those causes:

> The leading characteristic [of the period] was an extraordinary willingness to borrow money for the purposes of new real investment at very high rates.... This free borrowing was duly accompanied by capital expansion [programs].
>
> While some part of the investment which was going on in the world...was doubtless ill judged and unfruitful, there can...be no doubt that the world was enormously enriched by the constructions of the quinquennium from 1925 to 1929; its wealth increased in these five years by as much as in any other ten or twenty years of its history. The expansion centered round building, the electrification of the world, and the associated enterprises of roads and motor cars. In those five years an appreciable change was effected in the housing, the power plant, and the transport system of a large part of the world. But it was not unduly specialized. Almost every department of capital development took its share....
>
> It is not necessary for my present purpose to decide exactly how far this investment boom was inflationary.... But I think that the evidence suggests that the savings were

11 *CW of JMK, Vol. XIII* (1973), p. 343.

in fact abundantly available and were adequate to finance a very large part of the investment....

Some austere and puritanical souls regard it both as an inevitable and a desirable nemesis on so much over-expansion, as they call it; a nemesis on man's speculative spirit.... We need, they say, what they politely call a 'prolonged liquidation' to put us right. The liquidation, they tell us, is not yet complete. But in time it will be. And when sufficient time has elapsed for completion of the liquidation, all will be well with us again.

I do not take this view. I find the explanation of the current business losses, of the reduction of output, and of the unemployment which necessarily ensues on this not in the high level of investment which was proceeding up to the spring of 1929, but in the subsequent cessation of this investment. I see no hope of a recovery except in a revival of the high level of investment.... I suggest to you, therefore, that the questions to which we have to bend our intelligence are the causes of the collapse of investment and the means of reviving investment....

My assumption is this: I have taken it for granted so far that if the volume of investment falls off, then of necessity the level of business profits falls away also.... It will be my duty, therefore, to endeavor in my next lecture to give you an outline of this reasoning in terms as well adapted as I can find for the medium of oral exposition. [12]

In Keynes's second lecture, entitled, "The Abstract Analysis

12 Ibid., p. 345-51. We have quoted Keynes exactly as he wrote in *CW of JMK,* including his use of British spelling and some instances of words no longer in common usage.

of the Slump," he began by describing what he called "the costs of production," including wages, rents, interest, etc. He then explained "[t]he value of current investment" as being what businesses pay for "various kinds of currently produced capital goods" (we would add "and associated services."). To Keynes, the costs of production equaled the incomes of the public which consisted of what they 1) spent on consumption plus 2) what they saved. Thus, one part of business income is derived from the sale of goods and services to consumers while another part of business income is derived from the sale of capital goods (and associated services) to businesses. Keynes elucidated on this idea:

> It follows, if you have been able to catch what I am saying, that when the value of current investment is greater than the savings of the public, the receipts of the entrepreneurs are greater than their costs, so they make a profit; and when, on the other hand, the value of current investment is less than the savings of the public, the receipts of the entrepreneurs will be less than their costs, so that they make a loss....
>
> The whole matter may be summed up by saying that a boom is generated when investment exceeds saving and a slump is generated when saving exceeds investment. But behind this simplicity there lie, I am only too well aware, many complexities, many pitfalls, many opportunities for misunderstanding. You must excuse me if I slide over these, for it would take me weeks to expound them fully. Indeed, let me simplify further, for I should like for a moment to leave the variations in saving out of my argument.... I shall concentrate on the variability of the rate of investment. For that is, in fact, the element in the economic situation which is capable of sudden and violent change.... [I]t is out of the disequilibriums of savings and investment, and out of nothing else, that the fluctuations of profits, of output, and

of employment are generated.

> It is important to notice that so long as output is declining the effect of any decline of fixed investment is aggravated by disinvestment in working capital.... [This] ceases as soon as output ceases to decline further even though the level at which output is steady is a very low one. And as soon as output begins to recover, even though it still remains at a very low level, the tide is turned and the decline in fixed investment is partly offset by increased investment in working capital.[13]

After discussing the effect of variations in savings, Keynes concluded his second lecture:

> There can, therefore, I argue, be no secure basis for a return to an equilibrium of prosperity except a recovery of fixed investment to a level commensurate with that of the national savings in prosperous times.[14]

Keynes began his final lecture, optimistically entitled, considering what yet lay ahead, "The Road to Recovery," by assuredly stating his views regarding causation of the slump:

> Whether or not my confidence is justified, I feel, then, no serious doubt or hesitation whatever as to the causes of the world slump. I trace it wholly to the breakdown of investment throughout the world. After being held by a variety of factors at a fairly high level during most of the post-war period, the volume of this investment has during the past two and a half years suffered an enormous decline — a decline not fully compensated as yet by diminished savings or by government deficits.

13 Ibid., pp. 352-5.

14 Ibid., pp. 355-8.

> The problem of recovery is, therefore, a problem of re-establishing the volume of investment. The solution of this problem has two sides to it: on the one hand, a fall in the long-term rate of investment [interest?] so as to bring a new range of propositions within the practical sphere; and, on the other hand, a return of confidence to the business world so as to incline them to borrow on the basis of normal expectations of the future. But the two aspects are by no means disconnected. For business confidence will not revive except with the experience of improving business profits. And… business profits will not recover except with an increase of investment….We need, therefore, to work meanwhile for a drastic fall in the long term rate of interest so that full advantage may be taken of any recovery of confidence. (square brackets and question mark in original)

> The problem of recovery is also, in my judgment, indissolubly bound up with the restoration of prices to a higher level…. [T]he raising of prices is an essential ingredient in my policy…. My own conclusion is that there are certain fundamental reasons…for wishing prices to rise…. The first reason is on grounds of social stability and concord…. [T]he Second reason for wishing prices to rise is on grounds of social justice and expediency…. [f]or the burden of monetary indebtedness in the world is already so heavy that any material addition would render it intolerable…. If our object is to remedy employment it is obvious that we must first of all make business more profitable. In other words, the problem is to cause business receipts to rise relatively to business costs…. [15]

By 1931, as the price indexes of the period show, prices were

15 Ibid., pp. 358-362.

falling dramatically and deflation was occurring.[16] On an un-restated monthly basis, the WPI fell 24.2% over a period of twenty-one months from 95.1 in October 1929 to 72.1 in June 1931, the very month that Keynes made his trip to Chicago.[17] The Consumer Price Index was 11.3% lower in 1931 than it had been in 1929. It was in these circumstances that Keynes spoke in Chicago. He continued within his third lecture:

> The cumulative argument for wishing prices to rise appears to me, therefore, to be overwhelming, as I hope it does to you.
>
> Let us now return to our main theme. The cure of unemployment involves improving business profits.... The problem resolves itself, therefore, into the question as to what means we can adopt to increase the volume of investment, which you will remember means in my terminology the expenditure of money on the output of new capital goods of whatever kind.
>
> When I have said this, I have, strictly speaking, said all that an economist as such is entitled to say. What remains is essentially a technical banking problem. The practical means by which investment can be increased is, or ought to be, the bankers' business, and preeminently the business of the central banker. But you will not consider that I have completed my task unless I give some indication of the methods which are open to the banker.
>
> There are, in short, three lines of approach. The first line of approach is the restoration of confidence both to the lender and to the borrower.... The borrower...must have sufficient confidence in the business prospects to believe that he has a reasonable prospect of earning sufficient return from a

16 See *The Deflation of 1930* for further discussion, including showing the price indexes restated for 1929=100.

17 *HSUS, 1789-1945,* p. 344 (App. 23).

new investment proposition.... Failing the restoration of confidence, we may easily have a vicious circle set up in which...the lender requires...a higher rate than the borrower believes he can earn.... The second line of approach consists in new construction [programs] under the direct auspices of the government or other public authorities. Theoretically, it seems to me, there is everything to be said for action along these lines.... The third line of approach consists in a reduction in the long-term rate of interest....[A] sufficient change in the rate of interest must surely bring within the horizon all kinds of projects which are out of the question at the present rate of interest....

As I look at it, indeed, the task of adjusting the long-term rate of interest to the technical possibilities of our age so that the demand for new capital is as nearly as possible equal to the community's current volume of savings must be the prime objective of financial statesmanship. It may not be easy and a large change may be needed, but there is no other way out.

Finally, how is the banking system to affect the long-term rate of interest? For *prima facie* the banking system is concerned with the short-term rate of interest rather than the long.

In the course of time I see no insuperable difficulty....I suggest to you that there are three ways in which it is reasonable to hope to exercise an influence in this direction.

The first method is to increase the quantity of liquid assets—in other words, to increase the basis of credit by means of open-market operations ... on the part of the central bank.... The second course is to diminish the attractions of liquid assets by lowering the rate of deposit interest....[I]t seems to me that the rate of interest allowed on liquid assets should be reduced as nearly as possible to the vanishing-point.

The third method is to increase the attractions of non-liquid assets, which, however, brings us back again in effect to our first remedy, namely, methods of increasing confidence.

For my own part, I should have thought it desirable to advance along all three fronts simultaneously. But the central idea that I wish to leave with you is the vital necessity for a society, living in the phase in which we are living today, to bring down the long term rate of interest at a pace appropriate to the underlying facts. As houses and equipment of every kind increase in quantity we ought to be growing richer on the principle of compound interest.... Thus we need to pay constant conscious attention to the long-term rate of interest for fear that our vast resources may be running to waste through a failure to direct our savings into constructive uses...which should, if everything was proceeding smoothly in a well-governed society, lead us within a few generations to the complete abolition of oppressive economic want.[18]

Having reached the end of Keynes's three lectures, we think it desirable to summarize his "wish list." Keynes wanted to:

- Raise fixed investment to a level commensurate with that of savings in prosperous times,
- Restore confidence and raise business profits,
- Initiate new construction programs under public authorities,

18 *CW of JMK, Vol. XIII* (1973), pp. 362-7.

- Reduce the *long-term rate of interest* and achieve equilibrium of investment with saving, and

- Raise prices to achieve social stability and concord, manage the heavy burden of indebtedness, and raise business receipts relative to business costs.

While we these few generations later still await that "complete abolition of oppressive economic want" he had hoped for, we now leave Keynes, but not Chicago, and turn to University of Chicago professor and influential early economist, Jacob Viner.

An Early Deficit Financing Policy Proposal

While analyzing the complex factors that cause a depression was important, addressing conditions requiring specific actions was becoming an increasingly urgent necessity. Hoover's Economic Stabilization Strategy suggested smoothing the business cycle by engaging in public works projects during slumps. Such a policy that would cause even temporary deficits outside of war was a controversial idea. Economists and many elected officials of the time rigidly adhered to the mandate of "sound finance" which included a balanced federal budget as one of its bedrock components. J. Ronnie Davis, economics professor and author of *The New Economics and the Old Economists* weighed in on one such proposal put forward by Professor Jacob Viner of the University of Chicago in 1933. By then, economic thinking was expanding rapidly in response to the obdurate economic conditions, experience with the Reconstruction Finance Corporation and other programs, and a new political philosophy in the White House. While the Chicagoans did not depart from the position that a drop in business investment precipitated the current depression (Davis cited Paul Douglas who in 1934 "clearly pointed to changes in the rate of investment as the initiating cause of depression."[19]), Davis wrote of Professor Viner's bold recommendation that the most promising method of combating a depression was "governmental expenditures financed by borrowing from the banking system, with the hope that what the banks lend is newly created credit or credit which otherwise would have remained idle."[20] Davis continued:

> [Professor] Viner made it clear that sound principles of public finance justified unbalanced budgets. During depression, government clearly should incur an excess of expenditures over revenues, the deficit being financed either by creating new bank credit or resorting to the printing press.…
>
> Then Viner advanced a notion which, by 1933, Chicago economists had helped to make familiar. If the budget was to be balanced it should be balanced over the business cycle as the outcome of using public spending to compensate for changes in private spending.…

---

19 Davis (1971), p. 49.

20 Ibid., p. 44-5. Davis cited in a footnote Jacob Viner, "Inflation as a Remedy for Depression," Proceedings of the Institute for Public Affairs, Seventh Annual Session (Athens, GA: University of Georgia, 1933). Viner, 1930s Chicago School mentor and adviser to Milton Friedman and Paul Samuelson, also advised Treasury Secretary Henry Morgenthau and helped in the initial planning of the Social Security system.

> Within the profession Jacob Viner was an economist of no little influence by the early 1930s.... Well known as a theoretician, Viner was, moreover, concerned with economic policy. Along with his colleagues at the University of Chicago, he launched more than one attack on the sponsors of retrenchment. Viner recognized that at less than full employment outputs, expansionary fiscal policy should be administered to induce movements toward increased output and employment of productive factors. The whole notion of balancing the budget over the business cycle, for that matter, was linked directly to the notion of full employment output.[21]

The Evolution of the Keynesian Income-Expenditure Approach in the Real World

The Keynesian income-expenditure approach has evolved in many ways since the publication of Keynes's *General Theory.* One way is in the application of Keynesian concepts to the field of econometric modeling, which has evolved in complexity with the steady progress in statistical methods and computing capabilities. Lawrence Klein (1920-2013), for example, received the Nobel Prize in 1980 "for the creation of econometric models and their application to the analysis of economic fluctuations and economic policies." Klein's Ph.D. dissertation became the 1946 book, *The Keynesian Revolution.* Twenty years later, in 1966, he published a second edition in which he reassessed his thinking regarding the development of the Keynesian approach. In a new chapter entitled "The Keynesian Revolution

---

21 It is not within the scope of this book to provide a comprehensive survey of the thinking of professional American economists in the period 1929-33. For this we urge readers to refer to the very fine books of Professors Barber and Davis. While Keynes's *General Theory* has had a profound effect on the thinking of professional economists, explaining his theories set forth in his *General Theory* is also beyond the scope of this book. We also encourage readers interested in exploring Keynes's thinking to consider *Keynes: Useful Economics for the World Economy,* written by Peter Temin and David Vines and published in 2014.

Revisited," Klein wrote:

> For most of [the last 20 years], I have concentrated my attention on statistical studies of the consumption, investment, and liquidity preference functions and on economy-wide models. It is now time to turn this attention, to some extent, at least, to the interpretation of empirical findings....
>
> The primary contentions of Keynesian theory as set down in this book can be summarized in a form that gives us scientific agreement on our terms of reference. The Keynesian system is
>
> - A theory of the determination of total income (output or employment).
> - A theoretical explanation of the possibility of under-employment equilibrium.
> - A group of doctrines in public policy about how to control the economy at the desired levels of economic activity.
> - A long-run view on the historical trend of capitalism.
>
> I shall consider all these main contentions of Keynesian theory, but principally, I am concerned with the first and second. I want to re-examine the theory of income determination in the light of our knowledge of the actual functioning of the economy, a knowledge that has been built up by econometrics studies....
>
> The pillars of the model of income determination are widely recognized as the marginal propensity to consume (or save), the marginal efficiency of capital, and liquidity preference.... I want to emphasize that this is only a crude

> framework for thinking and illustrating main ideas. It has teaching attributes but obscures so much of life that it cannot be thought of as a *working* model.
>
> The trouble with this simple model is that it cannot be extended from a theory of income determination to a theory of employment without making it more complicated.[22] (emphasis in original)

Professor Klein devoted the remainder of his book to elaborating on processes and conclusions of econometric analysis. As regarding the work of Keynes, he stated:

> My feeling now is that the *General Theory* is an intellectual breakthrough, but that it is too simple for judging the real world.... The theory must be regarded as a *core* theory with *kernels* of truth. It needs substantial amplification for reaching the whole truth. Also, it does not rest on a carefully laid and well-documented statistical base.[23] (emphasis in original)

We join Professor Klein in acknowledging the *General Theory* as an intellectual breakthrough. We, indeed, sought and identified evidence of the empirical findings Klein referenced and will introduce this evidence in Chapter 6.

Guidance, a Caution and Several Hints

Since Keynes, as well as before, many economists have considered the level of business investment as the pivotal factor in the fluctuation of business cycles. Klein and Temin both pointed to statements Keynes made back in 1930. According to Klein, "Briefly, the argument of the Treatise ran as follows: The business cycle is caused by fluctuations in the rate of investment relative to the rate

22 L. Klein (1966), pp. 191-3.

23 Ibid., pp. 197-8.

of savings." Temin called attention to Keynes's statement that, "I attribute the slump of 1930 primarily to the deterrent effects on investment...greatly aggravated...in the United States, by...a disinvestment in working capital.

We have been guided by eminent economists who have warned against relying on a single factor as "the cause" of cyclical fluctuations in business. As Professor Haberler wrote, "Such a complex phenomenon as the business cycle, which embraces almost all parts of the economic system, does not easily lend itself to explanation by any one factor." As a crucial example, we believe we should sound a note of caution as to Professor Mitchell's concluding statement, "All that is needed to complete the explanation is...an analysis of the way in which cyclical fluctuations *originate in the business realm*"[24](emphasis ours)

"Core" thinking of the income-expenditure approach focuses on a collapse in investment, which certainly does originate in the business sector and definitely took place in 1929-33. Decreased spending by businesses is an important causal factor (among others) of the Great Depression. But we consider this core thinking as a kind of bias in Mitchell and others that inhibited researchers from looking *outside the business realm* for other potential causal factors. For this book, we have done just that. Even Keynes failed to take into account this economic thrust outside the business realm. As we have seen, Keynes's focus was on "the variability of the rate of investment.... For that is, in fact, the element in the economic situation which is capable of sudden and violent change."

Our research revealed documentary evidence indicating that a major cause of the Great Depression actually originated outside the business realm. In fact, based on our analysis, it is evident that the great majority of the activity of this outside factor arose in the *consumer sector of the economy* and that the Crash brought about a sudden and radical reversal in the behavior of a significant portion

24 Mitchell, (1931), pp.398-400.

of the American population largely made up of consumers. In the chapters ahead, we will thoroughly explore this consumer-based behavior as very possibly the major cause of the severity and long duration of the Great Depression.

Meanwhile, since the 1960s, another highly influential explanation of the cause of the Depression has held sway: the major school of economic thinking known as monetarism. Questioning the effectiveness of government intervention and advocating remedies focusing instead on monetary policy, including action by the Federal Reserve, monetarism is the subject of our next chapter.

CHAPTER 4

The Monetary Approach

We now turn to Milton Friedman and Anna J. Schwartz and their seminal, highly influential work, *A Monetary History of the United States, 1867-1960* (hereafter referred to as *Monetary History*), published in 1963. In this widely relied upon analysis, they argued that failures of the Federal Reserve System led to the Great Depression. They set a somber tone for their approach to the period they called "The Great Contraction"—instead of the generally used Great Depression—in Chapter 7 of their *Monetary History*:

> THE CONTRACTION from 1929 to 1933 was by far the most severe business-cycle contraction during the near-century of U.S. history that we cover and it may well have been the most severe in the whole of U.S. history. Though sharper and more prolonged in the United States than in most other countries, it was worldwide in scope and ranks as the most severe and widely diffused international contraction of modern times. U.S. net national product in current prices fell by more than one-half from 1929 to 1933; net national product in constant dollars by more than one-third; implicit prices by more than one-quarter; and monthly wholesale prices by one-third.[1]

1 Milton Friedman and Anna Schwartz, *Monetary History of the United States,* Princeton University Press, 1963, p. 299. In 2008, Chapter 7 was published by Princeton University Press in a standalone volume *The Great Contraction, 1929-1933* with a New Preface by Anna Schwartz and a New Introduction by Peter L. Bernstein. *Monetary History* hereafter referred to as Friedman and Schwartz (1963a)

Friedman and Schwartz's Approach

The essential core of Friedman and Schwartz's approach was the idea that money matters. First, they believed that money creation determines the level of prices. Secondly, they believed, based upon extensive empirical work, that the circulation of money bears a closer relationship to income than the relationship between expenditures and income focused on by the Keynesians as discussed in the prior chapter. It is illuminating to read from the introduction to their Chapter 7 in *Monetary History:*

> The 1929-33 contraction had far-reaching effects in many directions, not least on monetary institutions and academic and popular thinking about the role of monetary factors in the economy....
>
> The contraction shattered the long-held belief, which had been strengthened in the 1920's, that monetary forces were important elements in the cyclical process [of business fluctuations] and that monetary policy was a potent instrument for promoting economic stability. Opinion shifted almost to the opposite extreme, that "money does not matter"; that it is a passive factor which chiefly reflects the effects of other forces; and that monetary policy is of extremely limited value in promoting stability.[2]

Friedman and Schwartz chose to call the period "The Great Contraction" because the money stock, which they defined as currency in circulation plus demand deposits and time deposits at commercial banks—M-2—contracted very sizably throughout the period. Using their own money stock estimates stated in an appendix, one can calculate their estimated money stock's rates of growth and contraction: After growing at a compound growth rate of +1.6% per year over the four-year period of 1926-1929; M-2 contracted -4.0%

2 Ibid., p. 300.

in 1930, -15.5% in 1931, -8.9% in 1932, and -9.4% in 1933 for a total contraction of -32.8% over the four-year period 1930-1933, which corresponds to an annual compound rate of contraction of -9.5% per year for those four years.

Arguing against the income-expenditure-oriented views prevailing during the Depression/Contraction as "not valid inferences from experience," [3] their introduction continued:

> The monetary collapse was not the inescapable consequence of other forces, but largely an independent factor that exerted a powerful influence on the course of events....
>
> The contraction is in fact a tragic testimonial to the importance of monetary forces. True, as events unfolded, the decline in the stock of money and the near-collapse of the banking system can be regarded as a consequence of the non-monetary forces in the United States, and monetary and non-monetary forces in the rest of the world. Everything depends on how much is taken as given. For it is true also, as we shall see, that different and feasible actions by the monetary authorities could have prevented the decline in the stock of money — indeed, could have produced almost any desired increase in the money stock. The same actions would also have eased the banking difficulties appreciably. Prevention or moderation of the decline in the stock of money, let alone the substitution of monetary expansion would have reduced the contraction's severity and almost as certainly its duration. The contraction might still have been relatively severe. But it is hardly conceivable that money income could have declined by over one-half and prices by over one-third in the course of four years if there had been no decline in the stock of money.[4]

3 Ibid..

4 Ibid., pp. 300-1.

The first of these two paragraphs is quite important, and we find it astonishingly insightful as to Friedman and Schwartz's ideas. But it is the second paragraph that is really vital because it expresses in many ways the core of their thinking. Accordingly, we deal with the second paragraph first.

There is much in the second paragraph that we agree with. Our most enthusiastic agreement is with its final sentence: "[I]t is hardly conceivable that money income could have declined by [significant amounts] if there had been no decline in the stock of money." This statement is headed toward asserting that the Hoover administration, had it had a better understanding of the causes of deflation, could have taken steps to reduce deflation and, in so doing, regain higher levels of money income and consumption. This we agree with and will elaborate on in the last chapter of *The Deflation of 1930* which is entitled "Incipient Conclusions."We should observe that we agree with Friedman and Schwartz that money matters. Our goal from the outset was — and definitely remains — to provide a persuasive *synthesis* in which both the Monetary and Income-Expenditure Approaches make essential contributions. Both play valuable and complementary parts. There is also much in the second paragraph that makes us uncomfortable. An example is the sentence: "Everything depends on how much is taken as given." As historians we are quite loyal to facts. Thus, we take the presidency of Herbert Hoover during 1929-33, with all his flaws and limitations, as an unavoidable "given." We suspect that for Friedman and Schwartz "a given" meant a governing *assumption*. Milton Friedman was a major proponent of the efficiency of markets. We believe that the notion arose at the Chicago "school" during his time there that some markets, most specifically "financial markets," operated with "perfect efficiency." Arguing that anything "operates with perfect efficiency," causes us to hear alarm bells sounding.

A Noteworthy Absence of the Use of Bank Loan Repayment Statistics

In her paper entitled "Understanding 1929-1933," included in economist Karl Brunner's 1981 compilation, *The Great Depression Revisited*, Anna Schwartz summarized the approach she and Milton Friedman chose to take. (Brunner is said to have coined the term monetarism.) According to Schwartz, "What we did illuminate was the process by which the decline in the quantity of money was produced." They did so by focusing on an intermittent series of what they called "bank crises," but they did so without making any reference to statistics regarding the aggregate volume of bank loans or of the repayment over time of bank loans, both of which troubled us considerably. As leading monetarists, they must have known that using a check written on a demand deposit to pay off some or all of a bank loan causes the volume of bank loans and the volume of demand deposits both to fall by the same amount, which is the amount of the check. In Chapter 10, we use Friedman and Schwartz's own month-end money stock estimates to examine what caused the money supply to fall — as it did — by almost $2.8 billion in the one-month period from the end of October 1929 to the end of November. (In November 1929 the "downside" of what Friedman and Schwartz called "the sharp wiggle" occurred.)

Of course, normally when some bank borrowers pay off their bank loans other parties turn to banks for new bank loans, thereby causing the money supply to grow. But when bank loans are paid off *en masse,* the volume of bank deposits shrinks. Thus, the first place one should look when seeking to determine what caused a decline in the money supply is to examine whether the volume of bank loans declined at the same time. We were pleased to see Anna Schwartz's comment that "there was no attempt by banks to liquidate loans or by depositors to shift from deposits to currency" in the period from August 1929 to October 1930, but we were disappointed to find that she did not call attention to any corresponding bank loan statistics.[5]

5 Schwartz (1981) pp. 6-7.

Banking and Monetary Statistics Tell the Real Story

BMS's statistics tell a different story. First, we look at Friedman and Schwartz's own statistics for M-1 and M-2 in 1930:

- M-1 declined -5.7% from $26,434 million for December 1929 to $24,922 million for December 1930.
- M-2 declined -4.0% from $45,867 million on December 31, 1929 to $44,054 million on Dec. 31, 1930.[6]

Schwartz would have found that BMS's statistics for bank loans shrank over 1930 at a dramatic and accelerating rate:

Year-End 1929 to year-end 1930:

- Loans at All Member Banks declined -8.7% from $26,150 million on December 31, 1929 to $23,870 million on Dec. 31, 1930.
- Loans at *All Commercial Banks* declined -10.9% from $35,966 million on December 31, 1929 to $32,034 million on December 31, 1930. [7]

In the second half of 1930:

- Loans at *All Member Banks* declined at an annualized compound rate of -10.4%. (Over 6 months the

6 Friedman and Schwartz (1963a) pp. 712-713.

7 *BMS*, pp. 19 and 72-74.

decline was -5.3% from $25,214 million on June 30, 1930, to $23,870 million on Dec. 31, 1930.)

- Loans at *All Commercial Banks* declined at an annualized compound rate of -14.0 %. (Over 6 months the decline was -7.3% from $34,539 million on June 30, 1930, to $32,034 million on December 31, 1930.)[8]

In the last quarter of 1930:

- Loans at *All Member Banks* declined at an annualized compound rate of -13.3%. (Over 3 months the decline was 3.5% from $24,738 million on Sept. 24, 1930, to $23,870 million on Dec. 31, 1930.)[9]

What Caused the Monetary Collapse?

Friedman and Schwartz's answer to this question was given previously, which, with its ellipsis filled in, reads:

> The monetary collapse was not the inescapable consequence of other forces, but *largely an independent factor* that exerted a powerful influence on the course of events. The failure of the Federal Reserve System to *prevent* the collapse reflected not the impotence of monetary policy but rather the particular policies followed by the monetary authorities and, in smaller degree, the *particular monetary arrangements in existence.*[10] (our emphasis)

Explicitly, Friedman and Schwartz did not answer the question; they simply called it "largely an independent factor" without

8 Ibid. and authors' calculations.

9 Ibid.

10 Friedman and Schwartz (1963a) p. 300.

further clarification. As we can see, what Friedman and Schwartz did say was that the Fed did not "prevent" the collapse. (We believe another highly-thought-of monetarist gave the answer as we will explain later in this chapter.)

We will comment on at least some of "the particular monetary arrangements in existence." However, before doing so, it is important to expose the exact components of Friedman and Schwartz's thinking for clarification. First:

> [A]s events unfolded, the decline in the stock of money and the near-collapse of the banking system can be regarded as a consequence of *non-monetary* forces in the United States. (our emphasis)

But Friedman and Schwartz viewed this as changing strikingly in the fourth quarter of 1930:

> In October 1930, the character of the contraction changed dramatically.... Before October 1930, deposits of suspended banks had been somewhat higher than during most of 1929 but not out of line with experience during the proceeding decade. In November 1930, they were more than double the highest value recorded since the start of monthly data in 1921. A crop of bank failures particularly in Missouri, Indiana, Illinois, Iowa, Arkansas, and North Carolina, led to widespread attempts to convert demand and time deposits into currency.... A contagion of fear spread among depositors starting from the agricultural areas, which had experienced the heaviest impact of bank failures in the 20s. But such contagion knows no geographical limits.[11]

11 Ibid., p. 308.

After a discussion in *Monetary History* of aspects of the first banking crisis (some or all of which included what they called "the first liquidity crisis"), Friedman and Schwartz reasoned:

> The onset of the first liquidity crisis left *no clear imprint* on the broad economic series [shown in a graph of prices, personal income, and industrial production].... All in all, the figures for the first four or five months of 1931, ... have many of the earmarks of the bottom of a cycle and the beginning of a revival. (Our emphasis)
>
> Perhaps if those tentative stirrings of revival had been reinforced by a vigorous expansion of the stock of money, they could have been converted into sustained recovery. But it was not to be.... A month or two later, a renewed decline started in economic activity in general, and the hope of revival that season was ended.[12]

Now we can turn our attention to "the particular monetary arrangements in existence." But before doing so, we must once again focus on the exact components of Friedman and Schwartz's thinking. In the second paragraph on page 103 they state:

> Everything depends on how much is taken as given. For it is true also, as we shall see, that different and feasible actions by the monetary authorities could have prevented the decline in the stock of money — indeed, could have produced almost any desired increase in the money stock[13].

When one considers how our government "could have produced almost any desired increase in the money stock," the thought is inescapable that the German government did exactly that by simply printing and circulating paper currency in the early 1920s when hyperinflation resulted. But we think it "a given" that the Federal

12 Friedman and Schwartz (1963a), pp. 308-313.

13 Ibid., pp. 300-301.

Reserve *cannot* print and circulate paper currency. In the 1920s and 1930s, as today, the authority to print and paper currency did not reside with the Federal Reserve. Paper currency was produced by the Bureau of Printing and Engraving which reported (then as now) to the Treasury Department. Furthermore, this specific arrangement is only one of a great many "particular monetary arrangements in existence" that establish how this nation operates and funds all levels of government — federal, state and local.

Collectively, we believe these arrangements were (and are) core considerations in what is known as "sound finance." One needs to look no further than the presidential election of 1932, where both Republicans and Democrats strongly supported avoiding deficit financing, to see how strongly concepts of sound finance gripped the American psyche. In fact, many of these arrangements were established in our Constitution.

Praise for the Work of Milton Friedman

Much praise for the work of Milton Friedman, who died in 2006, has come forth, and his influence on government policy-makers, business leaders and the study of economics has been widely recognized, if also, as widely, debated. In his eulogistic 2007 tribute, Robert L. Hetzel, an economist in the Research Department at the Richmond Federal Reserve, wrote in the Richmond Fed's *Economic Quarterly:*

> Milton Friedman died November 16, 2006, at the age of 94. Any attempt to put his contributions to economics into perspective can only begin to suggest the vast variety of ideas he discussed. [John] Burton…commented that ""attempting to portray the work of Milton Friedman…is like trying to catch the Niagara Falls in a pint pot." At the beginning of his career, Friedman adopted two hypotheses that isolated him from the prevailing intellectual mainstream.

> First, central banks are responsible for inflation and deflation. Second, markets work efficiently to allocate resources and to maintain macroeconomic economic equilibrium. Because of his success in advancing these ideas in a way that shaped the understanding of the major economic events of this century and influenced public policy, Friedman stands out as one of the great intellectuals of the 20th century.[14]

In a footnote, Hetzel observed:

> In contrast, the Keynesian orthodoxy of the day assumed that inflation arose from an eclectic collection of causes and the price system did not work to maintain aggregate demand at a level sufficient to maintain full employment. The appeal of these assumptions, an appeal made irresistible by the Depression, rested on their apparent descriptive realism rather than on the optimizing behavior assumed by neoclassical economics.[15]

Further in his article, Hetzel continued:

> Even though written for economists, *A Monetary History* was one of the most influential books of the 20th century because of the way it radically altered reviews of the cause of the Depression. Economists had interpreted the Depression as evidence of market failure and the impotence of monetary policy to deal with that failure. They believed the near-zero level of short-term interest rates on Treasury bills meant that an "easy" monetary policy could not bring the economy out

---

14 Robert L. Hetzel, "The Contributions of Milton Freidman to Economics," FRB Richmond, *Economic Quarterly*, Winter 2007, p. 1.

15 Ibid.

> of recession.
>
> In contrast, Friedman and Schwartz explained the Depression not as a failure of the free enterprise system that overwhelmed monetary policy, but rather as a result of misguided actions of the Fed.[16]
>
> Friedman defended free markets indefatigably and in every forum. Like Adam Smith, he explained how markets and the price system harness the efforts of individuals to better themselves in a way that improves the general welfare. More than any other individual over the post-war period, Friedman moved the intellectual consensus away from the belief that a rising standard of living rested on central planning to the belief that it rested on free markets.
>
> Friedman advanced public understanding of the operation of markets through his free-market proposals to solve problems. His first collection of such proposals came in *Capitalism and Freedom*. Although inevitably controversial, many of Friedman's proposals came to fruition. Examples are flexible instead of pegged exchange rates, elimination of the 1970s price controls on energy, a volunteer army, and auctions for government bonds. Some of his proposals have met with partial success.... Some of his proposals have met with failure but have provoked useful debate.[17]

In his 2019 book *The Economists' Hour,* Binyamin Appelbaum, economics and business writer for the editorial page of *The New York Times*, lists a number of prominent economists who were in accord with aspects of Milton Friedman's views. Not all were, though, as

---

16 Ibid., p. 15.

17 Ibid., p. 22.

Appelbaum makes clear, quoting several of these economists, including Nobel Prize winning economist Robert Solow:

> "Prevailing economic doctrine has only recently—prodded by Professor Friedman, among others—swung around from the view that monetary phenomena are not very important to the view that perhaps they are," the Keynesian economist Robert Solow wrote in an open-minded review of *A Monetary History.*
>
> But Friedman's triumph was incomplete. Two important differences remained. First, while Keynesians increasingly accepted the importance of monetary policy, they did not accept the impotence of fiscal policy. "The issue is not whether money matters — we all grant that — but whether only money matters," said Walter Heller [Chairman of President Kennedy's Council of Economic Advisors]. Paul W. McCracken, the first chairman of Nixon's Council of Economic Advisers, described his views on macroeconomic policy as "Friedmanesque" — the quantity of money was important, but it wasn't the only thing.[18]

To honor his contributions, Friedman received the Nobel Prize in economics in 1976, well ahead of Ronald Reagan's presidency during which Friedman's influence gained dominance, for "the renaissance in the role of money in inflation and the consequent renewed understanding of the instrument of monetary policy."[19] The Nobel Committee obviously concurred that money matters, and economic policy in the United States since the Reagan admin-

18 Binyamin Appelbaum, *The Economists' Hour,* Little, Brown and Company, 2019, p. 62.
19 Ibid., p. 71.

istration has mostly leaned in that direction as well, if with widely contested results.

Irving Fisher's Monetarism and Thoughts on the Depression

Though they are today perhaps the best-known and most influential monetary economists who have delved into the Depression, Milton Friedman and Anna Schwartz were not the first American economists to pursue a monetary approach. One of the most prominent economists of the early 20th century was Yale University's Irving Fisher, a well-respected early proponent of monetary theory. Fisher, already well established as an economist, author and even inventor, is notoriously remembered for his very public—and spectacularly wrong—predictions about stock market performance. On September 5, 1929, *The New York Herald Tribune* quoted him as saying, "There may be a recession in stock prices, but not anything in the nature of a crash." He followed this up in *The New York Times* on October 16 with, "Stock prices have reached what looks like a permanently high plateau."[20]

His reputation marred, Fisher and his wife also proceeded to lose a great deal of their money in the Crash due to his speculation. This personal tragedy served to motivate him to attempt to understand the unprecedentedly dire events that had taken place. Turning inward, Fisher reflected most productively. First, he wrote *Booms and Depressions; Some First Principles* published in the depths of the Depression in 1932 (and dedicated to business-cycle expert Wesley Clair Mitchell). In this book, Fisher articulated his pioneering theory and introduced certain ideas regarding the cause or causes of the Depression. In a follow-up article, "The Debt-Deflation Theory of Great Depressions," published in October 1933 by The Econometric Society, he further expanded his thinking. We consider Fisher's

---

20 Edward Angly, *Oh Yeah?*, The Viking Press, 1931, pp. 37-8.

monetary approach in these two publications well worth further elaboration and do so in Chapter 1, "Irving Fisher's Debt Factor Approach"in *The Deflation of 1930.*

Curious to find out how Fisher might have influenced Friedman and Schwartz's thinking—his name appeared only in footnotes in their writings—we turned to Rutgers University economists Michael Bordo and Hugh Rockoff, who made it clear in a 2011 paper in the NBER Working Paper Series, "The Influence of Irving Fisher on Milton Friedman's Monetary Economics," that Fisher's influence, in their view, extended far beyond footnotes. [21] In the introduction to their paper, Bordo and Rockoff declared, "Irving Fisher was the most prominent American economist of the early twentieth century. Milton Friedman was the most prominent economist of the later twentieth century.".[22] They delineated extensive references indicating Fisher's influence throughout *Monetary History* and offered the following as evidence:

> Fisher's influence on Friedman was both indirect through the Chicago School and direct. Regardless of the weight attached to the two influences, Fisher's impact on Friedman was profound.
>
> Both Fisher and Friedman, moreover, were advocates of 100 percent reserves. Fisher's debt-deflation theory of the depression and his stamped money proposal were temporary departures from his earlier emphasis on the supply of money which Friedman did not embrace. Both Fisher and Friedman blamed the Federal Reserve for creating the Great Depression

21 One footnote in *Monetary History* (p. 413) had Fisher opining in the *Annals of the American Academy of Political and Social Science* (Vol 171, Jan. 1934, p. 151), "I thoroughly believe that if [New York Fed Governor Benjamin Strong Jr.,] had lived and his policies continued, we might have had the stock market crash in a milder form, but after the crash there would not have been the great industrial depression."

22 Michael D. Bordo and Hugh Rockoff, *The Influence of Irving Fisher on Milton Friedman's Monetary Economics,* NBER Working Paper Series, Working Paper 17267, August 2011.

> and both believed that had Benjamin Strong lived that the outcome would not have been nearly as dire.
>
> In sum, Irving Fisher was a pioneer Friedmanian; and Milton Friedman was a latter day Fisherian.[23]

Influence does not necessarily imply agreement, of course. Bordo and Rockoff commented on several lines of thinking where Friedman diverged from Fisher's views, for instance in pointing out that "Fisher's debt-deflation theory of the depression and his stamped money proposal were temporary departures from his earlier emphasis on the supply of money which Friedman did not embrace'."[24]

Whatever Friedman's views were on the debt-inflation theory and the stamped money proposal, we have found no evidence that Fisher considered either of them as temporary, nor were they a departure from his long-held monetarist views. Nonetheless, whether overt or subtle, Fisher's groundbreaking works undoubtedly left their mark on the thinking of Friedman and Schwartz.

Friedman Talks to a Man About a Horse

Debate between Keynesians and Monetarists has gone on for decades in the halls of academia and the halls of Congress. Joining in on the discussion, we now look into two well-utilized sources for Depression-era data: the *Annual Report of the Board of Governors* (*ARBG*) of the Federal Reserve System for 1931 and 1932 and the Federal Reserve Board of Governors' *Banking and Monetary Statistics 1914-1941* (*BMS*) published in 1943. Using both of these sources we address a statement of Friedman's, which Temin called attention to, as to why the quantity of money in the United States fell by one-third

23 Ibid., pp. 40-2.

24 Ibid., p. 41.

in the course of the 1929-1933 period.[25] Using the proverbial metaphor about a horse being led to water, Friedman explained the fall:

> [I]t fell not because there were no willing borrowers—not because the horse would not drink. It fell because the Federal Reserve System forced or permitted a sharp reduction in the monetary base, because it failed to exercise the responsibilities assigned to it in the Federal Reserve Act to provide liquidity to the banking system.[26]

By the end of 1931, it was clear that the quantity of money in the United States was dropping drastically. The Federal Reserve System recognized explicitly the important role in the fall of bank loans in this process. In their *Annual Report of the Board of Governors of the Federal Reserve System for 1931 (ARBG 1931,* p. 5*),* a chart was included that is reproduced on opposite page as Chart 4.1.

ARBG 1931 described the conditions regarding bank loans, bank credit and bank loans and investments that prevailed through the end of 1931:

> The decline in bank loans *which had begun in the autumn of 1929* continued throughout 1930 and 1931. (emphasis ours)…. [W]hile there was some reduction in bank credit in the last quarter of 1929 and in the first quarter of 1930, it was not until the latter months of 1930 that the volume of bank credit showed a rapid decline, either for member or for nonmember banks. After the middle of 1930, however, the reduction became pronounced and continuous and after the middle of 1931 extremely rapid…. At the end of 1931 loans *and investments* of all banks in United States, amounted to

25 Temin (1976), p. 15.

26 Milton Friedman, *Dollars and Deficits: Inflation, Monetary Policy and the Balance of Payments,* Prentice-Hall, Inc., 1968, p. 3.

Chart 4.1

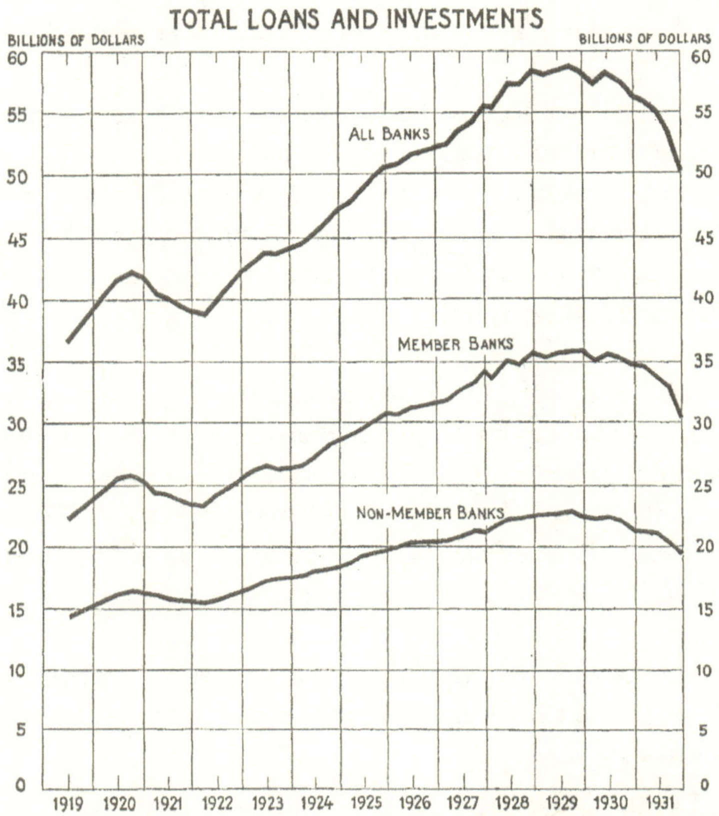

Figures beginning with June, 1920, are for all dates on which member banks made call reports; for earlier period they are for June only

[$49.7 billion], were about [$9.1 billion] less than in the autumn of 1929 and at about the same level as the autumn of 1925.[27] (emphasis ours)

Perhaps it might be understandable for bank borrowers to pay back their bank loans if bank interest rates were rising sharply, but they weren't. *ARBG 1931* continued:

Continued liquidation of bank loans during the first half of 1931 was accompanied by a further decline in short-term

27 *ARBG 1931,* pp. 4-5. Growing or shrinking investments does not change bank credit.

> money rates[28] .... During the summer reserve bank rates wereat the lowest levels that have ever prevailed.[29]

The following year, *ARBG 1932* reported:

> Volume of member bank credit outstanding continued to decline during 1932, rapidly during the first half of the year and less rapidly thereafter, reflecting a further liquidation of loans, partially offset by an increase in investments.[30]

According to these Federal Reserve sources and other money supply statistics that Friedman and Schwartz painstakingly measured in *Monetary History*—which they presented as M-2—the money supply totaled $45,867 million at year-end 1929, and $30,807 million at year-end 1933, a fall of 32.8% or $15,060 million.[31]

Since it is bank loans and the use of those borrowed funds that determine the size of the money supply as the concept of the bank credit multiplier explains, bank borrowing statistics provide critical insights. The Federal Reserve's *BMS* revealed that loans outstanding of All Banks *totaling $35,966 million at year-end 1929 had dropped 54.8% to $16,246 million at year-end 1933, almost the level of 1916.*[32] It was this repayment of $19,720 million in prior bank borrowings that caused the money supply⁻M-2 for Friedman and Schwartz, M-1 for others⁻to shrink.

Returning to Friedman's metaphor of the horse, there was a brief period from March 27 to June 30, 1930, when the Fed considered itself to be pursuing policies of monetary ease, and bank

28 Ibid., p. 5

29 Ibid., p. 6

30 *ARBG 1932*, p. 5.

31 Friedman and Schwartz (1963a), pp. 712-4.

32 *BMS*, p. 19. Only growing or shrinking bank loans changes bank credit.

loans at All Member Banks increased by $95 million.[33] Friedman's horse did indeed drink, at least a small amount as provided by the Fed. But otherwise bank loans fell, and the overall statistics from the end of 1929 to the end of 1933 do not show Friedman's horse drinking. Instead, the horse may have gone to the trough, but rather than drinking, the horse actually *returned a major part of what it had already drunk* before December 31, 1929.

We will see how and why this and much more came to pass in the chapters ahead as we reveal the untold story found in contemporary annual data unchanged over the years and held securely for so long within the archives of our trustworthy Treasury Department source.

33 *BMS,* p. 74.

CHAPTER 5

Peter Temin's Invitation and Our R.S.V.P.

The work of MIT economist and economic historian Peter Temin provides an excellent foundation upon which to develop the story of the Great Depression/Contraction/Deleverage. A prodigious writer of books, articles and NBER working papers on topics ranging from industrialization in Britain and America, pre-World War I banking systems, the post-bellum economy of the American South, the 2008 recession to the grain trade in the early Roman Empire, Temin was moved to make a specific response to Milton Friedman and Anna J. Schwartz's argument in *Monetary History* that failures of the Federal Reserve System led to the Great Depression. In his 1976 *Did Monetary Forces Cause the Great Depression?* (hereafter shortened to *Did Monetary Forces*), Temin asked two questions:

- What caused the Great Depression of 1929-1933?

- Why was the Great Depression so severe and so protracted?

In this chapter, we focus on Temin's pioneering analysis in *Did Monetary Forces* for a number of reasons. First, his book gives an excellent and highly cogent review of the Depression and especially of what occurred (or didn't occur) in the pivotal year of 1930. But he also raised enticing questions—especially as to the "unexplained" drop in consumption in 1930—which stimulated our own thinking because we had the great fortune to encounter (and, we might add, eagerly devour) *Did Monetary Forces* early on in our research. Most pertinent, Temin made it very clear that Friedman and Schwartz provided neither an appreciation of nor an explanation for any demand for borrowed money to spend. In fact, Temin described important aspects of their work as "seriously incomplete"[1] and "unproven."[2]

Introducing the benefits of using information from aggregate balance sheets—another way his book fueled our research—Temin highlighted studies from the 1950s and 1960s conducted by economic statistician Raymond W. Goldsmith of Yale, who, beginning with financial support provided by the Life Insurance Association of America and with guidance and staff support supplied by NBER, served as lead author of the impressive three-volume *A Study of Saving in the United States* and, separately, *Studies in the National Balance Sheet of the United States.*[3] Though acknowledging that "[m]ost of the literature on the Depression… is replete with assertions about unobserved and unpredictable magnitudes,"[4] Temin proceeded with a detailed analysis of the magnitudes—or numerical quantities—shown in certain statistics, but including those from the Department of Commerce, the Federal Reserve's *Banking and Monetary Statistics (BMS), Historical Statistics of the U.S. (HSUS),* as well as Goldsmith, but from 1929-33. Thus, not only was he challenging himself to analyze the data he could find, he was also issuing an invitation to future researchers like ourselves.

Temin's Method of Inquiry

Throughout his book, Temin engaged in a debate between the two schools of economic thought that, as we have seen, offered opposing explanations for what caused the Great Depression and for why it lasted so long. To facilitate comparison with publica-

1 Temin (1976), p. 22.

2 Ibid., p. 31.

3 Goldsmith (1956 and 1963).

4 Temin (1976), p.174.

tions other than Temin's book, we have chosen to call Temin's "money hypothesis" the "monetary approach" and Temin's "spending hypothesis" the "income-expenditure approach." About the different theoretical approaches of these two schools, Temin provided clear distinctions, (we substitute our preferred terminology in the following quote):

> [E]xplanations of the Depression can be classified into two groups, one group offered generally by those who believe that monetary policy would have been the best tool to alleviate the Depression and the other by adherents of fiscal policy.... The two... explanations for the Depression have different events at their cores. What I have called [the monetary approach] asserts that the collapse of the banking system was the primary cause of the Depression, while [the income-expenditure approach] asserts that a fall in autonomous aggregate spending lay at the root of the decline.[5]

"The collapse of the banking system was the primary cause of the Depression" refers, of course, to the four serious banking crises that began in November and December of 1930. As for affirming Temin's statement that "a fall in autonomous aggregate spending lay at the root of the decline," we merely need to return to Table 1.1 from Chapter 1, repeated here on the following page for ease of reference.[6]

In this seminal table, not available until well after the Great Depression, we see the National Income and Product Account (NIPA) statistics showing the fall in GNP, Personal Consumption, and Fixed Investment for 1929-33 that clearly confirm the "fall in...autonomous aggregate spending."

5 Ibid., p. 7.

6 NIPA 1929-1976, table 1.1, p. 1.

Table 1.1						
Gross National Product: Annually, 1929-1934 ($ million)						
	1929	1930	1931	1932	1933	1934
Gross national product	**103,420**	**90,700**	**76,073**	**58,280**	**55,818**	**65,291**
Personal consumption expenditures	**77,251**	**69,916**	**60,482**	**48,591**	**45,811**	**51,344**
Durable goods	9,243	7,166	5,483	3,641	3,464	4,219
Nondurable goods	37,686	34,022	28,956	22,741	22,257	26,691
Services	30,322	28,728	26,043	22,209	20,090	20,434
Gross private domestic investment	**16,197**	**10,249**	**5,620**	**965**	**1,406**	**3,328**
Fixed investment	14,483	10,601	6,768	3,445	2,970	4,063
Non residential	10,610	8,325	5,031	2,705	2,390	3,177
Structures	5,118	4,145	2,388	1,245	954	1,079
Producers' durable equipment	5,492	4,180	2,643	1,460	1,436	2,098
Residential	3,873	2,276	1,737	740	580	886
Nonfarm structures	3,620	2,078	1,602	667	497	783
Farm structures	175	131	78	38	43	52
Producers' durable equipment	78	67	57	35	40	51
Change in business inventories	1,714	-352	-1,148	-2,480	-1,564	-735
Nonfarm	1,836	-83	-1,608	-2,590	-1,370	195
Farm	-122	-269	460	110	-194	-930
Net exports of goods and services	**1,149**	**1,032**	**516**	**407**	**358**	**601**
Exports	7,035	5,448	3,641	2,474	2,402	2,975
Imports	5,886	4,416	3,125	2,067	2,044	2,374
Government purchase of goods and services	**8,823**	**9,503**	**9,455**	**8,317**	**8,243**	**10,018**
Federal	1,441	1,552	1,613	1,578	2,122	3,123
National defense	----------	----------	----------	----------	----------	----------
Nondefense	----------	----------	----------	----------	----------	----------
State and local	7,382	7,951	7,842	6,739	6,121	6,895

Source: *The National Income & Product Accounts of the United States 1929-76; Table 1.1*, p.1.

Temin's use of the word "autonomous" here and throughout his book is a key concept. Autonomous means not only that the various category entities—that is, consumers with respect to Personal Consumption and businesses with respect to Fixed Investment—operated independently from each other, but also that each separate consumer or business operated independently from all others. In other words, each party, for its own reasons and without coordinating, collaborating or conspiring with others, decided independently how much to spend and on what. As Table 1.1 reveals, when the stories behind each autonomous action merged in aggregate, however, we find one dismal spending trend.

While Table 1.1 (opposite) shows enormous drops in demand, the NIPA numbers lack a narrative to explain autonomous decisions by either individuals or businesses. But other data did leave evidence, as we will see.

A Large "Unexplained" Drop in Personal Consumption

In *Did Monetary Forces* Temin aggressively questioned virtually every facet of both the income-expenditure and the monetary approaches to the causes of the Depression. Digging into these very complicated subjects, he searched for an explanation for the significant and unexplained drop in consumption. In Chapter III of *Did Monetary Forces* entitled "Precipitating Factors," Temin called attention to "sharply falling consumption… in 1930" and attempted a careful explanation based on the evidence he had at hand: [7]

> The fall in consumption must be regarded as truly autonomous, which in this case means also unexplained. The unexplained component of consumption, therefore, was approximately $3 billion in 1929 prices (out of a total fall of $4.3 billion). When added to the smaller falls in exports and in consumption due to the fall in asset prices, this implies a fall in autonomous spending of about $4 billion in 1929 prices. Compared to a total Gross National Product of approximately $100 billion, this fall—if it was indeed an autonomous fall—could have had multiplier effects large enough to explain the continued downward path of national income.
>
> It is somewhat unsatisfactory to say that the Depression was caused by an unexplained event, but this alternative is

7 Temin (1976), p. 65.

> preferable to statements that are inconsistent with the data. The [income-expenditure approach] is consistent with the data if we accept the autonomous nature of a large part of the fall in consumption in 1930. It is not, however, a complete story.[8]

Through careful exposition, analysis and logic, Temin succeeded in picking apart the various lines of argumentation in both the monetary approach and the income-expenditure approach to arrive at his overall evaluation expressed in the book's concluding paragraph:

> This study has shown that the [income-expenditure approach] fits the observed data better than the [monetary approach], that is, that it is more plausible to believe that the Depression was the result of a drop in autonomous expenditures, *particularly consumption*, than the result of autonomous bank failures.[9] (emphasis ours)

His last chapter offered the following explanations that he admitted were incomplete and which inspired us to seek further evidence and to attempt our own narrative:

> In addition to the fall in income, the collapse of the stock market, and the poor harvest in 1929, something else happened to depress consumption in 1930. At the current stage of our knowledge, the unexplained fall in consumption is larger than the part we can explain....
>
> The large fall in consumption in 1930, deriving from a variety of diverse and as yet still incompletely delineated sources prevented recovery that year. Goods that could not

8 Ibid., p. 83.

9 Ibid., p. 178.

> be sold were not produced. The fall in aggregate demand spread throughout the economy. And as the fall of 1930 wore on and business did not recover,... businessmen lost the confidence that underlies private investment. The economy continued to decline.[10]

A consummate economist, Temin was extending an invitation for further research in the hope that others might tap into an incontrovertible source, or sources, that would yield a convincing explanation. We believed that if we could identify Temin's "unexplained component of consumption... of about $4 billion," we could provide a focal element of the "precipitating factors" of the Great Depression. Temin's questioning approach created a fertile environment that helped us to pursue our own case.

How the Crash Caused constitutes our grateful acceptance of Peter Temin's invitation.

Our R.S.V.P. to Temin—in a Nutshell

In the next chapter, we relay the story of how the statistics that confirm our answer to Professor Temin came into our hands. For now, we hint at what those statistics show and what future chapters will discuss in detail in response to Temin's questions.

As Temin posited in *Did Monetary Forces*, "something... happened to depress consumption in 1930" and "the unexplained component of consumption... implies a fall in autonomous spending of about $4 billion."[11] The data we found is that in 1930 individuals in the U.S.—i.e., consumers—paid back to corporations (which include almost all banks and much of the retail industry) debt obligations that exceeded $4 billion in total. Consumers, in order to pay back this amount, made personal, autonomous decisions to diminish their

10 Ibid., p. 172.

11 Ibid., p. 83.

consumption by the amount of this debt repayment. In other words, paying back $4+ billion in debt obligations caused consumers to reduce their consumption expenditures by $4 billion—a bull's-eye on Temin's target.

The year 1930 proved to be just the first year to hit Temin's target. Our analysis allows us to conclude that individuals in the U.S.—i.e., consumers—paid back another $7+ billion in 1931. Looking further at our statistics covering the full period of 1929-1933, we see a repercussive reduction of debt obligations of a startling almost $31 billion. Paying back $4+ billion in debt in 1930 equaled roughly 4.4% of GNP that year. Paying back $7+ billion in debt, equaled roughly 9.2% of GNP in 1931. Consumers then paid off about 11% of GNP in 1932 and more than 4% in 1933. The dual action of depressing consumption in order to repay debt depresses—indeed contracts—the entire economic structure.

How Does Repaying a Bank Loan Cause the Money Supply to Shrink?

It is beyond controversy that the money supply shrank, as monetarists have observed, and the massive amount of loan repayments had a major impact on the size of the economy, with all the attendant effects including unemployment. All else being equal, repaying bank loans (with checks drawn on banks) causes the money supply to shrink in a very specific way. As a matter of course, lending banks almost always require their borrowers to maintain money on deposit at their banks. To repay a bank loan, a borrower writes a check payable to the bank in the amount of the loan repayment. The bank then reduces the amount of the loan by the amount of the check, and also debits the borrower's bank account by the amount of the check. Simultaneously the bank's loan assets are reduced by the amount of the repayment, and the bank's deposit liabilities are reduced by the amount of the check payment. The money supply shrinks with the reduction of the bank's deposit liabilities.

While Temin did not choose to note this, it is curious to us that in their analysis, Friedman and Schwartz failed to mention or discuss the fact that bank loan repayments, by themselves, would reduce the money supply. It is hard to imagine that they didn't understand this mechanism. Perhaps they overlooked the fact because in normal times, as the money supply was growing, some other party would take out bank loans, thus offsetting any drop in the money supply resulting from any particular loan repayment. During the long period from 1867 to 1960 that Friedman and Schwartz covered in their *Monetary History,* the money supply was almost always growing. During the Depression, however, it wasn't growing, and the question is, why? Though in an economy that is expanding, a new borrower generally turns up to enter into a new bank loan, when an economy is contracting a new borrower may not turn up. Friedman and Schwartz did not explain that, absent such a new borrower, paying off bank loans causes an economy to shrink. And repaying bank loans at a growing rate causes the money supply to shrink at a growing rate, as ample data show.

Temin on Friedman and Schwartz's Lack of a Meaningful Demand-for-Money Function

Professor Temin's questioning of key missing elements in Friedman's and Schwartz's analysis also spurred our own examination of their approach. Among the fundamental elements of economic thinking, concepts of supply and demand are perhaps the earliest ideas introduced to beginning students. In MIT professor Paul Samuelson's *Economics*, his respected and long-utilized basic textbook, he devoted an early chapter to "Supply and Demand: The Bare Essentials." His chapter included the concepts of a downward-sloping demand curve, an upward-sloping supply curve and the idea that where the two curves intersect is the equilibrium market price.[12] But, as Temin pointed out in *Did Monetary Forces*, Friedman and Schwartz did not include any thoughts or considerations regarding *a demand curve for borrowed money to spend* in their thinking about the determinants of the size of the money supply.

As we have seen, the analysis of the Great Depression by Friedman and Schwartz was dependent on their theoretical approach to the determinants of the size of the money stock. Temin began his discussion with a clear explanation of Friedman and Schwartz's approach:

> Friedman and Schwartz identified three determinants of the stock of money. They are the quantity of high-powered money or the monetary base (that is, those kinds of money that can be used either as currency or as bank reserves), the ratio of bank deposits to bank reserves, and the ratio of bank deposits to currency held by the public.[13]

Friedman and Schwartz argued that the stock of money is a function of these three determinants by formulating, and deriving mathematically, an equation that expresses this function, which they described in an appendix to their book.[14] The equation shows how these three measures— 1) the quantity of high-powered money, 2) the ratio of bank deposits to bank reserves, and 3) the ratio of bank deposits to currency held by the public—determine the amount of the stock of money. The argument underlying the equation is that each of these three measures results from the behavior of an identifi-

---

12 Paul Samuelson, *Economics*, (Seventh edition, 1967), McGraw Hill.

13 Temin (1976), p. 16.

14 Friedman and Schwartz (1963a). The pertinent appendix, entitled "Proximate Determinants of the Nominal Stock of Money," begins on page 776. The equation that Temin labels "Equation (1)" on page 16 of *Did Monetary Forces,* appears on page 791 of *Monetary History* where it is labeled "equation (12)."

able group acting on the basis of identifiable influences. Furthermore, each measure is determined by a group that is separate from, and acts independently of, other groups—that is, autonomously, to use Temin's word.

Temin presented Friedman and Schwartz's equation in his book and labeled it "equation (1)," but he questioned its fundamental adequacy. As Temin explained it, in his view, the stock of high-powered money is determined by "monetary authorities, that is, the Federal Reserve System"; the deposit-reserve ratio is "determined by the actions of banks"; and the deposit-currency ratio is "determined by individuals."[15] Temin then speculated:

> This separation of influences appears to be rather different than the normal separation used by economists. A more traditional decomposition of influences determining prices and quantities of economic goods separates them into supply and demand components. It is appropriate, therefore, to ask if the behavioral relations underlying equation (1) relate to the supply of or the demand for money to see if this equation can be identified either with the supply of or the demand for money.[16]

After further analysis, especially of writings by Friedman and/or Schwartz other than *Monetary History,* Temin concluded:

> Equation (1) then is a supply function for money. To the extent that the analysis of changes in the stock of money is conducted in terms of this equation, it treats only the supply side of the market for money. There is no reason not to detail changes in the supply of any good over time, but we do not normally speak of the supply alone as the determinant of

15 Temin (1976), p. 17.

16 Ibid.

> quantities on the market.
>
> Yet Friedman and Schwartz consistently referred to the variable on the left-hand side of equation (1) as the stock of money, not the supply of money. And they referred to the arguments on the right-hand side of equation (1) as the determinants of the money stock. They clearly assumed that the stock of money was determined by supply alone.[17]

Temin's conclusion was unambiguous:

> Friedman and Schwartz's description of the determinants of the stock of money... is seriously incomplete. It looks only at one side of the market and ignores effects coming from the demand for money. An account of the supply alone cannot tell how much of the variation in the quantity came from changes in supply conditions and how much from demand conditions.[18]

Perhaps their lack of apprehension of and understanding for "effects coming from the demand for money," to quote Temin, might explain how Friedman and Schwartz could argue in the passage quoted on page 104:

> For it is true also, as we shall see, that...feasible actions by the monetary authorities...could have produced almost any desired increase in the stock of money.

Perhaps it could also explain how Friedman and Schwartz could use the proverbial metaphor about a horse being led to water to infer and argue in the passage quoted on page 117 that the Federal

17 Ibid., p. 18.

18 Ibid., p. 22.

Reserve System was to blame for the Great Depression because "it failed ... to provide liquidity to the banking system."

Unobserved and Unpredictable Magnitudes and Inadequate Data

Professor Temin was well aware of the need for economists and others to derive their theories and base their policy recommendations on solid economic data. His comments on this subject in *Did Monetary Forces* began with a focus on macroeconomics and the effectiveness of policy recommendations:

> What can we say about the role of macroeconomic policy in this story? It is clear from the fact that the Depression occurred that effective countermeasures were not used. Those countermeasures that were tried clearly were ineffective; the Depression took place. To show that a macroeconomic policy can be effective, a historian is forced into the uncomfortable position of attempting to prove that it was not used. Only if it was not used can it emerge from the debacle of the 1930s unscathed.
>
> But it is hardly the same thing to say that a policy was not discredited and to say the policy has been shown effective. It is for this reason that the position of the historian of policy is uncomfortable. The historical record can only show that a policy was not shown to be ineffective policy; the record does not show how the Depression was cured by the administration of this or that prescription.
>
> A totally different kind of analysis is needed to show that a policy would have worked had it been tried and—by extension—that it will work today. To show this, the structure

> of the economy needs to be exposed. One cannot answer the question of what might have been from the narrative of historical events alone. One must make inferences from these events about the underlying structure that tied them together. But as shown in Chapter II, the data for the inter-war period are not rich enough to indicate a unique underlying structure.[19]

We followed with fascination Professor Temin's admonitions regarding the need for knowledge of this underlying structure. One of us shares a background with Professor Temin that includes a stint served as an Officer of the Deck for Fleet Operations on the bridge of a U.S. Navy destroyer. In such a capacity, there is no action taken without clear, visceral knowledge of the structure of the ship and how it would react, for example, to its helm and engines and, indeed, to its fire control and damage control systems. Also necessary was extensive experience with the capacities and performance of the ship's internal communications systems as well as its external communications with other ships—in other words, knowledge of an underlying structure is crucial.

In our book, we write not as theorists but as historians with particular experience in examining data. Just as forensic teams in various fields do, our objective is to determine—through a narrative revealed in the data—what happened. We believe that the period of contraction began before the Great Crash and that what started it was largely endogenous to the operating of the U.S. economy in the period 1922-1929. Our aim is not to identify precisely what started the period of contraction but rather, as was Professor Temin's, to identify how the Great Crash *transformed* that contraction into what became the Great Depression with its calamitous severity and long duration.

---

19 Ibid., pp. 173-4.

As to unobserved and unpredictable magnitudes, Professor Temin continued with what amounted to modest self-criticism:

> More than one structure can be used to explain the data for [the inter-war] period, and the choice between these structures must be made upon other grounds.
>
> Two separate attributes of macroeconomic theory contribute to this difficulty. The first characteristic of the theory is its extensive use of unobserved variables whose behavior is not assumed to be governed by strict laws. Many theories depend critically on the behavior of variables which cannot be observed, such as expectations and interest rates on non-marketed assets, and which are not clearly functions of observed magnitudes.
>
> The discussion of consumer expectations in Chapter III, of the risk perception in Chapter IV, and of the real interest rate in Chapter V, all represent attempts to come to grips with unobserved variables in this study….
>
> Most of the literature on the Depression, however, is replete with assertions about unobserved and unpredictable magnitudes…. There is no way to prove these statements wrong…. It follows that one cannot choose between competing explanations of the same events.[20]

Having accepted Professor Temin's invitation, we now discuss our "treasure trove," a vast archive of statistics that includes our "evidentiary Rembrandt"—the aggregate U.S. corporate balance sheets for the years 1927-1933—as we continue trying to solve a longstanding mystery.

20 Ibid., pp. 174-5.

CHAPTER 6

An Evidentiary Treasure Trove in the Attic

> [T]he first duty of an economist is to describe correctly what is out there: a valid description without a deeper explanation is worth a thousand times more than a clever explanation of nonexistent facts.
>
> —Paul Samuelson (*Papers*, p.1543)

IT BEHOOVES THOSE who conduct research into any topic to do more than just become familiar with the thinking of people who have already gained expertise in the field. Becoming familiar with sources of data is also important.

We have already introduced the two leading American schools of economic thought, the Keynesian income-expenditure school and the more recent monetary school, centered preeminently around Milton Friedman at the University of Chicago, that challenged the earlier income-expenditure approach.[1] We have introduced the National Bureau of Economic Research (NBER) and Professor Temin, a thoughtful critic of Professor Friedman's monetarist approach. We have also presented several vital sources of data. In Chapter 1, we considered the National Income and Product Accounts (NIPA), maintained by the U.S. Commerce Department. In Chapters 4 and 5 we have used

1 We acknowledge Irving Fisher, of course, as an early monetarist.

data gathered by the Federal Reserve System and published by the Fed in *Banking and Monetary Statistics 1914-1941* (*BMS*).

One purpose of this chapter is to showcase a division of the U.S. Treasury Department that is a major source of data on 1929-33—the Internal Revenue Service (IRS). This chapter focuses on those extensive IRS archives and on specific data that we have found essential in telling the story of the Great Depression. We also consider how professional economists have made little use of this IRS data over the decades.

The IRS Archives: A Source of Valuable Evidentiary-Grade Data

The pedigree and integrity of the IRS data were, and remain to this day, incontestable. From the beginning, the IRS mandate enacted in 1913 by passage of the 16th Amendment required the careful standardization of submitted data—via income tax returns—as needing to stand up in court. In fact, the data became concrete evidence when it was submitted to the Federal government and admissible evidence in court cases and all kinds of government inquiries.

Every year, including from 1929-33, autonomous entities who met the income requirements within the IRS codes submitted their portions of this data to the U.S. Department of the Treasury's tax bureau known by all as the Internal Revenue Service or IRS. For example, in 1929, 4.0 million individuals and 509,000 corporations filed income tax returns. Upon receiving each submission, IRS staff evaluated the data it contained and audited the return, if necessary, to ensure maximum accuracy and completeness. After finishing this yearlong evaluation and auditing process, all the data were turned over to statisticians in the IRS Statistical Section for tabulation. The IRS then published and made available to the public an extensive, detailed annual document called *Statistics of Income*

(SOI) for the designated year—*SOI for 1930*, for example.[2] This is the kind of information that historians love to find and make use of. It is comprehensive rather than comprising statistical samples. It is also contemporary, uniform and as accurate as legal reporting requirements and careful auditing can make it. Furthermore, now every annual *SOI*, beginning with 1916, is available on the IRS website for public scrutiny and use and is carefully preserved in an archive without change over the ensuing years.[3]

This pedigree is why we consider the IRS data our evidentiary treasure trove.

The Unheralded Evidentiary "Rembrandt" at the Heart of Our Research

In August 2018, motivated by a statement made by Keynes in 1930 in the *Treatise on Money* (cited in Chapter 3 on p. 80), we began a search for statistical evidence as to what was actually happening economically around the period of the Crash and after. We asked our very able data researcher if he could find data on aggregate corporate balance sheets for the years 1929-33, and especially statistics on aggregate corporate working capital. As Keynes had written:

> I attribute the slump of 1930 primarily to the deterrent effects on investment of the long period of dear money which preceded the stock-market collapse and only secondarily

2 When we cite statistics from the *Statistics of Income* series, we present them without making any corrections, so as to enable our readers to verify them readily if they choose to do so. For instance, the statistics that are based on numbers close to 100% of corporations are not corrected to estimate them for exactly 100% of corporations. If the numbers are not "close enough" to 100% and thus need correction, we explain why on an as-needed basis.

3 www.irs.gov/statistics/soi-tax-stats-irs-data-book

> to the collapse itself. But the collapse having occurred, it greatly aggravated matters, especially in the United States, by causing a disinvestment in working capital.[4]

Within days, our data researcher showed us one particular page of *Statistics of Income for 1929*, an impressive 429-page document compiled by the IRS Statistical Section. That page presented nothing less than an aggregate corporate balance sheet for year-end 1929, comprising tabulated statistics from 398,815 corporate tax filings submitted for that year.[5] (The page also included statistics that gave us a high degree of confidence in the completeness and accuracy of the data.) While studying the aggregate balance sheet data for 1929, an undertaking that stemmed from years of working with financial management tools, we sensed we were onto something important and called for more data. The result—our Table 6.1 (on next page)—shows the corresponding IRS corporate data for 1929-33.[6] With mounting curiosity as befits our prior professional experience, we created a rudimentary outline of our ultimate, still-hypothetical objectives and commenced the challenging endeavors of conducting the necessary research and analysis and then writing this book, with its unique takes on the Crash and Great Depression thanks to the IRS.

Table 6.1 presents the Aggregate U.S. Corporate Balance Sheet for each of the years 1929-33.[7] When working with data, clear definitions are essential. To the extent that any line items under Assets and Liabilities required further elucidation, the IRS provided thorough definitions in each *SOI* yearly publication, usually on

4 Keynes (1930, Vol. 2), p. 196. (In The Royal Economic Society 1971 edition this is p. 176.)

5 *SOI for 1929*, p. 25.

6 Ibid. Of the 509,436 corporations that submitted tax returns in 1929, 53,415 were inactive and 57,206 declined to submit balance sheets voluntarily. Of the corporations that declined voluntarily to submit balance sheets, 88% had a net income of less than $5,000 or a deficit less than $5,000.

7 *SOI for 1930*, p. 27; *for 1931*, p. 30; *for 1932*, p. 30; *for 1933*, p. 30.

Table 6.1					
Aggregate U.S. Corporate Balance Sheet, 1929-1933					
Assets and liabilities-Statement prepared from U.S. income tax returns of corporations submitting balance sheets showing major assets and liabilities as of December 31 each year or at the close of business of the fiscal year nearest thereto ($ million)					
Assets and liabilities	1929	1930	1931	1932	1933
Assets:					
Cash (in till and deposits in banks)	22,371	21,012	15,880	15,917	15,236
Notes receivable and accounts receivable (less reserve for bad debts)	66,810	59,675	48,667	39,564	35,835
Inventory	21,911	18,771	15,140	12,372	13,597
Tax-exempt investments:					
Obligations of States and Territories or political subdivisions; securities issued under the Federal farm loan act and obligations of the U.S. or its possessions	10,338	10,228	10,667	11,917	13,571
Investments other than tax-exempt:					
Stocks, bonds, mortgages, loans, real estate, etc.	55,844	83,809	74,305	75,630	70,474
Capital assets: Real estate, buildings, equipment etc. (less depreciation)	116,446	120,994	115,303	108,553	104,958
Misc. assets not distributed	42,057	19,511	16,534	16,129	14,535
Total assets	335,778	334,002	296,497	280,083	268,206
Liabilities:					
Notes and accounts payable	29,453	26,870	23,251	20,562	19,362
Bonded debt and mortgages	46,643	50,282	48,101	47,310	45,883
Misc. liabilities not distributed	94,714	95,768	81,882	78,642	75,384
Capital stock:					
Preferred	19,738	19,117	19,117	19,076	18,394
Common	90,120	87,067	79,794	78,413	74,088
Total capital stock	109,858	106,184	98,911	97,489	92,482
Surplus	60,699	61,632	51,976	45,664	44,792
Less deficit	5,588	6,734	7,624	9,584	9,696
Net surplus	55,111	54,898	44,352	36,080	35,096
Total liabilities	335,778	334,002	296,497	280,083	268,206

Source: *SOI for 1929-33*: *1929* p.25, *1930* p.27, *1931* p.30, *1932* p.30, *1933* p.30.

the page or two on which the year's balance sheet appeared. For instance, *SOI for 1930* provided the following extensive definitions of "miscellaneous assets" and "miscellaneous liabilities" and the accompanying commentary:[8]

8 *SOI for 1930* also provided information on a significant change in accounting treatment that occurred in 1930. Other *SOI* editions noted changes of this sort as needed.

• *Miscellaneous assets.*—Copyrights; formulas; goodwill; patents; trade-marks; sinking funds; other funds; deferred charges; organization expenses; suspense items; prepaid items; interest discount, coupons, and dividends receivable; guaranty deposits, and deposits on contracts, meters, and leaseholds; cash value of life insurance; and real estate by foreclosure.

• *Miscellaneous liabilities.*—All reserves other than surplus reserves and reserves for depreciation and bad debts, accrued expenses, deferred and suspense items, funds held in trust, borrowed securities, discounts and dividends payable, outstanding coupons and certificates and overdrafts. Some miscellaneous liabilities of life insurance companies include policy claims and value of outstanding policies and annuities. Miscellaneous liabilities of banks include deposits (time, saving, demand, etc.) and bank notes in circulation.

The amounts for 1930 shown under "Miscellaneous assets not distributed" and "investments other than tax exempt, etc.," are not comparable with the data under corresponding classifications in 1929 due principally to the fact that stocks, bonds, loans, mortgages, etc., owned by life insurance companies in 1929 that were classified as "Miscellaneous assets not distributed," have been tabulated as "Investments other than tax-exempt, etc." Moreover, the returns of corporations become more complete each year with respect to the definite allocation of their forms of assets and thereby permit a more accurate classification of the data according to the principal forms of assets, thus steadily decreasing the proportion tabulated as "Miscellaneous assets not distributed."[9]

Acknowledging the care taken and the level of detail offered by the IRS Statistical Unit, we will revisit these Aggregate Corporate Balance Sheets often in future chapters as we consider changes in strategies in corporate financial funding during these turbulent

9 *SOI for 1930,* p. 26.

years, as well as the dramatic financial actions taken by American individuals, as consumers, at the time.

Working Capital Statements Drawn from Our Evidentiary "Rembrandt"

One objective of this chapter is to present the analytical framework that we used to understand the financial activities of businesses and consumers over the course of the Great Depression. One critical focus, for instance, is on working capital.

As the all-important difference between a corporation's current assets and current liabilities, working capital, also known as "net working capital," measures a corporation's liquidity, near-term operating efficiency and overall financial well-being. Current assets include cash, accounts receivable (customers' unpaid bills), financial notes receivable within the next year and inventories. Current liabilities include accounts payable (the corporation's own unpaid bills) and financial notes payable (due within a year). These measures and their movement have proved hugely illuminating.

Table 6.2

Aggregate U.S. Corporate Working Capital 1929-1933

($ million)

Current assets:	1929	1930	1931	1932	1933	Percent (%) change from 1929
Cash	22,371	21,012	15,880	15,917	15,236	-31.9
Notes & Accounts Receivable	66,810	59,675	48,667	39,564	35,835	-46.4
Inventory	21,911	18,772	15,140	13,597	13,507	-38.4
Total	111,092	99,459	79,687	69,078	64,578	-41.9
Less						
Current liabilities:						
Notes & accounts payable	29,453	26,870	23,251	20,562	19,362	-34.3
Net working capital	81,639	72,589	56,436	48,516	45,216	-44.6

Source: *SOI for* 1929-33.

Table 6.2, above, presents Aggregate U.S. Corporate Working Capital for the years 1929-1933 using the data from Table 6.1.

Clearly, U.S. corporate working capital diminished materially year by year in 1930 through 1933. In fact, the final column of Table 6.2 shows that Total Current Assets declined 41.9% and Working Capital declined 44.6% over the period.

Three of the four components of working capital—cash, notes and accounts payable and inventories—are relatively controllable by corporations, at least large corporations. Large corporations have a measure of decision-making ability as to the amount of cash and inventory they want on hand to make their businesses run efficiently, and they also have control over the speed at which they pay their bills. As a result, while these three components declined materially, each declined less than 40.0%.

For one component, however, the decline was greater than the rate of decline of Working Capital overall. In fact, the major influence propelling the diminishment of working capital was in the fourth component—Notes Receivable and Accounts Receivable. Table 6.2 shows this fourth component declining 46.4% over the four-year period. This component is usually less controllable because, at least in the case of accounts receivable, it depends on the speed with which customers want to, or can, pay their bills. Since one entity's payable is another entity's receivable, entities that slow down the speed with which they pay bills directly impact the working capital of those entities owed the money as receivables.

Certain accounting principles are worthwhile to go into here, as they reveal important realities about the 1929-33 period. When working with aggregated data, this two-sided reality—assets and liabilities—can and inevitably does lead to the issue of double counting. For example, in considering aggregate corporate notes and accounts receivable, given that almost all banks provide their balance sheet statistics to the IRS as corporations, virtually all Notes Payable by non-bank corporations to banks are included in the Aggregate Corporate Balance Sheet on both sides of the ledger. As Notes Payable of non-bank corporations, they appear as liabilities. As Notes Receivable of corporate banks, they appear as assets. Further, since the customers of many corporations are other corporations, a meaningful proportion of the Accounts Receivable at U.S. corporations is included in Accounts Payable at other U.S. corporations. To restate the obvious, one corporation's liability can be, and most often is, another corporation's asset.

Taking this idea one step further, nowhere that we have found in *SOI for 1929* or *SOI for 1930* were there statistics on the proportions of corporate receivables that were payable by other corporations or payable by entities that were not U.S. corporations. This distinction was of particular interest to us. Who might these entities that were not U.S. corporations be? To our thinking, we presumed some were likely various governmental entities at local, state and federal levels; others were foreign or non-U.S. entities. However, as we will see, a significant number were individuals—those who had come to be thought of economically as consumers. These individuals owed money to various corporate entities—for instance, banks, consumer finance companies, automobile manufacturers who financed their dealers by buying their dealers' receivables, department stores and other retailers. We will focus on this key group of debtors below, as well as in *The Deflation of 1930*.

For the moment, however, we put individuals' financial activity to the side to focus on corporations. We make the assumption that all corporate notes payable and accounts payable on the balance sheets for 1929-33 shown in Table 6.1 and the working capital statements shown in Table 6.2 were payable to other corporations. We have based our assumption on the fact that many corporations obtain much, if not all, of their financing by borrowing from banks. Furthermore, most corporations that produce and sell finished consumer goods buy raw materials and partially finished goods from other corporations. In addition, since corporations, when taken in aggregate, hold far more as corporate notes and accounts receivable than the total amount of corporate notes and accounts payable, assuming that all corporate notes payable and accounts payable are held as receivables by other U.S. corporations also enabled us to isolate and concentrate on sums that were payable to U.S. corporations by entities that were not U.S. corporations, including individuals.

As we continue our focus on U.S. corporations, neither Peter Temin nor John Maynard Keynes, who cited the importance of "a disinvestment in working capital," had statistics to support their suppositions. We, however, have found concrete numbers in the IRS statistics for the values (or magnitudes) year by year of the components of working capital in 1929-33.

As we saw in Chapter 5, Temin pointedly declared in his conclusion to *Did Monetary Forces*, "Most of the literature on the Depression...is replete with assertions about unobserved and unpredictable magnitudes." In response, we created Table 6.3 to

Table 6.3

Rates of Change - 1929-1933

(Assumes **100%** of Corporate payables are owed to Corporations)

($ million in current dollars)

1929	1930	1931	1932	1933	% Change from 1929
Fall in GNP					
103,420	90,700				-12.3
		76,073			-26.4
			58,280		-43.6
				55,818	-46.0
Fall in notes and accounts receivable *held by* U.S corporations					
66,810	59,675				-10.7
		48,667			-27.2
			39,564		-40.8
				35,835	-46.4
Fall in notes and accounts payable *owed by* U.S. corporations					
29,453	26,870				-8.8
		23,251			-21.1
			20,562		-30.2
				19,362	-34.3
Fall in notes and accounts payable *owed by others* to U.S. corporations					
37,358	32,805				-12.2
		25,416			-32.0
			19,002		-49.1
				16,473	-55.9

Source: Commerce Department; IRS *Statistics of Income 1929-1933*.

show Rates of Change for 1929-1933 in current dollars in various aggregate balance sheet components or magnitudes.

The first component or magnitude in Table 6.3 is GNP (taken from Table 1.1, page 53) which fell 46.0% from $103.4 billion in 1929 to $55.8 billion in 1933.

The second magnitude is "Notes and accounts receivable *held by* U.S. corporations" which fell 46.4% from $66.8 billion in 1929 to $35.8 billion in 1933. When measured in then-current dollars, both GNP and Notes and accounts receivable held by U.S. corporations fell over the four years at almost the same rate.

The third magnitude is "Notes and accounts payable *owed by* U.S. corporations" which for now we are assuming is 100% on both sides of the aggregate U.S. corporate balance sheet—as payables on the liabilities side and as a portion of receivables on the assets side. Table 6.3 shows that this amount fell 34.3% from $29.5 billion in 1929 to $19.8 billion in 1933. In other words, when considered as a portion of the liabilities side of the aggregate U.S. corporate balance sheet, this asset-side sum also fell, although at a rate well within the capacity of the corporations themselves to manage.

Subtracting corporate payables from corporate receivables derives the amounts in the fourth component, labeled in Table 6.3 as "Fall in Notes and accounts payable *owed by others* to U.S. Corporations." We contend that it is this component of "by others" that offers a critical insight into the behavior of these unspecified "others," most of whom were, in actuality, individuals, i.e., consumers. For example, for 1929, $66,810 million minus $29,453 million gives $37,358 million in Notes and accounts payable owed by others to U.S. Corporations. Calculated in this same fashion, the amounts for 1930, 1931, 1932 and 1933, namely $32,805 million, $25,416 million, $19,002 million and $16,473 million respectively, show a rate of change in this component from 1929 to 1933 of -55.9%.

Based on our assumption that all corporate notes payable and accounts payable on the balance sheets and the working capital statements for 1929-33 —i.e. ,100% as shown in the heading of Table 6.3 were payable to other corporations, we assert that American consumers repaid their collective debts—loans on securities, mortgages, consumer finance debts, loans from banks, etc.—much more aggressively than the rate at which GNP fell, indicating their strong motivations to reduce indebtedness, i.e., to deleverage.

Using Sensitivity Analysis Based on an Alternative Key Assumption

Before proceeding, in order to look at how realistic our earlier assumption was that all corporate notes payable and accounts payable are held as receivables by other U.S. corporations (including banks) and what impact it had on the apparent rate at which consumers sought to repay their debt obligations, we first consider an alternate basic assumption.

Table 6.4, on next page, presents Rates of Change that appear in Table 6.3 based on an alternative assumption, namely that 90% of corporate payables were owed to U.S. Corporations rather than 100%. Comparing the two tables reveals that the numbers under "Fall in Notes and accounts payable *owed by* U.S. Corporations to U.S. Corporations" in Table 6.4 are smaller than the numbers in Table 6.3, while the numbers under "Fall in Notes and accounts payable *owed by others* to U.S. Corporations" are larger. These changes are to be expected given our newly suggested reduction in the percentage of corporate payables due to other corporations.

Comparing the two tables also reveals that the "Change From 1929" reflecting the "Fall in Notes and accounts payable owed by others to U.S. Corporations" is slightly less than those that appear in Table 6.3. Most particularly, in Table 6.4 the four-year rate of change became -54.3% compared to -55.9% in Table 6.3. The 90% assumption showed consumers still highly motivated to get out of debt even if not by quite as much as the 100% assumption did. The

Table 6.4					
Rates of Change - 1929-1933 (Assumes **90%** of Corporate payables are owed to Corporations) ($ million in current dollars)					
1929	1930	1931	1932	1933	% Change from 1929
Fall in GNP					
103,420	90,700				-12.3
		76,073			-26.4
			58,280		-43.6
				55,818	-46.0
Fall in notes and accounts receivable *held by* U.S Corporations					
66,810	59,675				-10.7
		48,667			-27.2
			39,564		-40.8
				35,835	-46.4
Fall in notes and accounts payable *owed by* U.S. Corporations					
26,508	24,183				-8.8
		20,926			-21.1
			18,506		-30.2
				17,426	-34.3
Fall in notes and accounts payable *owed by others* to U.S. Corporations					
40,302	35,492				-11.9
		27,741			-31.2
			21,058		-47.7
				18,409	-54.3

Source: IRS *Statistics of Income 1929-1933*.

fall based on the 90% assumption still exceeded the drop in GNP.

How realistic are these two assumptions of 100% and of 90%? For us to try to ascertain concretely what amount or proportion of the payables of corporations were in fact owed by consumer households in 1929 was unnecessary because, fortunately, we could turn to economist Raymond W. Goldsmith's estimated Balance Sheet of Corporations for confirmation of the reasonableness of our approach. Goldsmith, whom we'll discuss further below, determined that the total payables of corporations in 1929 equaled $29,100 million compared with the equivalent IRS statistic of $29,453 million. Since Goldsmith also concluded that the payables owed to other corporations equaled $27,900 million, his estimate indicated that 95.9% of corporate payables in 1929 were owed to other corporations.[10] Thus,

10 Raymond William Goldsmith, Dorothy S. Brady and Horst Mendershausen, *A Study of Saving In The United States*, Volume III, Princeton University Press, 1956, p. 79.

the soundness of either our original 100% assumption or our 90% alternative assumption is supported by prior research.

Where did consumers get the money they used to repay their debts? Simply stated, they tightened their belts, month-by-month, then year-by-year. They spent less and less on all manner of consumer goods and services (as statistics and anecdotes verified, tobacco and bootleg alcohol were exceptions) in order to pay off their debts as fast as they could. It is our view that it was the top priority for indebted American consumers to get out of debt.

It is this story *How the Crash Caused* tells—the story of how prosperity led first to speculation that grew completely out-of-hand and led to the Crash, with its sudden disappearance of a huge cushion of wealth, and then ushered in the Great Depression/Contraction that followed.

How Have Economists Made Use of the IRS Data Over Time?

Once the IRS statistics came into focus for us, our logical first step was to see who else had made use of this official data and how they had used it. Launching a search for publications by academicians and others referencing the IRS archive in relation to their studies of the period, we came to the unexpected conclusion that it appears the data had been mostly unexplored. While we found a few credible references, discussed below, none of the references offered what we regarded as critical insights into the factors that led to the Crash and the causes and duration of the Great Depression.

One economist who did make some use of this prodigious information was the aforementioned Raymond W. Goldsmith (1904-88) in his sweeping works *A Study of Saving in the United States* and *Studies in the National Balance Sheet of the United States*.[11] In

11 Ibid., p. 471 as an example.

both publications, besides providing voluminous statistics, the IRS reports supplied a vital framework on which to organize and array his compiled statistics and estimates. This framework included, for example, such IRS breakdowns as "Nonfarm households," "Unincorporated business," "Nonfinancial Corporations," "Unincorporated brokers and dealers," etc. However, Goldsmith's focus was strictly on presenting the data. Other than assessing the relevance of the data to the statistics he sought to collect, Goldsmith did not interpret or analyze the implications of the data so as to explain economic developments, nor did he attempt to gain potential insights into the causes and duration of the Great Depression.

In our research, we also learned from cultural critic Gilbert Seldes in his 1933 work *The Years of the Locust (America, 1929-1932)* that J. Edward Meeker, the economist of the New York Stock Exchange, called Seldes' attention to the IRS data in order to enable Seldes to attempt an estimate of the number of Americans speculating in stocks in 1928-30. [12] About the IRS data, Seldes, as a cultural observer and not an economist, merely commented, "What impresses me is that 4 million people filed income tax returns and that less than one tenth of them showed either profit or loss in the stock market in their returns."[13]

We found a brief third reference to the IRS reports within a sourcing footnote in the second volume of *Business Cycles: A Theoretical, Historical, and Statistical Analysis of the Capitalistic Process* by pioneering economist Joseph Schumpeter (1883-1950). The footnote supported his statement, "[N]et earnings of all corporations (excluding tax-exempt ones and life insurance companies) before deduction of

---

12 Gilbert Seldes, *The Years of the Locust*, Little, Brown and Company 1933, p. 312. Reprinted in 1977 by Da Capo Press.

13 Ibid., p. 313 in pp. 310-316. We believe Seldes was using statistics from *Statistics of Income for 1929.* In Chapter 4 in *The Deflation of 1930*, readers can see that the proportion of tax returns showing profit or loss was higher than 10%.

income taxes were by over 78 per cent below the 1929 figure ($1,960 million)…."[14] However, Schumpeter offered no further commentary.

An Exciting Discovery, with Caveats

That lone Schumpeter footnote also fortuitously led us to a brief but dense twelve-page publication of the National Bureau of Economic Research from 1935, *Bulletin 55* entitled "Profits, Losses and Business Assets, 1929-1934." NBER had been founded in 1920 as, to quote their website, "a private, nonpartisan organization that facilitates cutting-edge investigation and analysis of major economic issues."[15] Dated April 11, 1935, *Bulletin 55* was authored by a then young economist named Solomon Fabricant (1906-89). Fabricant went on to a distinguished career teaching, conducting research and writing on productivity, growth and recessionary conditions and became NBER's third director of research from 1953 to 1965. (Wesley Clair Mitchell, whom we met in Chapter 3, was the first director, and Arthur Burns, who was Chairman of the Federal Reserve System from 1970-1978, was the second.) Looking back on economic conditions in the early 1930s as it related to businesses, Fabricant began *Bulletin 55:*

> The large business losses in 1932, the decline in annual deficits in 1933, and the further improvement in 1934 are already well known. So much have we learned from current financial reports of large corporations. But the figures that relate to business profits constitute a peculiarly significant index in an industrial economy. Profits represent, at once, gains of enterprise arising from the conjunction of past events and decisions, and influences upon current judgments

14 Joseph Schumpeter, *Business Cycles: A Theoretical and Statistical Analysis of the Capitalist Process*, Volume II, McGraw-Hill Book Company, Inc., 1939, pp. 912-3.

15 www.nber.org.

> concerning the future. It is well, therefore, to check conclusions derived from samples and estimates by the data on corporate profits issued by the Treasury Department. These comprehensive figures cover all the taxable corporations in the United States, small as well as large.
>
> What was the earnings position of business enterprise as a whole at the bottom of the severest depression of the last half-century? How did the net incomes of large and small companies, of different industrial groups, compare in 1932? How did corporate incomes respond to the complex of factors active in the first and second years of recovery? What effect did the drain upon business resources have upon the assets and condition of business between the end of 1929 and 1932? It is these questions that concern us in the present *Bulletin.*
>
> There are now available complete and final reports covering profits and balance sheets of all corporations in the United States for 1932 (and earlier years), and preliminary data that make possible reliable estimates of net income of all corporations in 1933. Also, many large companies have already published reports covering 1934 operations. This Bulletin presents these figures, based chiefly on the official Statistics of Income issued by the United States Treasury Department, with emphasis on the course of profits and the condition of business enterprise since 1929. [16]

We admit that we were initially pleased finally to find an analysis of the IRS statistics that aimed to be even somewhat thorough, and we studied it with some expectation. However, while we would like to confirm that the bulletin was right on the money, we curiously found a certain selectivity—even discrepancies—in the bulletin when compared with the IRS's own reports. NBER *Bulletin*

---

16 Solomon Fabricant, "Profits, Losses and Businesss Assets, 1929-1934" *Bulletin 55,* NBER, 1935, p. 1.

Table 6.5 **Aggregate Balance Sheet, 1929-1932** (All Corporations Other Than Finance, Real Estate and Service Companies)[1]								
	($ million)				Percent (%) of 1929			
	1929	1930	1931	1932	1929	1930	1931	1932
<u>Assets</u>								
Cash	7,460	7,513	6,283	6,106	100.0	100.7	84.2	81.8
Notes & accounts receivable (net)	21,849	19,831	16,829	14,281	100.0	90.8	77.0	65.4
Inventories	20,799	18,070	14,692	12,077	100.0	86.9	70.6	58.1
Capital assets (net)	94,813	98,322	93,947	88,307	100.0	103.7	99.1	93.1
Investments								
Tax-exempt	2,913	2,572	2,561	2,677	100.0	88.3	87.9	91.9
Other[2]				26,246				
Misc. assets	39,400	40,140	34,586	11,157	100.0	101.9	87.8	94.9
Total	187,234	186,448	168,898	160,851	100.0	99.6	90.2	85.9
<u>Liabilities and capital</u>								
Notes and accounts payable	19,845	18,268	15,411	13,954	100.0	92.1	77.7	70.3
Bonded debt and mortgages	34,944	37,485	35,465	34,907	100.0	107.3	101.5	99.9
Misc. liabilities	15,368	14,436	11,982	12,464	100.0	93.9	78.0	81.1
Capital stock								
Preferred	15,352	14,793	15,166	15,200	100.0	96.4	98.8	99.0
Common	63,705	64,461	59,734	59,576	100.0	101.2	93.8	93.5
Surplus and undivided profits less deficit	38,020	37,005	31,140	24,750	100.0	97.3	81.9	65.1
Total	187,234	186,448	168,898	160,851	100.0	99.6	90.2	85.9

[1] Excluding tax-exempt corporations and companies not reporting balance sheets.

[2] Figures for 1929-31 are not given here since there is evidence that some investments were not separated from miscellaneous assets in the earlier reports.

Source: NBER *Bulletin* 55, p.8.

55, published in 1935, is, of course, a historical document, written within a time period and serving objectives directly related to the events and needs of that period. Later in this chapter, we will comment on what we consider to have been NBER's main objective in addressing the needs of its time and give our thoughts on the success of their efforts. But, first, we delve into *Bulletin 55* more deeply.

When we examined *Bulletin 55*, we quickly noted that it presented only a *subset* of the available balance sheet information the IRS published (our Table 6.1 on p. 138) Table 6.5 (above) shows the NBER bulletin's selective, or reduced, Aggregate Balance Sheet, which accounted for *only 55.8%* of the total assets and total liabilities shown in the complete IRS Aggregate Balance Sheet in Table 6.1 (page 140) for 1929 and 57.4% for 1932. We regarded NBER's omissions as conspicuous and deserving of explanation. Yet *Bulletin*

55 offered neither reasoning as to why NBER chose its limited focus on this subset nor even an acknowledgment that NBER had, in fact, ignored data of potential importance. In the text, *Bulletin 55* stated simply, "We confine ourselves to the total, omitting the finance, real estate and service groups." A footnote added the following:

> It is desirable to omit realty concerns, banks and other financial institutions from the present discussion. Owing to certain changes in classification this makes it necessary also to exclude service companies.[17]

To us these editorial decisions—without a stated rationale as to why Fabricant was being selective—resulted in serious and deliberate omissions, considering what was going on in the period. In our view, the omission of these critical sectors was questionable. For instance, why would NBER exclude the highly influential finance sector, consisting of banks, as well as brokerage firms and insurance companies? Why exclude financial intermediaries, such as finance companies, that raised funds from consumers through installment loan payments and conveyed those funds (likely from consumers' savings accounts) to business concerns that in turn would invest the funds?[18]

Consumer sector liabilities appeared as major assets on finance sector balance sheets—e.g., bank loans to consumers appeared as

---

17 NBER *Bulletin 55*, p. 7.

18 One suspicion we had was that *Bulletin 55* omitted the finance sector to focus on the "industrial" side of the business economy in keeping with Wesley Mitchell's point-of-view expressed in Chapter 3: "All that is needed to complete the explanation is treatment of several other random factors in addition to those here discussed, and an analysis of the way in which *cyclical fluctuations originate in the business realm.*" (emphasis ours). However, analysis of the components of the subset balance sheet in Table 6.5 indicates that "Agriculture and related industries" remains in the balance sheet of Table 6.5, which leads one to consider this subset balance sheet as including somewhat more than just the industrial side of the business economy.

assets—and consumer sector assets appeared as major liabilities—e.g., bank deposits of consumers appeared as bank liabilities. In omitting the finance sector, *Bulletin 55* failed to acknowledge the economic significance of the actions of consumers in the Depression period. In fact, as we will see, instead of engaging in thrift by committing their funds to savings, consumers were committing those funds very aggressively to pay off their own financial obligations of notes and accounts payable to the Aggregate of U.S. corporations shown in Table 6.1. Thus *Bulletin 55* failed to note or even to consider the financial behavior that IRS figures in Tables 6.3 and 6.4 reveal.

Furthermore, while *Bulletin 55* did consider working capital, the statistics that were included necessarily reflected their selected subset of U.S. corporations as shown in Table 6.5. For example, about a core component of working capital, *Bulletin 55* stated, "While receivables (notes and open accounts) exceeded notes and accounts payables by two billion dollars in 1929, the balance was but a seventh of that figure at the end of 1932."[19] From this, *Bulletin 55* drew its conclusions:

> But in any event working capital, in the form of liquid assets, was insufficient to finance the requirements that an upturn would bring....T]he credit-making mechanism of our banking system was needed to quicken it into life.[20]

To us there is considerable irony in this statement considering their omission of the banking system from their data set. It suggests that NBER regarded itself as responsible for examining and reporting on the economics of the *industrial* side of the U.S. economy but not for considering and reviewing the economics of the *financial* side, despite acknowledging their declared need of that omitted banking system to "quicken" the economy back into life. Did the staff of NBER not understand the importance of what could appear on

19 Ibid., p. 10.

20 Ibid., p. 11.

balance sheets or the importance of credit analysis in the finance sector's process of making its own autonomous investment decisions, or did the staff choose to ignore or omit it?

Most important to us is that *Bulletin 55* also failed to address the large volume of information in the *Statistics of Income* series on individuals, the other—and equally significant—breakdown of tax filers the IRS used. Notably, *SOI for 1929* reported that individuals bore a tax liability of $1,002 million, only slightly less than the $1,193 million tax liability of corporations.[21] In 1932, the tax liability of individuals was $330 million, actually exceeding the tax liability of corporations of $286 million.[22] *Bulletin 55* limited its focus to corporations despite the significance of the available data on individuals, including important business activities engaged in by sole proprietorships and partnerships. (For some other, lesser caveats particularly regarding certain definitions and statistics used in *Bulletin 55* see the Endnote to this chapter.)

Did NBER Achieve Its Objective in Publishing *Bulletin 55?*

Bulletin 55 was written and published in 1935, in the middle of the longer Depression period, 1929-39, as most Americans experienced it. The first three paragraphs of *Bulletin 55* that we quoted on page 148, included a series of questions that culminated with the following passage intended to state the *Bulletin's* objectives:

> What effect did the drain upon business resources have upon the assets and the condition of business between the end of 1929 and 1932? It is these questions that concern us in the present *Bulletin*. [23]

21 *SOI for 1929,* p. 4 and p. 17.

22 *SOI for 1932,* p. 5 and p. 21.

23 NBER *Bulletin 55,* p. 1.

Reading this might lead us to think that the primary objective of NBER was to foster research into the causes of the Great Depression. Certainly, informing economists and others of the value of the *SOI* series as a source of voluminous, highly meaningful data might have been one objective of NBER.

We believe, however, that NBER's primary objective—in 1935—was actually to show that the U.S. economy had turned the corner and was on an upswing. When *Bulletin 55* was published in April 1935, the statistics available in the *SOI* series were available only through the end of 1932. The tables on earnings in *Bulletin 55* presented preliminary estimates for 1933 earnings and further for 1933 and 1934, and these estimates consistently pointed towards improved conditions. For instance, the *Bulletin 55* Summary includes the following telling statement:

> At the bottom of depression, in 1932, only four industries were making profits: public utilities, foods, tobacco products, and chemicals[24].... In brief, 1932 was definitely the low point in the average earnings of business enterprise. The year 1933, with a few exceptions, showed considerable improvement over 1932 (chiefly in the form of a reduction in losses), and it is probable that 1934 was more favorable. Here are reflected the effects, upon the business enterprise, of the interaction between the situation created by the preceding years of decline and the new factors injected into the scene of 1933. While business in the aggregate was not yet on a profitable basis in 1933, or perhaps even in 1934, fears of the end of the profits system must, in light of the figures, be modified. Industry has always revealed great powers of adaptation and recuperation. What we find today constitutes no exception to this experience.[25]

24 Actually, *SOI for 1932,* pp. 148 and 150, show that foods and chemicals were in aggregate deficit.

25 NBER *Bulletin 55,* p 11.

If we are correct that NBER's primary objective in publishing *Bulletin 55* was to show that—at least on the corporate side—the U.S. economy had turned the corner in 1933 thanks to "new factors injected into the scene" and was on an upswing, we consider NBER to have succeeded commendably. However, *Bulletin 55* had its limitations as to revealing broader realities going on in the Depression, and it made far less than full use of what the IRS archive had to offer.

Some Further Thoughts

As discussed, *Bulletin 55*, as pleased as we were to discover it, focused on only some of the data in the *SOI* series: corporate net earnings/income statistics and a subset of aggregate corporate balance sheet statistics. In neglecting the individual sector data altogether, the NBER's bulletin missed key forces at play that our analysis of IRS data on individuals will provide for a fuller picture, including compelling and poignant details about how individual Americans handled their finances and managed their lives during the Depression years.

The broader story of the Great Depression was about how overall demand for all manner of goods and services fell year after year then picked up somewhat in 1933. Everywhere the *SOI* series presented "net income less deficit" statistics for corporations, it also presented gross income/revenue statistics. The contours that these gross income/revenue statistics painted constituted a vital part of the story of the Great Depression, which we will examine in Chapter 11 in *The Deflation of 1930*.

The full data set in the IRS archive has always been there with the capacity to reveal more, but scant evidence exists that this rock-solid source has ever been scoured for the depths of the insights it contains. In the coming chapters, a revised story of the origins, scope, scale and impact of the Great Depression as it befell the United

States will unfold before us, with the estimable, long-neglected IRS archive emerging from the shadows to play a leading role in our look at the notorious phenomenon of speculation, as well as in expanding our understanding of the effects of the 1929 Crash on Americans as they responded to unfolding events over the months that followed.

Endnote

In this Endnote we examine in detail aspects of *Bulletin 55* that appear to differ from the information that we actually found in the IRS Statistics of Income publications for 1929-33. (We were unable to find in *Bulletin 55* explanations for these differences.) We make these observations in an Endnote because many readers may not wish to go into this level of detail.

As a start, we found that Fabricant and the NBER staff used definitions for measures of earnings and rates of earnings that differed from the way the IRS defined "net income" for their statistics, but did not make clear how SOI definitions related to the NBER definitions. In a footnote, *Bulletin 55* gives the following definitions:

> "Net income" is the net earnings after payment of all business expenses and fixed charges including Federal income taxes.... "Capitalization" is book value of stockholders' equity.[26]

Because we make frequent use of the *Statistics of Income* series, we cite the contrasting definition of net income from *SOI for 1932* as the IRS applied it to their statistics:

> *General definitions.*—Throughout this report, "net income" represents the amount of the gross income, as defined in the revenue act effective for the year for which the income is returned, in excess of the deductions claimed by the taxpayer under the provisions of the respective acts, and "deficit" means the excess of deductions over gross income.[27]

---

26 Ibid., p. 2.

27 Ibid., p.3.

Upon careful review, we also found inaccuracies in the actual statistics *Bulletin 55* cited as attributed to the *Statistics of Income* series. Table 6.6, presents a comparison.

Table 6.6

Net Earnings Of All Corporations In the United States, 1929-1933

($ million)

	1929	1930	1931	1932	1933*
NBER *Bulletin 55*					
Net income before payment of income taxes	9,130	1,960	-2,850	-5,200	-2,110
Income taxes	1,180	700	390	270	410
Net income after payment of income taxes	7,950	1,260	-3,240	-5,470	-2,520
	1929	1930	1931	1932	1933
IRS Historical Statistics					
Net income before payment of income taxes	8,740	1,551	-3,288	-5,644	-2,547
Income taxes	1,193	712	399	286	416
Net income after payment of income taxes	7,547	839	-3,687	-5,930	-2,963

* Preliminary estimates.

Sources: *SOI for 1929-33*: *1929* pp.19-20, *1930* pp.21-22, *1931* pp.22-23, *1932* pp.22-23, *1933* pp.23-24. NBER *Bulletin 55* pp.6, 7.

Consistently, the *Bulletin 55* Net Earnings figures are about $400 million greater than figures shown in the corresponding *Statistics of Income* reports. With current dollar GNP figures of $103.4 billion in 1929 and $55.8 billion in 1933, as seen in Table 1.1 (p. 52), that $400 million excess was a material sum, enough to raise an eyebrow.

Table 6.7 shows another discrepancy, in this case with regards to what *Bulletin 55* presented as "Rates of Earnings on Book

Table 6.7

Rates of Earnings On Book Value Of Capital 1929-1933

(All Corporations In The United States)

	1929	1930	1931	1932	1933
Net income (after taxes)					
as a percentage of capitalization[1]	6.6%	2.4%	-0.7%	-2.9%	-1.2%
Net income (after taxes)					
as a percentage of capitalization[2]	4.7%	0.5%	-2.5%	-4.4%	-2.3%
Capitalization[2]	($ million)				
Common stock	85,520	87,067	79,794	78,413	74,087
Preferred stock	19,738	19,117	19,117	19,076	18,394
Surplus and dividend profits					
less deficit	55,111	54,898	44,352	36,080	35,096
Total capitalization	160,369	161,082	143,263	133,569	127,577

[1] Source: NBER *Bulletin 55*, p.4.

[2] Source: *SOI for 1929-33*: *1929* pp.19-20, *1930* pp.21-22, *1931* pp.22-23, *1932* pp.22-23, *1933* pp.23-24.

Value of Capital, 1929-1933." Here we compared the as-is *Bulletin 55* statistics with our calculations based on actual IRS statistics to show that the IRS statistics were materially lower than the *Bulletin 55* statistics. We found no explanation in *Bulletin 55* as to why this was so.[28]

Table 6.8

Rates of Earnings of Corporations in The U.S.,1929-1933

Classified By Industry

(% percentage)

	Ratio of net income to capitalization					Ratio of total profits to total capital				
Industrial group	1929	1930	1931	1932	1933	1929	1930	1931	1932	1933
Mining and quarrying	2.9	0.0	-2.8	-2.8	-2.9	3.2	0.6	-1.8	-1.8	-1.9
Manufacturing	8.6	2.7	-1.0	-3.6	0.7	8.3	3.0	-0.3	-2.6	1.2
Construction	7.8	5.7	-0.9	-7.8	-4.6	7.4	5.6	0.3	-5.2	-2.6
Public utilities and transport	6.5	4.0	2.3	0.7	0.6	5.6	4.1	3.1	2.2	2.1
Trade	5.1	-0.5	-4.4	-7.2	-0.3	5.2	0.0	-3.3	-5.9	0.4
Service	4.3	2.0	-2.2	-10.0	-7.6	4.6	3.0	0.2	-3.2	-1.8
Finance and real estate	5.8	1.8	-1.5	-3.8	-5.2	5.7	2.6	0.2	-1.5	-2.6
Grand total	6.6	2.4	-0.7	-2.9	-1.2	6.2	2.9	0.7	-0.9	0.4

Source: NBER *Bulletin 55*, p.4.

Table 6.8, reproduced directly from *Bulletin 55*, presents "Rates of Earnings...Classified by Industry" and focuses on NBER's selection of seven of the eight industry groups used by the IRS for its most general level of economic evaluation. While we question all *Bulletin 55* statistics for Net Income (after taxes) and Rates of Earnings shown in Table 6.7, including the grand totals repeated in Table 6.8, our particular discomfort with Table 6.7 is with losses the table fails to show for 1930, in particular. Of the eight industry groups that the

28 NBER *Bulletin 55*, p. 1-2. Footnotes in *Bulletin 55* stated, "Tax-exempt corporations and life insurance companies are excluded." In the *Statistics of Income* reports, we found no information on any tax-exempt corporations to exclude, no reasons for excluding life insurance companies and no reason *Bulletin 55* made these exclusions. In our tables above we made no exclusions, corrections or adjustments. The statistics shown in Tables 6.5 and 6.6 are just as they appeared in *Bulletin 55* or in the *Statistics of Income* reports.

SOI series reported on, four experienced aggregate losses in 1930. According to the IRS groupings, Agriculture and related industries experienced an aggregate loss of $46 million; Mining and quarrying, $44 million; Trade, $88 million; and Finance and real estate, $502 million.[29] But Table 6.8, as it appeared in *Bulletin 55*, showed only one industry, Trade, experiencing a loss in 1930, and one key category, Agriculture, was missing altogether.[30] Using the NBER procedure for calculating rates of return on book capital on the IRS statistics (including the Federal income tax figures), we concluded that the 1930 statistics shown in Table 6.8 should be -0.8% for Mining and quarrying rather than zero; -1.5% for Finance and real estate rather than +1.8%; and -0.4% for Trade rather than -0.5%. Furthermore, Agriculture and related industries, declined -3.9% and should have appeared for the sake of completeness.

29 *SOI for 1930*, p. 214.

30 Ibid., p. 217.

CHAPTER 7

Leverage—The Financial Fuel for Prosperity and Speculation

(Through Year-End 1928)

IN THIS CHAPTER, as we begin our history of the Crash and on into the Great Depression, we follow up our Prologue to delve more deeply into how credit expansion—particularly the willingness of buyers and sellers to enter into debt relationships—fueled the prosperity of the 1920s. That same willingness led stockbrokers' customers to speculate—via indebtedness using margin accounts—which, with the Crash, led to disastrous consequences for so many.

The Growing Prosperity of the 1920s

In November 1930, one unsettling year after the Crash, the *Quarterly Journal of Economics* published an article entitled "Credit Expansion, 1920 to 1929, and its Lessons" by economist Charles E. Persons. Persons taught economics at Boston University and Harvard before joining the Census Bureau as Expert on the Economics of Unemployment. This valuable, and, for us, insightful piece of contemporaneous scholarship was almost certainly begun well before a disagreement as to how statistically to handle certain, temporarily unemployed workers led to his resignation from the Bureau.

In the opening paragraph of his article, Persons bemoaned the inadequacy of supporting data covering his topic that existed at the time:

> The thesis of this paper is that the existing depression was due essentially to the great wave of credit expansion in the past decade. There is a lamentable lack of comprehensive and accurate data concerning this process of debt creation. But highly suggestive information may be assembled regarding the growth of bank loans and investments; the increase in mortgage indebtedness, urban and rural; the increasing volume of securities outstanding; and the expansion of installment credit.[1]

Undeterred, Persons—writing in the present tense as befitted his 1930 account — pursued statistics from a variety of sources. Members of the Federal Reserve Board staff, for example, supplied him with data for his discussion about banks. This data showed a 40.2% growth in loans and investments at All Banks from $41,658 million on June 30, 1920, to $58,417 million on December 31, 1929, with that growth divided almost evenly between Member banks (40.6%) and Non-member banks (39.4%) over the decade.

Of this growth in credit offered by banks—as well as by other financial institutions—Persons determined that "[t]he great field of credit expansion in the last decade lies in the realm of urban real estate mortgages."[2] Urban simply meant all "non-farm," and with the explosion in development of suburbs nationwide during the 1920s, urban real estate mortgages offered by various types of financial institutions burgeoned. Persons supported his claim by providing pertinent statistics. One table showed that urban real estate mortgages held by commercial banks, mutual savings banks,

1 Persons, (1930), pp. 94-5.

2 Ibid., p. 96.

life insurance companies, building and loan associations, as well as in mortgage bonds (or "real estate bonds," a term used for these debt instruments in the 1920s) more than doubled in the 1920s, from $11,070 million in 1920 to $27,107 million in 1929.[3] The mutual savings bank, in particular, was a type of financial institution that was especially active in mortgage lending at the time. Of this type, Persons estimated, "[i]t is probable that the Mutual Savings Banks held over 5 billions of non-farm real estate loans in 1928"[4] or about 20% of the total mortgages.[5] He observed:

> The essential point is that indebtedness of this character, accepting the totals as they stand, increased from 11 to 27 billions of dollars in ten years. This is nearly 150 per cent increase. The absolute gain of 16 billions over tops by 5 billions the entire debt of this character amassed in all the earlier years of our urban development. It should be noted that the period of most rapid increase lies in the three years 1925, 1926, and 1927. Each of these years shows roughly 3 billions of new urban real estate debt.[6]

Elaborating on this growth in mortgage debt, Persons continued, "To this data for urban mortgage loan expansion may be added evidence of an increased debt burden imposed on farm lands [7].... A general statement for the decade shows a rise of 1.5 billion in the first four years, and a very gradual rise of less than one half billion in the following five years."[8]

---

3 Ibid., p. 104

4 Ibid., p. 101.

5 Of the statistics he assembled on urban real estate mortgages, Persons qualified his estimations by pointing out that, in general, the statistics only included first-mortgage obligations.

6 Ibid., p. 104.

7 Ibid.

8 Ibid., pp. 107.

There was also tremendous growth in the availability of financial instruments, particularly public offerings of stock. Persons included another data source— Moody's estimates of the total volume of Securities Outstanding—that showed what was taking place within the securities industry. This growth in public securities is where the explosion in the call loan market (and the attendant brokers' loans) came from. Persons's table with Moody's data showed that "Corporate bonds and notes," "Public securities," and "United States bonds" grew 60.9% from $61.9 billion in 1920 to $99.6 billion in 1928.[9] As Persons argued, the growth in any market occurred due to credit availability. The reality was that an expansion of a market meant more opportunities for people to become indebted, and some forms of debt, like speculation, carried outsized risks if prices fell, a topic we will cover in greater detail.

Finally, Persons turned to various industry trade sources to explore the dramatic increase in installment sales to individuals in the 1920s as covered in the Prologue. Persons explained:

> It so happened that this new credit method coincided in the time of its introduction with the origination of new consumption goods of the widest popular appeal. Its enthusiastic adoption in the marketing of these new commodities as well as the simultaneous development of new and very effective advertising organizations and methods have resulted in the very rapid increase of outstanding consumer credit. The round number total of 3 billion is probably a highly conservative estimate.[10]

The new consumer goods that Persons focused on included vacuum cleaners, radios, electric irons, ironing machines, washing machines, sewing machines and electric refrigerators—some of the many products that used electricity. He estimated that the total

9 Ibid., pp. 107-8.

10 Ibid., p. 118.

expenditures on these goods almost tripled from $145.0 million in 1922 to $422.4 million in 1929.[11] For radio purchases alone, Persons approximated that the volume sold on credit grew staggeringly from $3 million in 1922 to $412 million in 1929.[12] He also cited the NBER's 1929 publication *Recent Economic Changes*. The NBER estimated that "70 to 80 per cent of furniture" and "140 million dollars worth of clothing is sold on installments annually."[13]

However, for Persons it was one particular acquisition by individuals that was the primary driver, so to speak, of total installment debt: the automobile. In fact, it was his well-considered estimate that of total installment indebtedness "about half results from the sale of automobiles and trucks, both new and in the used car market."[14] We drew the statistics in Table 7.1 from the Commerce Department's Survey of Current Business series to show how the production of

Table 7.1

Cars and Trucks Produced Annually

(In Thousands)

Year	Amount	(%) Gain or Loss
1922	2,571	
1923	3,854	49.9
1924	3,500	-9.2
1925	4,153	18.7
1926	4,256	2.5
1927	3,394	-20.3
1928	4,357	28.4

Source: Department of Commerce, *Survey of Current Business*

11 Ibid., p. 111.

12 Ibid., p. 113.

13 Ibid., p. 109.

14 Ibid., p. 115.

cars and trucks grew from 1922 through 1928. Although slowed by two contractions principally in 1924 and 1927, production grew 69.5% from 2.6 million cars and trucks in 1922 to 4.6 million six years later in 1928. As one measure of how these vehicle sales affected consumer debt expansion, Persons pointed to the notes receivable held by General Motors Acceptance Corporation or GMAC, founded in 1919, which handled the major part of the financing of General Motors vehicles. In 1922, GMAC held $26.2 million in notes receivable. By 1928, its total of notes receivable had increased 12.3 times to $322.6 million. Obviously, while vehicle production was growing rapidly, installment debt supporting the sales of cars and trucks was expanding much more rapidly.

While Persons lamented the inadequacy of available data, he still felt confident in the credibility and the reasonableness of the conclusions he drew, based as they were on the diverse statistics he had intrepidly tracked down and then carefully analyzed. He went on to summarize succinctly what he determined had caused the "temporary bulge" of consumption of the prior decade:

> The evidence as to debt expansion here presented is fragmentary. It is often incomplete. We have no data as to junior liens on urban real estate, which, in the aggregate, amount to enormous sums. There is no record of loans extended by individuals or of personal loans to small borrowers.... No general total may be attempted. But the evidence is consistent and cumulative. The [1920s] witnessed a great volume of credit inflation. Our period of prosperity [in the 1920s] was based on nothing more substantial than debt expansion....[15]
>
> The essential point here is that during the period of the introduction of these new financial devices and while the newly opened reservoirs of credit are filling, we have a temporary increase in the nation's purchasing power.... While

15 Ibid., p. 116.

> the new credit is expanding to its justified limits, more than the normal amount of commodities may be sold. The industries affected are stimulated to expand their productive capacity and to build up their labor force to the level set by this temporary bulge in consumption. In the working out of competitive forces their great prosperity leads to expansion even beyond this limit as over-eager producers seek an enlarged share of the market and profits. [16]

In the prosperity-minded 1920s, credit offerings to consumers had extended beyond homes, automobiles and radios. While credit-offering entities had once exercised moral suasion through "credit men" to control indebtedness, they now saw the moneymaking opportunities, stimulated by increasingly nuanced advertising and sales techniques that encouraged buyers to go into debt to have what they wanted and even what they may not have known they wanted. For some consumers of cars and refrigerators, it was a mere sidestep to begin buying shares of stock "on credit." We now focus on the speculation in stocks from the perspective of the lenders, who—via the call loan money market—stimulated the stock market expansion leading up to the Crash.

Speculation: "Another Day Older and Deeper in Debt"

If asked to describe in one word the cause of the devastating stock market Crash of 1929, most Americans would likely choose "speculation." The wildfire of stock speculation in the latter years of the 1920s had no exact precedent, though speculation had certainly happened before. For example, the Florida real estate boom and bust that had taken place only a few years earlier definitely presaged the Great Bull Market. Combining a combustible blend of influences

16 Ibid., pp. 129-30.

and forces, speculation drew fuel from two directions at once: the sell side and the buy side. On the sell side, Wall Street firms used sophisticated new marketing methods to encourage people to invest in stock, in addition to providing them with the means to do so—leverage—via brokers' loans for margin accounts. On the buy side, many of these stock buyers, as distinguished from the far smaller group of knowledgeable investors who had participated in the stock market for years, were new to the stock market. If sadly short on trading savvy, these novices were long on enthusiasm and eager to participate in what, at the time, looked like a sure thing because of steadily rising stock prices and robust industrial growth.

To understand the development of this volatile situation, we use statistical evidence to reveal how the supply of credit—the ready availability of what the NYSE listed as "call loans" that brokerages borrowed then passed through to their margin customers as "brokers' loans"—enabled NYSE members to fund, and profit handily from, their customers' speculation as stock prices rose.

The Period Up To 1925

We start with passage of the Federal Reserve Act of 1913. The mere creation of the Federal Reserve banking system expanded the nation's availability of credit, setting the stage for what was to come on Wall Street. According to the 1937 classic *Banking and the Business Cycle: A Study of the Great Depression* in the United States, credit availability expanded (presumed to be inherently inflationary) due to the fact that the reserve requirement set by the new Fed for its member banks was approximately 50% lower than prior levels—from approximately 21% before the Act, to 11.61% under the original Act and 9.76% under the June 21, 1917 Amendment to the Act.[17] Upon becoming Fed members, banks could lend more with their freed-up reserves, expanding the available credit nationwide.[18] As we have noted, credit seeks borrowers. Borrowers go into debt for reasons,

17 Chester A. Phillips, Thomas F. McManus and R. W. Nelson, *Banking and the Business Cycle: A Study of the Great Depression in the United States*, Macmillan and Co., 1937, p. 23.

18 Ibid, p. 137.

and stock speculation—in an environment where banking and investment banking were joined at the hip—became one big reason.

Volumes have been written about the evolution of the Fed as an institution, but of particular value to our book is that in the early years of the Fed's existence—beyond its mandate to control inflation and interest rates—it began to play a central role as a reliable source of statistics on the U.S. banking system. Of importance throughout our research, this included statistics on member banks, non-member banks outside its jurisdiction and, fortuitously, on call loans as offered on the NYSE, as well as the attendant brokers' loans. Charles Persons made use of statistics he solicited from Fed staff members for his 1930 article, and this book would have been inconceivable without making use of Fed data.

Just before World War 1, influential leaders both in and outside government regarded the establishment of a central bank, already a fixture in European countries, as a critical step towards managing the nation's monetary instability as had played out in one recession after another. The National Banking Act of 1863 fell short of that role because, while the National Banking Act regulated those banks designated as national banks, other, generally smaller, local banks were regulated inconsistently at the state level.

The Federal Reserve System, or the Fed as it quickly became known, took up the central bank mantle. Once established, the Fed, with headquarters in Washington and comprising twelve regional banks across the country, became an important force in gathering and disseminating accurate and reliable statistics. This data included the activities and financial well-being not only of member banks that paid membership fees, had an ownership stake and got preferential treatment including influence over Fed decisions, but also of the thousands of non-member local banks and, by extension, of the economy as a whole.

To give a picture of U.S. banking before the tumultuous events of the Crash and subsequent Depression, we take one point in time—for instance, December 31, 1924. There were 28,185 commercial banks in the country of which 9,587 were Fed members and 18,598 were non-members. Although non-member U.S. banks far outnumbered member banks, they tended to be considerably smaller in size, with one office in small towns and cities. Of the total of $44,068 million deposited at U.S. commercial banks, member banks had 73.5% on deposit versus 26.5% at non-member banks. [19]

The Fed, Bank Lending, the Call Money Market and Brokers' Loans

While bank lending was monitored and regulated at the federal level and also by state governments, there turned out to be a regulatory gap in lending activities. The NYSE, outside any federal regulation before or even after 1914 when the Fed system went into operation, also offered what it called "call loans," an entire money marketplace for investors from which brokerage houses could obtain funds to lend to its margin customers. Once established, the Fed had an ill-defined, basically non-regulatory relationship with the NYSE. The Fed controlled neither the volume of the call money market as traded on the NYSE nor the rates at which those day-loans traded. As the 1920s progressed, the call money market ballooned, and, at times, the attractive interest rates on those loans lured funds from what the Fed termed "non-bank others," well outside the purview, much less the control, of the Fed. Fed attention on the call money market at this time has been much analyzed and discussed over the years, as we will be seeing in future chapters.

In 1943, the Fed issued its landmark compilation *Banking and Monetary Statistics, 1914-1941 (BMS)*, which included statistics back to its founding. This credible source made it clear that the NYSE call loan money market offering brokers the quick, but callable, funds that enabled them to make brokers' loans was well established before the legislation that created the Federal Reserve System. For instance, statistics in *BMS* on "Short-Term Open-Market Rates in New York

19 *BMS,* pp. 19, 72, 23 respectively.

City" actually began prior to 1914 and showed that in 1890 the "Prevailing rate on Stock Exchange time loans, 90 days" that year was 5.31% and the "Average rate on Stock Exchange call loans… Renewal" was 5.84 %.[20] Time loans, another borrowing option for certain qualified borrowers, were generally for 90 days and locked in at a specific rate, whereas call loans, true to their name, could be "called"—demanded back by lenders or paid back by brokers—on one day's notice. Call loans also carried renewal risk both in terms of rates and credit availability. The risks inherent in the call loan market proved disastrous to many speculators.

As to rates, then as now, the search for yield played a key role in the expansion of participant lenders in the call loan money market beyond, and, more importantly, outside the control of the powerful New York banks that, pre-Fed, comprised the New York Clearing House banks. The contention among them at the time the Fed was formed was that outsider lenders had created instability in the banking system that eventually led to the Panic of 1907. This catalyzed the growing movement to create a central bank. However, there were limits to the Fed's mandate with regard to regulating non-member banks and certainly not regulating lenders who were not banks, namely, the non-bank others who feature prominently among late-1920s call loan participants. The call loan money market, as we noted, was the prime example of such a regulatory gap.

Along with the Fed's *BMS*, another important source for examining the dynamics of speculation has been *Stock Exchange Practices* (*SEP*), the 1934 report hearings held by the U.S. Senate Committee on Banking and Currency that provided a summary of over nine thousand pages of revealing, at times explosive, testimony from what became known as the Pecora Commission (or Hearings or Investigation) begun on March 4, 1932. As stated on the first page of the committee report, the hearings' overall purpose was "to investigate stock exchanges with respect to the buying and selling

---

20 Ibid., p. 448.

and the borrowing and lending of listed securities." We will return more than once to this rich information source.

The Senate committee's *SEP* explained how brokers' loans came about: "When a customer purchases stock on margin, the broker is required to increase his borrowings in order to finance the transaction, and thereupon a broker's loan arises."[21] In other words, the customer's stock purchase caused the broker to do two things. The broker simultaneously increased both his margin lending to the customer and his own borrowing in the call loan money market on the floor of the NYSE. Thus, the broker's loan to the customer actually represented two loans: first, a third party's loan to the broker through the NYSE call money market and second, a broker's margin loan to the customer covering the difference between the stock price and the amount of cash the customer came up with.

For additional context, we return to the Fed in *BMS* for their description of the call money market:

> *Nature of the market for brokers' loans.* The market for brokers' loans, as it is generally conceived, is centered around the New York Stock Exchange. Although some of these loans grow out of a customer relationship between banks as lenders and brokers and dealers as borrowers, the majority are made in the open market on a strictly impersonal basis. The market in which these loans are made was until recent years the most active and the most sensitive of the money markets of the country. It was the market where surplus funds of banks, and sometimes of other lenders, could generally be readily placed or from which funds could be quickly withdrawn as needed. Because of the dominance of call loans, the branch of the money market dealing in brokers' loans has been frequently designated as the call money market.[22]

21 *Stock Exchange Practices: Hearings Before the Committee on Banking and Currency, United States Senate (1932-1934),* p. 12.
22 *BMS,* p. 434.

In contrast with then, our most active money market by *volume* today is for U.S. treasury bills. (*BMS* reported the first $100 million in issued government bills in December 1929.) At present, the Treasury bill market exceeds $14 trillion.

Another difference is that our most closely watched money market *rate* today, and hence the most sensitive rate as to broad impact, is the fed funds rate. As those who follow financial markets know, Fed funds are required deposits held by each member bank at their regional Federal Reserve Bank, and they represent a proportion of each member bank's demand deposits, day by day. On any given day, some member banks have excess fed funds reserves on deposit, which means that their reserves exceed what they are required to hold. Simultaneously the reserves of other member banks fall short of what those banks are required to hold. In the fed funds market—and in return for interest payments—banks that hold excess reserves trade their excess reserves to banks whose reserves fall short. The rate of interest that forms the basis upon which those interest payments are made is known as the "fed funds rate." It is the fed funds rate to which virtually all market participants in debt markets pay closest attention when formulating their own expectations as to how broader market interest rates—short-term, intermediate term and long-term rates on government, municipal and corporate securities—will behave. Thus, to put things in perspective, the call money market in the 1920s and early 1930s was the equivalent *in terms of influence* of today's fed funds market, and call money rates then had the same broad impact that fed funds rates have today, though this impact was then outside of government regulation.

Historically, most lenders in the call money market were banks, but during periods when speculation drove rates to high levels, other entities became lenders in the call money market. As we shall see, this segment of non-bank "others," which included both non-bank corporations and wealthy individuals, grew hugely during the prosperity of the late 1920s.

Speculators Embrace Margin Accounts Financed in the Call Money Market

So who was borrowing to purchase stock in the late 1920s? With stock prices that seemed to keep rising, the short answer is just about anyone who had even a bit of cash could get a loan from a broker because the call money market was a robust source of funds that enabled brokers to meet the demands, via brokers' loans, of buying stock on margin.[23] This ready credit brought stock purchasing within the reach of growing numbers of people.

As is the case today, margin accounts with brokerage firms enabled customers to purchase shares of stock at less than the full cash purchase price by borrowing from their brokers, with the stock serving as collateral for the loan. For example, customers required to put up 50% of the purchase price in cash could borrow the remaining 50% from the broker at a certain spread above the call loan rate the broker was paying in call loans to finance the customers' margin loan. Brokers determined margins, as well as the interest rates they charged their customers for margin loans, based on their business relationships with the customers and the customers' creditworthiness. Highly creditworthy customers with histories of large trading volumes enjoyed lower cash margin requirements and lower loan rates on their brokers' loans. Less creditworthy customers with histories of lower trading volumes or who were new to the firm had higher margin requirements and paid higher brokers' loan rates. There is

23 The brokerage held the shares as collateral against the margin customers' brokers' loans.

substantial evidence from many sources that these vague lending standards grew increasingly lax as stock prices continued to climb.

Customers who put down margins equaling at least 50% of the market value of their accounts were considered investors. Investors obviously had more skin in the overall game, so to speak, and were thought of as being more sophisticated.[24] Customers with lesser margin requirements comprised a mixed bag of speculators, including many novices—for example, Groucho Marx with his familiar story of speculation misfortune (see p. 232)—and opportunists, as well as, many would say later, suckers.

By the late 1920s, virtually all speculators and even many investors were using borrowed funds to leverage their stock purchases. In the later half of the decade, some customers had margin requirements as low as 10%, which meant they were eligible to borrow 90% of the price of the stock. If the stock price went up, as was common then, such customers had a portion of available funds in their account with which they could acquire more stock, again via borrowing, so long as they maintained the agreed-to margin on the value of their portfolio. However, if a stock price went down, the broker could, and likely would, issue margin calls requiring these customers to top up their accounts in order to maintain their margin, be it 10% or higher, or be forced to liquidate enough of their positions to return to their agreed upon margins.

As to the brokers' cost of borrowing in the call money market, at any given time two rates applied, those on new loans and those on renewals (see Table 7.2, (page 179), and Table 7.3 (page 180). New call loan rates applied to loans only on the day they were initiated. Renewal rates applied to loans already initiated and renewed each

24 Some borrowers maintained time accounts as well as day-by-day margin accounts with their brokers. With a time account, customers could secure borrowed funds for a fixed period of time at a fixed interest rate. Time accounts appealed to investors who held onto stock but had less appeal to speculators who were interested in getting in and out of their securities purchase rapidly and didn't want to carry unnecessary debt.

subsequent day with the consent of both the lender (bank or other non-bank party) and the borrowing broker. Whether the rate on renewals was higher or lower than the new loan rate depended on market conditions. In the period just before the Crash, the renewal rate tended to be slightly higher, a reflection of the perception of additional carry risk by lenders.

As the 1920s progressed, the amount of speculation that a broker's customers were willing to engage in directly determined the volume of borrowing by brokers in the call money market. Demand led supply. Brokers had little incentive, secured as their loans were by the shares, to place limits on the volume of call loans they took out on any given day.

Brokers' Loans—Interest Rates and Loan Volumes Rise

Why stock market activity increased throughout the 1920s became a critical plot twist in the lead-up to the Crash. The search for return was one key factor for both lender and borrower, so we turn first to rates and then to volumes to delve deeper into the market's momentum at the time.

Table 7.2

Call Money Rates on the NYSE

(% Percent)

Week Ending	Renewals		New Loans	
	High	Low	High	Low
Dec. 27, 1924	4.5	3.0	5.0	3.0
Dec. 26, 1925	6.0	5.5	6.0	5.5
Dec. 25, 1926	6.0	5.0	6.0	5.0
Dec. 31, 1927	5.5	5.0	5.5	5.0
Dec. 28, 1928	12.0	9.0	12.0	9.0

Source: *NYSE Year Book 1929-1930*, pp.84-87.

Table 7.3					
Short-Term Open-Market Rates in New York City (% Percent)					
Week Ended	Prevailing rate on-			Average rate on Stock Exchange call loans	
	Prime comercial paper 4 to 6 months	Prime bankers' acceptances, 90 days	Stock Exchange time loans, 90 days	New	Renewal
Dec. 27, 1924	3.6	3.0	3.6	4.4	3.9
Dec. 26, 1925	4.4	3.5	4.9	5.9	5.9
Dec. 25, 1926	4.5	3.9	4.8	5.6	5.5
Dec. 31, 1927	4.0	3.3	4.3	5.5	5.4
Dec. 29, 1928	5.4	4.5	7.8	10.8	10.0

Source: *BMS*, pp.454-455.

The call money market provided lenders, like the repo market today, with a liquid, day-to-day lending instrument—a place to park, even if briefly, idle cash. Rates offered in the call money market to banks and others who financed brokers' loans were posted at the NYSE and were avidly watched by lenders or potential lenders. Over the course of a trading day, call money rates would vary. To give an idea of how rates rose and fell, Table 7.2, previous page, drawn from the *New York Stock Exchange Yearbook—1929-1930,* shows the NYSE-recorded high-and-low rate fluctuations for the year-end weeks from 1925-1929. The 1928 peak was noteworthy because all four rates—the two highs and even the two lows—represented 1928 highs for their four categories. (Even higher highs would be experienced in 1929 for all four categories.)

By comparison, Table 7.3, above, is drawn from the Fed's *BMS* and includes NYSE call money rates, as a subset of the broader category of Short-Term Open-Market Rates in New York City, for the year-end weeks of 1925-1929. Although the Fed recorded "prevailing rates" and "average rates" rather than highs, lows and closing rates, it is still obvious that rates paid on brokers' loans in the NYSE call loan money market generally rose over the course of these years, making them an increasingly attractive short-term investment opportunity for banks, but also, more significantly, for unrelated non-bank entities with investable cash who were seeking return through an instrument that seemed liquid and safe—callable, as it was, day by-day and backed by what seemed to be increasingly valuable, and easily liquidated, collateral.[25]

Turning from rates to loan volumes, Table 7.4 shows the

Table 7.4

Call Loans By Groups of Lenders

(Figures partly estimated. In millions of dollars)

Date	Total	By New York City banks	By outside banks	By others
1925, 31-Mar	2,420	1,040	700	680
30-Jun	2,660	1,150	770	740
30-Sep	2,930	1,060	950	920
31-Dec	3,550	1,450	1,050	1,050
1926, 31-Mar	3,000	1,030	905	1,065
30-Jun	2,930	1,060	780	1,090
30-Sep	3,220	960	1,000	1,260
31-Dec	3,290	1,160	830	1,300
1927, 31-Mar	3,290	960	910	1,420
30-Jun	3,570	1,130	970	1,470
30-Sep	3,910	1,170	1,060	1,680
31-Dec	4,430	1,550	1,050	1,830
1928, 31-Mar	4,640	1,270	1,070	2,300
30-Jun	4,900	1,080	960	2,860
3-Oct	5,510	880	1,020	3,610
31-Dec	6,440	1,640	915	3,885

Source: *BMS*, p.494.

25 In Chapter 9, we recount that during the core week of the stock market Crash, the week ending October. 30, 1929, the New York banks that represented out-of-town banks and non-bank others in the NYSE call money market received instructions from a large portion of these customers calling their loans to brokers. Despite a huge volume of withdrawn call loans, Friedman and Schwartz stated, "The adjustment was orderly, thanks largely to prompt and effective action by the New York Federal Reserve Bank." (Friedman and Schwartz (1963a), pp. 305-6)

volume of the call money market (not "brokers' loans," as titled in the original *BMS* table) made on the floor of the NYSE. The volume almost consistently rose at an increasingly brisk pace from the end of the first quarter of 1925 through the end of 1928. In the twelve months ending October 3, 1928, alone, the total volume of call loans grew by a striking 40.9%, but that growth rate paled in comparison with the annualized growth rate experienced in the fourth quarter of 1928. The actual growth rate experienced in this three-month period was 16.9%, a 67.5% annualized rate of growth.

Table 7.4 clearly shows who, in particular, was responsible for the huge growth in call loans: labeled in the table "By others." And who were these others? They were non-bank entities including domestic corporations, wealthy individuals and even, if perhaps to a lesser extent, foreign entities. The statistics in *BMS* reveal that in the three years prior to the Crash, this segment of "By others" grew 33.3% by September 30, 1927, and another 114.9% by October 3, 1928. Notably, participation by these "others" grew another 83.9% by October 4, 1929. Some observed this huge increase in call loans made by nontraditional lenders as a red flag waving in front of Wall Street bulls. Indeed, those who ran and worked at the Fed argued against speculation and deemed these loans by non-bank lenders "bootleg loans" that constituted an "end run" around banks and therefore beyond the Fed's regulatory control.[26]

Altogether, the volume of call loans from all sources stood at $6.4 billion at the end of 1928. This was a huge amount of cash chasing the shortest short-term yield. There were some, including *New York Times* financial editor Alexander Dana Noyes, who pointed out that this cash could—and should—have been employed in more productive ways with regards to the economy, such as underwriting capital investments, instead of further fanning the flames of speculation. But most regarded those who made such public warnings as wet blankets, and clearly policymakers didn't act on those alarm bells.

---

26 Allan H. Meltzer, *A History of the Federal Reserve, Volume 1: 1913-1951*, The University of Chicago Press (June 2004 ed.), p. 251.

Another Speculation Source: Bank Lending Secured by Securities

Up to now we have focused on one source of funding for speculation—call loans, which then became brokers' loans made by members of the NYSE to their customers. We now turn to other sources of funding for speculation. Besides lending to brokers and dealers in the call money market, banks also made direct loans on securities to their own customers. In the case of brokers' loans, the brokers and dealers held their customers securities as collateral; however, in the case of loans on securities to their own customers, the banks held their customers' securities as collateral.

Table 7.5

All Member Banks-Classification of Loans On Call Dates

($ million)

Call Date	Loans on securities, except to banks			
	Total	To brokers and dealers		To others
		In New York City	Outside New York City	
1928, Oct. 3	8,545	1,899	850	5,796
Dec. 31	9,903	2,556	975	6,373

Source: *BMS*, p.76.

Table 7.5 presents statistics on the security loans made by All Member Banks of the Federal Reserve System. It wasn't until the autumn of 1928 that the Fed began quantifying the amount of lending made by member banks that arguably encouraged speculation. As a result, Table 7.5 shows statistics for only October 3 and December 31 but nothing prior.[27]

Before evaluating the data presented in Table 7.5, however, we consider it worthwhile to look at what was going on in U.S. banking in the mid-20s. Earlier in this chapter, we cited the 28,185 commercial banks in the United States and the $44.1 billion of deposits those commercial banks held as of the end of 1924. Because in the four

27 The information in *BMS*, pp. 62-4, describes the process.

succeeding years the number of banks declined and the volume of deposits grew, it is useful to look at those changes in more detail. From the end of 1924 to the end of 1928, the total number of commercial banks declined 11.4%; the number of Fed member banks declined 7.8%, and the number of non-member banks declined 13.3%.[28] In contrast, the money stock grew 19.6% over that four-year period. The proportion held by member banks rose modestly from 73.5% to 74.1%, while the proportion held by non-member banks fell modestly from 26.5% to 25.9%.[29] In summation, while non-member banks, most of which were country banks in rural areas, remained numerous at the end of 1928, their presence and their economic significance were slowly declining.

With this background in mind, we evaluate the information presented in Table 7.5. In contrast to Table 7.4, which presents statistics on lending to brokers and dealers in the call money market on the floor of the NYSE, Table 7.5 presents lending statistics for "All Member Banks" of the Federal Reserve System nationwide to their customers. Most of these customers were, as the table shows, brokers and dealers in New York City. Some were brokers and dealers outside New York City, and the remaining (or "others") were neither brokers nor dealers. However, in order to compare the statistics in Table 7.5 to those in Table 7.4 and thus quantify as broadly as possible the amount of lending from all sources funding speculation, we must, like accountants of yore, don green eye shades and avoid double counting.

Fortunately, avoiding double counting is actually quite easy. Careful analysis of several years of *BMS* statistics in Tables 7.4 and 7.5 reveals that Call Loans "By New York City banks" plus call loans "By outside banks," quarter by quarter, on Table 7.4 is virtually the same as the amounts reported, quarter by quarter, in Table 7.5 as loans by "All Member Banks…To brokers and dealers In New York City." Table 7.4 indicates that money lent to fund brokers' loans on Dec. 31, 1928, amounted to $1,640 million lent by New York City

28 *BMS*, pp. 19, 72, 23.

29 Ibid., pp. 19, 73, 23.

banks and $915 million lent by "outside banks." That total— $2,555 million— is virtually the same as the $2,556 million that Table 7.5 indicates was lent by All Member Banks nationwide to brokers and dealers in New York City precisely where their brokers' loans funded stock speculation.

Thus, we can use Tables 7.4 and 7.5 to estimate the volume of all lending to acquire and carry securities. We start by deducting the amount shown in Table 7.4 of $2,556 million as loans by "All Member Banks…To brokers and dealers In New York City" from the total of $9,903 million shown in Table 7.5 to get an adjusted total of $7,347 million. By adding this adjusted total to the total Brokers' Loans shown in Table 7.3 of $6,440 million, we get $13,787 million as an opening estimate of the amount lent to support the acquisition and carrying of securities in the United States on December 31, 1928— that is almost $13.8 billion in 1928 dollars—with many more months of speculation ahead.

As we have previously stated, the sum in Table 7.4 of Call Loans "By New York City banks" plus "By outside banks" is virtually the same as the amounts reported in Table 7.5 as loans by "All Member Banks… To brokers and dealers In New York City." But this is only part of the story, because the statistics shown in the tables do not include activity by non-member banks that also likely encouraged speculation. By this omission, the Fed made it clear that, in terms of assessing banks as to whether or not they were supporting speculation, non-member banks were outside their purview. With non-member banks holding over 25% of the nation's money stock, this was a large number to disregard.

Was There Any Other Unaccounted for Lending on Securities?

Another intriguing question looms as to who was lending to finance speculating in stocks, the answer to which must remain conjectural for lack of substantive supporting data: how many individuals lent money to other individuals for the purpose of purchasing and carrying securities? How much did they lend? And did these individual lenders know their borrowers or were they anonymous transactions? One obvious example of individual-to-individual loans was likely between family members. There are many reasons for lending within families, of course, such as parents or grandparents lending for the purpose of setting relatives up with a portfolio or for second mortgages to enable a home purchase, but such private and personal information was, and is, seldom made public and has left no readily gatherable and documentable record. Even without actual statistics on the volume of person-to-person loans—neither as to amounts nor what the relationships were between lenders and borrowers—it seems at least reasonable to suggest that the volume of these loans may have been quite large. If borrowers found themselves unable to repay, as surely occurred following the Crash, tensions within families could linger painfully, adding to the stockpile of woes and pressures then confronting so many. One pertinent anecdote that illustrated this kind of situation appeared in *My Father Irving Fisher* by Irving Norton Fisher written in 1956. The senior Irving Fisher, as we have mentioned earlier, lost a great deal of both his own and his wife's money in the Crash, and he resorted to borrowing from his wife's prudent sister who had not speculated.[30] Were it not for his son's memoir, we likely wouldn't know of that particular, and no doubt painful, individual-to-individual loan.

It is also worth pointing out that in 1929, unlike now, the great majority of brokerage firms were partnerships (or possibly sole proprietorships), that is, not organized as corporations. This means brokers and dealers were taxed as individuals and personally liable for any shortfalls. Of course, brokers' loans that financed their customers' margin accounts were collateralized by their customers' stock holdings. This arrangement worked fine during the boom

30 Irving Norton Fisher, *My Father Irving Fisher,* Comet Press Books, 1956, p. 266.

market, but when the collateral value tanked, the repercussions for brokers could be, and often were, dire.

We close this chapter with a reminder about the symbiotic relationship between credit and debt. Especially, we saw how the data on the growth in brokers' loans in the late 1920s confirm the ample supply of funds seeking quick return in the call money market, brokerages' readiness to use that call loan money to make brokers' loans and the steady stream of eager speculators who readily took advantage of those brokers' loans. Tragically, many of these parties lacked the wisdom of forethought to step back and get out of the way of the conflagration just ahead. The next chapter takes us deeper into the fray where common sense had been replaced by exuberant ambitions, starry-eyed aspirations and greed.

Endnote

Corporate Financial Statistics for 1927-29

What does the data from 1927-29 tell us about the pre-Crash period?

In Chapter 7, we examined the great wave of credit expansion that occurred during the 1920s. Credit expansion or debt expan-

Table 7.6

Aggregate U.S. Corporate Balance Sheet, 1927-1929

Assets and liabilities-Statement prepared from U.S. income tax returns of corporations submitting balance sheets showing major assets and liabilities as of December 31 each year or at the close of business of the fiscal year nearest thereto

($ million)

Assets and Liabilities	1927	1928	1929
Assets:			
Cash (in till and deposits in banks)	16,851	21,952	22,371
Notes receivable and accounts receivable			
(less reserve for bad debts)	50,959	62,804	66,810
Inventory	21,005	20,751	21,911
Tax-exempt investments: Obligations of States and			
Territories or political subdivisions;			
securities issued under the Federal farm loan act			
and obligations of the U.S. or its possessions	9,781	10,116	10,338
Investments other than tax-exempt- Stocks, bonds,			
mortgages, loans, real estate, etc.			55,844
Capital assets: Real estate, buildings, equipment etc.			
(less depreciation)	104,945	109,931	116,446
Misc. assets not distributed	84,001	81,663	42,057
Total assets	287,542	307,217	335,778
Liabilities:			
Notes and accounts payable	24,126	27,437	29,453
Bonded debt and mortgages	34,740	42,943	46,643
Misc. liabilities not distributed	96,274	93,950	94,714
Capital stock:			
Preferred	17,800	18,475	19,738
Common	74,081	77,256	90,120
Total capital stock	91,881	95,731	109,858
Surplus	45,415	52,069	60,699
Less deficit	4,893	4,913	5,588
Net surplus	40,522	47,156	55,111
Total liabilities	287,543	307,217	335,778

Source: *SOI 1927-29*: *1927* p.20, *1928* p.32, *1929* p.25.

sion—these two sides of the same coin were inseparable, as data research confirms.

Compiled from IRS reports, Table 6.1 covers the dramatic years 1929-33 when Aggregate U.S. Corporate Notes receivable and accounts receivable fell over 46%. Debtors repaid $30,975 million in current debt obligations over this four-year period of time with major economic consequences. That indebtedness built up over time. We found IRS data showing the growth in current receivables before the Crash. Table 7.6—formatted identically to Table 6.1—covers 1927-29 and shows that Aggregate U.S. Corporate notes receivable and accounts receivable totaled $50,959 million at the end of 1927, a measure, of course, of debt obligations entered into earlier in the 1920s. U.S. debtors added an additional $15,851 million in debt obligations in 1928 to arrive at the $66,810 million due at the end of 1929 and payable in 1930.

Delving into data prior to 1927 in order to compare that data with the subsequent years, however, proved difficult, due to changes in the way the IRS categorized data beginning with 1928. Specifically, the line item Notes receivable in the Aggregate U.S. Corporate Balance Sheet for 1927 included a footnote that read, "Includes loans and discounts from bank statements which for 1926 were included in 'Miscellaneous assets.'"[31] In addition, *SOI for 1929* explained, "Amounts under 'Miscellaneous assets' for 1929 are not comparable with preceding years due to the separate classification for the first time of 'Investments other than tax-exempt.'"[32] This classification change is why Table 7.6 shows Investments other than tax-exempt as $55,844 million in 1929, but no corresponding entries for the category in 1927 or 1928.

These obstacles to our research, however, did not deter us. We were still able to examine current accounts payable across the years because the IRS made no similar modifications in that category.

31 *SOI* for 1927, p. 20.

32 *SOI for 1929*, p. 24.

Table 7.7 shows that Aggregate U.S. Corporate Notes and accounts payable totaled $24,126 million at the end of 1927. To that base, borrowers added $5,328 million in current debt to obligations entered into earlier in the 1920s to arrive at $29,543 million due at the end of 1929 and payable in 1930.

Considering such robust borrowing, what did other economic indicators show? The Table 7.7 statistics confirm that the word "robust" also applied to other indicators of the broader economy in the buildup to the Crash:

Table 7.7

Rates of Change - 1929-1930

(Assumes 100% of Corporate payables are owed to Corporations)

($ million)

	1927	1928	1929	% change From 1927
Rise in GNP				
			103,420	8.7
		97,100		2.1
	95,100			
Rise in notes and accounts receivable **held** by U.S corporations				
			66,810	31.1
		62,804		23.2
	50,959			
Rise in notes and accounts payable **owed** by U.S. corporations				
			29,453	22.1
		27,437		13.7
	24,126			
Rise in notes and accounts payable **owed by others** to U.S. corporatic				
			37,357	39.2
		35,367		31.8
	26,833			

Source: *SOI 1927-29*: *1927* p.20, *1928* p.32, *1929* p.25:
The National Income & Product Accounts of the United States 1929-76, p.72.

• GNP rose 8.7% from $95.1 billion in 1927 to $103.4 billion in 1929.

• Notes and accounts receivable held by U.S. Corporations rose 31.1% from $51 billion in 1927 to $66.8 billion in 1929.

• Notes and accounts payable owed by U.S. Corporations rose 22.1% from $24.1 billion in 1927 to $29.5 billion in 1929.

• Notes and accounts payable owed to U.S. Corporations by "others" who were not U.S. Corporations rose 39.2% from $26.8 billion in 1927 to $37.4 billion in 1929.[33]

These corporate financial statistics from the IRS for this stage-setting period were consequential and helped us cover our main years of focus with a deeper understanding of the state of the economy just prior.

33 NIPA 1929-76 Statistical Tables, pp. 1 and 72; *SoI for 1927-1929*. These statistics assume that U.S. Corporations paid 100% of their Notes and accounts payable to other U.S. Corporations, an assumption we revise in Chapter 16, pp. 16-17.

CHAPTER 8

Furious Speculation Leads to Panic

(Through October 23, 1929)

THE EXTRAORDINARY NATURE of what Alexander Dana Noyes called the "furious stock speculation"[1] of the late 1920s continues to draw the attention of writers of all stripes and hues, including journalists, political and other economists, political leaders, historians, financial market experts, novelists, playwrights and poets. Rather than recreate an account of the forces at play, we continue in this chapter to rely on selections from writers who, over the years, have tackled one of the most analyzed and debated chapters in our nation's history, and most definitely its economic history.

Perhaps one reason for the topic's lasting fascination, obviously extant to this day, is the complexity of the factors involved and the unresolved and opposing views as to causes. With the benefit of decades of commentary and data, we turn for clarity to the numbers, while noting how little people focused on them then — beyond stock prices and their direction.

As we saw in Chapter 7, data-backed evidence showing the rapid growth in speculative lending was available at the time from both governmental and private sources. However, with the daily, even hourly, cheer leading on Wall Street, from some in government and in the press generally, rational minds to assess data and effectively warn of the danger were mostly absent. In fact, expressing reservations was

1 Noyes (1938), p. 311.

unpopular, unwelcome and mostly unheeded. There was, as Otto Kahn, the senior partner of Kuhn, Loeb and Company, called it during the Pecora hearings, an "absolute runaway feeling throughout the country."[2]

Putting 1929 in Context

Virtually all of the writers who have looked closely at the events of 1929 have agreed that financial markets in the U.S., especially stock markets and money markets, took leave of their senses. In order to understand this, we need contextual insight.

We begin with one of the rare detached and objective observers who warned of the collective delusion of the day and the dangers that likely lay ahead.[3] As we mentioned in the previous chapter, Alexander Dana Noyes, the respected financial editor of the *New York Times* for decades, including the 1920s and 1930s, was one of the few who spoke out. His contemporaneous red flags, however, went unheeded by those who might have been in a position to take action. Nearly a decade after the Crash, Noyes expressed his views in *The Market Place: Reminiscences of a Financial Editor*, published in 1938:

> For many years to come, history of the twenties and thirties, social and political as well as financial, will in retrospect be intimately interwoven with the furious stock speculation of 1929, the great Stock Exchange panic of October 1929,

2 *SEP*, p. 1010.

3 Noyes (1938), p. 51. Noyes stated, "The recourse taught by experience to newspaper writers of character was simple: to abstain altogether from personal speculation, which is the only way for preserving an unbiased mind; to see to it that the Stock Exchange fraternity should understand this attitude; to refuse all favors except being put in touch with legitimate news as a matter of professional duty; never to venture into the corridors of the Stock Exchange itself (where the very atmosphere unsettles sober judgment); to be scrupulously careful regarding habitual affiliations; to judge every rumor by the source from which it comes, but until the rumor, from whatever source, had been investigated, to receive it with cool skepticism."

> and the profound industrial depression of the three ensuing years. Our whole community's view of life and manner of living were in that period changed with the most violence, not once but twice. Ideas and convictions prevalent in 1929 were not those of 1927, and no more complete reversal of mental attitude could be imagined than the change in the opposite direction after 1929.[4]

The initial change in "our whole community's view of life and manner of living," was, in Noyes's view, precisely the development of the "furious" speculation about which he wrote even as things rapidly got out of hand. Of the timing and nature of this initial change, Noyes recalled, "Financial historians are apt to date the Stock Exchange boom from the autumn of 1927; but there was not apparent in that season, as I remember it, the least premonition of what was to happen."[5]

John Kenneth Galbraith, respected Canadian-American economist, public official and diplomat—who celebrated his 21st birthday on October 15, right before the Crash—later echoed Noyes in his 1954 classic *The Great Crash, 1929:*

> Until the beginning of 1928, even a man of conservative mind could believe that the prices of common stock were catching up with the increase in corporation earnings.... Early in 1928, the nature of the boom changed. The mass escape into make-believe, so much a part of the true speculative orgy, started in earnest.[6]

Noyes, who actually relied on data to offer important insights to his supposedly financially sophisticated readers, still wrapped his memoir's discussion in a curious apology for making ample mention and use of revealing "dry statistics," even though the data

4 Ibid., p. 311.

5 Ibid., p. 315.

6 Galbraith (1954), p. 11.

were practically screaming about the dangers of how quickly call loans were exploding:

> During most of 1927, outstanding "brokers' loans" did not vary greatly from the year before. But the total rose from $3,673,000,000 in September 1927 (double the monthly average of 1921 or 1922) to $4,432,000,000 at the year and, to $5,274,000,000 in the middle of 1928, and to $6,439,000,000 at its end; then, in rapid progression to no less than $8,549,000,000 on October 1 1929.
>
> Perhaps I owe the reader an apology for interpolating in my personal reminiscences these dry statistics; but without them it is impossible to understand what happened afterward. To those of us who knew our Wall Street, the "brokers' loan account" proved unmistakably that credit used on the stock exchange for speculative purchases, having already reached an unprecedented magnitude, was now doubling within the year. More than $1,000,000,000 of this increase was occasioned, not by banks and brokers, the customary lenders on the Stock Exchange, but by railway and industrial companies whose surplus funds in those prosperous times were exceptionally large, and which offered those funds directly on the speculative market, to get the benefit of the 9 to 15 per cent to which "call-money rates" had risen. The result was jubilant insistence by the speculators—one heard it on every side — that speculation, however far it might be carried, could not this time be checkmated, as in former great speculations it had in the long run usually been, by a "money squeeze." By this time, the spirit of illusion had spread beyond the ranks of infatuated speculators.[7]

7 Noyes (1938), pp. 320-1.

In one forthright *New York Times* column, Noyes himself felt strongly enough to shut out the madding crowds and issue warnings of what to him were "very visible signs of danger." But he reflected in *The Market Place* on the criticism he received when he expressed "disapproval or skepticism" as to what was taking place on Wall Street:

> The speculative mania seemed by 1929 to have neither geographical nor social bounds. Books were published and widely read, explaining how it was a sensible citizen's duty to "cash in" on the country's impregnable financial future; how investors in stocks had always fared better than investors in bonds; or even arguing that lavish personal expenditure, not thrift or saving, was the sure road to national prosperity. There were occasions, even in social conversation, when expression of disapproval or skepticism would provoke the same resentment as if the controversy had to do with politics or religion. It was not in all respects an agreeable task to point out in the *Times* what seemed to me very visible signs of danger. As in the similar circumstances of the short-lived speculative mania of 1901, expression of such judgment had to meet the denunciatory comment that the writer was trying to discredit or stop American prosperity.[8]

The View from the Fed

In its *Annual Report for 1929,* the Fed divided that eventful year into "two periods of unequal duration." During the first period, which lasted from the start of the year until late October, "[t]he problem was to find a suitable means by which the growing volume of security credit could be brought under orderly restraint without occasioning avoidable pressure on the commercial credit and business." Acting to achieve such restraint, the Board "set forth its views of how the Federal Reserve banks would best proceed" in a letter

8 Ibid., pp. 322-3.

to them dated February 2, 1929.[9] The letter, with a supplemental statement further elaborating the Board's position, was issued to the public February 7. In it the Board stated:

> When [the Board] finds that conditions are rising which obstruct Federal Reserve banks in the effective discharge of their functioning of so managing the credit facilities of the Federal Reserve system as to accommodate commerce and business, it is its duty to inquire into them and to take such measures as may be deemed suitable and effective in the circumstances to correct them; which, in the immediate situation means to restrain the use, either directly or indirectly, of Federal Reserve credit facilities in aid of the growth of speculative credit.[10]

Almost immediately after the issuance of the Fed's statement, the Bank of England raised the bank rate from 4½% to 5½%, aiming to reduce the flow of gold from London to New York. According to Galbraith, the result of the Fed's directive and the interest rate rise in England was "a sharp break in the market" from which the market recovered, though "for February as a whole, there was no gain."[11]

The View from the Brokerage Industry

As the Fed was acting to restrain speculation by reigning in the banks, the brokerage industry was prospering by pursuing its own course of action that circumvented the banks. As Barrie Wigmore has explained:

> The diversion of funds into the call loan market by corporations, foreigners, and individuals was prompted by the speculative mania of the period. The banks…maintained

9 *ARBG for 1929,* pp. 1-3.
10 *ARBG for 1929,* p. 3.
11 Galbraith (1954), p. 34.

> their call loans below $2.3 billion throughout 1929. Therefore, the brokerage community had to bid up call loan rates above competing rates and go beyond the banks to their [brokerage] customers to attract the funds the banks would not lend.[12]

In 1929, the NYSE member firms had more than 800,000 cash-paying customers to whom their brokers could explain the advantages of call money market lending—the high interest rates and high liquidity of one-day loans—whenever their customers sold some or all of the stocks they held in their portfolios. We will learn more about these customers and clients, many of whom were quite wealthy, in *The Deflation of 1930*, where we consider speculators and investors in depth.

These facts about standard business practices on Wall Street, however, weren't widely known in 1929. Instead, they emerged in 1933-1934 when the U.S. Senate Committee on Banking and Currency, investigating Wall Street excesses that led to the Crash and ensuing Depression, held hearings—known to history as the "Pecora hearings" after Ferdinand Pecora, the committee's dogged chief counsel. Activities on the New York Stock Exchange featured prominently. While there were altogether 29 stock exchanges in various cities across the U.S., the NYSE was far and away the dominant exchange. Of all the commissions received by the 29 exchanges for the period January 1, 1928, through August 31, 1933, 95.2% were paid to member firms and individual members of the NYSE. During 1929, the member firms of the NYSE had a total of 1,548,707 customers. Of these, 59.2% were of a cash character and 40.8% were of a margin character.[13] Those 631,872 margin customers mattered a lot in terms of NYSE member profitability.

In 1929, the brokerage industry was thriving and expanding quite aggressively across the U.S., even including offices aboard passenger ships at sea, as we will see. According to the Pecora hear-

12 Barrie A. Wigmore, *The Crash and Its Aftermath*, Greenwood Press, 1985, p. 94.

13 *SEP*, pp. 5-10.

ings, 447 NYSE member firms carried margin accounts, and each had a profit center that performed the accounting and back-office functions associated with managing margin customer relations. Each firm charged margin customers a spread above the call market rates at which the firm borrowed. The spreads varied considerably according to the risk categories into which the firm fit its margin customers, and the spreads varied over time depending on market conditions. Suffice it to say, servicing margin customers was almost always highly profitable.

A Noteworthy Warning and an Attempt by the Fed to Take Direct Action

Noyes was not the only one to issue clear warnings that were ignored or publicly disparaged. Another was long-time investment banker and a Vice Chair of the Federal Reserve Paul Warburg (1868-1932). Noyes quoted Warburg extensively in his book:

> In March of 1929 the late Paul Warburg, alone of all the eminent New York bankers, opened fire publicly on the speculative mania. He declared that the unprecedented rise in company stocks was "quite unrelated to respective increases in plant, property, or earning power"; that the "colossal volume of loans" had reached its existing height through "carrying unabsorbed securities." Unless what he bluntly called "the orgy of unrestrained speculation" could be stopped, not only would ultimate collapse cause personal disaster to the speculators, "but it would also bring about a general depression involving the entire country." This was plain language; it came from a high source, and the longer sequel proved it to be perhaps the most accurate prediction made in that strange era.... To the speculating public Warburg's warnings first caused alarm, then indignation, and

> presently, when the stock market resumed its upward rush, expressions of supercilious contempt.[14]

Accounting for the period almost to the end of March, the Fed reported, "For eight weeks following the issuance of the board's statement on February 7, security loans fluctuated irregularly without definite trend."[15] On March 4, Herbert Hoover took the oath of office.

Then, on Friday, March 22, six weeks and a day after February 7, when the Fed letter and statement went public, the Federal Reserve Board met for its regular monthly meeting and had to confront the call money market statistics. From February 6 to March 20, banks, both in New York City and "out of town," had reduced their lending to brokers by a total of $188 million. However, non-bank "others" had increased their lending by $313 million, enabling brokers actually to increase their loans to their margin account customers by $124 million. Despite a most unusual continuation of the Fed's Friday meeting into Saturday, the press received no hint of how the Fed reacted to this data.

In *Rainbow's End: The Crash of 1929*, Professor Maury Klein described what happened on the next day of trading when no one had any idea what the Fed would do:

> On Monday, March 25, the call rate soared 14 percent, the highest rate since 1920, and panic seized the market. Trading exceeded 5.8 million shares as the Dow dropped 8.71 and the *Times* average 5.87. "The speculative element shivered in fear of a drastic ultimatum from the Federal Reserve Board that never came...," reported the *Times*. "Many operators... were openly expressing the wish that the board would do its worst 'and get the agony over.'"[16]

---

14 Ibid., pp. 323-4.

15 *ARBG for 1929*, p. 7.

16 Maury Klein, *Rainbow's End: The Crash of 1929*, Oxford University Press 2001, pp. 178-9.

Taking the position that by acting aggressively the Federal Reserve could have diminished or perhaps even ended speculation in March 1929, while American business was still booming, Galbraith stated:

> On the next day, Tuesday, March 26, everything was much worse.... A wave of fear swept the market.... Prices seemed to drop vertically..... Thousands of speculators, in whose previous experience the market had always risen, now saw for the first time the seamy side of their new way of life. Each new quotation was far below the last one. Moreover, the ticker, unable to cope with the unprecedented volume, was far behind the market. Not only were things bad, but they had almost certainly become worse, yet one couldn't tell from the ticker how much worse. Before the day was out many of these thousands received a peremptory telegram from their brokers.... It asked [for] more margin promptly.
>
> Meanwhile the banks continued to trim sails for the storm. It is probable that some professional traders were selling because they foresaw the moment when there would be no money with which to carry stocks on margin. And that moment might be near, for the morning of March 26, the rate on call money [market loans] reached 20 per cent, its high for the 1929 boom.
>
> March 26, 1929, could have been the end. Money could have remained tight. The authorities might have remained firm in their intention to keep it so. The panic might have continued. Each fall in prices would have forced a new echelon of speculators to sell, and so forced prices down still more. It did not happen, and if any man can be credited with this, the credit belongs to Charles E. Mitchell.[17]

17 Galbraith (1954), pp. 36-7.

In other words, a crash—most hopefully a milder version of the Crash—could have occurred in March rather than October 1929, if the Federal Reserve Board had kept its nerve. Ah, but for "Sunshine Charley Mitchell". [18]

Charles E. Mitchell, to whom Galbraith gave "credit" for extending the boom and the speculation, was the chairman and chief executive of the National City Bank, one of New York City's two largest and most influential banks, as well as Chairman of National City Company, its securities affiliate. According to cultural historian William Klingaman in *1929: The Year of the Great Crash,* Mitchell was "the country's recognized leader in retail marketing of securities." [19] He had also become a director of the New York Federal Reserve Bank on January 1, 1929. As Galbraith told the story:

> During the day, as money tightened, rates rose, and the market fell, Mitchell decided to take a hand. He told the press, "We feel that we have an obligation which is paramount to any Federal Reserve warning, or anything else, to avert any dangerous crisis in the money market." The National City, he said, would loan money as necessary to prevent liquidation. It would also (and did) borrow from the New York Federal Reserve Bank to do what the Federal Reserve Board had warned against doing....
>
> Mitchell's words were like magic. By the end of trading on the 26th money rates had eased, and the market had rallied. The Federal Reserve remained silent, but now its silence was reassuring. It meant that it conceded Mitchell's mastery. [20]

---

18 Different sources spell his name as either Charley or Charlie. We will use Charles E.

19 William K. Klingaman, *1929: The Year of the Great Crash,* Harper & Row, 1989, p. 153.

20 Galbraith (1954), pp. 37-8.

Writing nearly fifty years after Galbraith, historian and professor Maury Klein told a slightly different story about the events of March 26, 1929, based on research unavailable to Galbraith, the most important of which was published in a paper entitled, "Charles E. Mitchell: Scapegoat of the Crash?" by Thomas F. Huertas and Joan L. Silverman. Upon consideration of Huertas' and Silverman's new research, Professor Klein summarized the events of March 26 as follows:

> [The stock market atmosphere] was a whirlpool of uncertainty that, with luck, might suck the bull market down while disturbing the economy itself with only mild ripples of contraction.
>
> But who would step forward at this critical juncture and smite or at least corral the groggy bull? The obvious candidate was the Federal Reserve Board. It held a prolonged session on March 26, the same day that call rates hit 20 percent, and again reached an impasse.... In New York a frustrated George Harrison [President of the Federal Reserve Bank of New York] called Charley Mitchell to tell him that "in circumstances...bordering on the 'panicky' the Federal Reserve Bank did not want and could not be in a position of arbitrarily refusing loans on eligible paper to member banks." He added that Mitchell should not interpret these words as encouraging or discouraging him from putting National City funds into the call market, but that "the call money market was now the problem of the New York money market, that is the member banks and the private bankers." Then Harrison dutifully called [Federal Reserve Board Governor] Young in Washington to inform him of

what he had told Michell.

> This remarkable piece of ambiguity thrust the burden squarely on Charley Mitchell.... He had no obligation to do anything, but Sunshine Charlie was not a man to shirk action when he thought it was necessary. Convinced that a market collapse could produce only widespread harm, he announced that National City would make $25 million available to squeezed borrowers "whatever might be the attitude of the Federal Reserve Board...rather than permit a complete demoralization of the money market." His action stabilized the call loan rate at 15 percent and sent the market sharply upward to recoup most of its losses before the day's end.
>
> When the board learned of Mitchell's action, it privately approved what he had done but professed outrage at what he was reported as saying...[21]

Based on their research, Huertas and Silverman gave the following account in their article:

> [T]he Federal Reserve Board agreed that Mitchell had done the right thing. One member of the Board, Charles S. Hamlin, noted in his diary, "None of the B[oar]d criticized what Mitchell did—it was merely what he said."[22]

---

21 M. Klein (2001), pp. 179-80.

22 Thomas F. Huertas and Joan L. Silverman, "Charles E. Mitchell: Scapegoat of the Crash?" *The Business History Review,* Spring 1986, p. 100. Charles S. Hamlin quote found in *Diary,* 29 March 1929, Library of Congress, Washington, D.C.

It is worth noting that while these comments from Klein and from Huertas and Silverman clarified the situation and the actions of Mitchell, they did nothing to lead us to think more highly of the resoluteness and effectiveness of the Federal Reserve Board. Galbraith's conclusion was, "Clearly the Federal Reserve was less interested in checking speculation than in detaching itself from responsibility for the speculation that was going on."[23] Klein and Huertas and Silverman hardly showed the Fed in a better light.

Watching how events developed, many speculators who had elected to sell their portfolios in late March and get out of the market then foolishly chose to get back in. Again, Noyes reflected:

> [W]hen, as happened [first] in December 1928 and [later] in March 1929, a sudden break in stocks was quickly followed by a tempestuous recovery to heights previously unattained, belief in an indefinitely continued rise seemed to be irresistible.
>
> Anyone who was close to the Wall Street scene could not mistake the psychological change which followed, even among seasoned professional speculators who had been through many similar illusions. Those of them who had sold short because of distrust at the general public's activities, or who had closed out their speculative accounts to take profits at the expansion of such outsiders, now surrendered to the public's own illusions. On the Stock Exchange, daring speculators were pointed out (some of them gave interviews to the newspapers) who…were declared by excited Wall Street to have accumulated paper fortunes running to $25,000,000 or $50,000,000[24]

---

23 Galbraith (1954), p. 35.

24 Noyes (1938), p. 324.

A Look at the Bond Market

Table 8.1 **Yield Curves** **Dec. 1927 - Oct. 1929** (% Percent)						
	Call Market loan renewals	Commercial Paper	Corporate Bonds (Moody's) By ratings			
			Aaa	Aa	A	Baa
1927						
Dec	4.38	4.00	4.46	4.62	4.92	5.32
1928						
Mar	4.46	4.10	4.46	4.59	4.92	5.32
Jun	6.18	4.75	4.57	4.75	5.07	5.55
Sep	7.30	4.55	4.61	4.79	5.07	5.59
Dec	8.28	5.38	4.61	4.77	5.08	5.60
1929						
Jan	7.58	5.41	4.62	4.79	5.10	5.63
Feb	6.83	5.53	4.66	4.86	5.14	5.66
Mar	9.01	5.78	4.70	4.92	5.24	5.79
Apr	8.48	5.97	4.69	4.91	5.23	5.80
May	9.90	6.00	4.70	4.91	5.24	5.80
Jun	7.36	6.00	4.77	4.98	5.31	5.94
Jul	9.25	6.00	4.77	4.97	5.32	5.95
Aug	8.40	6.08	4.79	4.99	5.39	6.04
Sep	8.50	6.22	4.80	5.01	5.43	6.12
Oct	6.70	6.25	4.77	5.01	5.38	6.11

Source: *BMS*, pp. 455-6 & 469.

Table 8.1 shows a succession of yield curves beginning with December 1927, and ending with October 1929, presenting monthly average Call Loan Renewal rates, Commercial Paper rates and Corporate Bond rates by Moody's ratings. The first yield curve ended 1927 with a moderate range of rates and an upward-sloping dispersion. Then, with call loan rates rising, the yield curve rose and flattened in mid-1928 and ended the year inverted. Next, yield curves are shown month-by-month for 1929. By May, 1929, the monthly average Call Loan Renewal rate had reached its high for the year and thereafter tended to decline, while the monthly average corporate bond rates rose in May and continued to rise thereafter, though more slowly. Meanwhile, the Commercial Paper rate was stable from May to July, then rose until October.

What drove these yield curves up? The "segmented markets theory" holds that short-term markets and long-term markets for debt instruments are different markets and are not necessarily related to each other, but we are not adherents of that theory. As Table 8.1 reveals, rapidly rising call loan rates aggressively "sucked" funds from other markets for competing instruments, thereby driving these yield curves up.

The phenomenon of rising yield curves was clearly a factor leading in the direction of recession. Many businesses have long financed their fixed investments in property, plant and equipment by issuing long-term debt instruments—bonds—much as home buyers finance their acquisitions with mortgages. In this regard, Barrie Wigmore stated:

> Before the crash, credit markets were dominated by events in the stock market. The call loan market which was used to finance stock purchases was the center of money market activity because it offered rates 4%-5% above competing short-term securities. Bond prices declined throughout the year [meaning bond rates rose] until October.... Corporate bond issues in 1929 were only $2.1 billion, of which over $1.1 billion were issues with convertible privileges or warrants attached. In prior years the volume of new annual corporate bond issues reached $4.5 billion, with a much lower proportion of equity-related issues. New bond issues of all types in 1929 were the lowest since 1924.[25]

25 Wigmore (1985), p. 105.

Corporate financial managers were clearly not contemplating plant expansion in the 1929 environment.

Back to the Frenzied Stock Market

We return to Galbraith as he continued telling the unfolding story of the speculative scene:

> By the summer of 1929 the market not only dominated the news. It also dominated the culture. That *recherché* minority which at other times has acknowledged its interest in Saint Thomas Aquinas, Proust, psychoanalysis, and psychosomatic medicine then spoke of United Corporation, United Founders, and Steel. Only the most aggressive of the eccentrics maintained their detachment from the market and their interest in autosuggestion or communism. Main Street had always had one citizen who could speak knowingly about buying or selling stocks. Now he became an oracle.[26]
>
> That much of what was repeated about the market—then as now—bore no relation to reality is important, but not remarkable. Between human beings there is a type of intercourse which proceeds not from knowledge, or even from lack of knowledge, but from failure to know what isn't known. This was true of much of the discourse on the market.[27]

The "Work" of Speculators

What were speculators reading and whom did they listen to? Noyes described the circumstances in late summer of 1929:

> Ringleaders of the professional speculation, whose original purpose had been to "unload" at a propitious moment on

26 Galbraith (1954), p. 74.

27 Ibid., p. 75.

the public, who now had themselves yielded unreservedly to the mania, came personally into the limelight, giving out interviews and radio broadcasts which the newspapers printed, declaring the stock exchange prices were too low, rather than too high. They denounced volubly the Federal Reserve's unsuccessful efforts to inspire some sense of caution....

Those curious productions known as "brokers' bulletins"—printed effusions of speculative houses, professing to predict the market's daily course—had gone quite beyond general assurances. The "morning letter" had already adopted the plan of informing clients stocks would rise that day and how far—sometimes 10 or 20 points.

Now they improved on that formula sufficiently to notify customers that at 2 P.M., Radio or General Motors would be "taken in hand." Brokers' offices were crowded from 10 A.M. to 3 P.M. with seated or standing customers who, instead of attending to their own business, were watching the blackboard. In some "customers' rooms" it was difficult to get access to a spot from which the posted quotations could be seen; no one could get a chance to inspect the tape.[28]

Galbraith described the atmosphere of the market among Wall Street insiders as the summer of 1929 ended:

The conviction that the market had become the personal instrument of mysterious but omnipotent men was never stronger. And indeed, this was a period of exceedingly active

28 Noyes (1938), pp. 327-8.

> pool and syndicate operations—in short, of manipulation.[29]
>
> People did not believe they were being shorn. Nor were they. Both they and the pool operators were making money with the difference, only, that the latter were making more. In any case, the public reaction to inside operations was to hope it might get some inside information.[30]

Hindsight is golden, as the saying goes. During the Pecora hearings held in 1933, Otto Kahn reflected on the early days of September 1929 and on the collective delusion:

> They were determined that every piece of paper would be worth tomorrow twice what it was today. I do not believe the whole banking community could have prevented it.... When it had taken full sway of the people and there was an absolute runaway feeling throughout the country, I doubt whether anyone could have stopped it before calamity overtook us.[31]

Later, Noyes, with his decades-long, up-close knowledge of the American stock market and its participants, contrasted the experience of 1929 with the bursting of earlier bubbles:

> The end of the great speculation came at the moment when the whole community seemed to have convinced itself that the end would never come, but it did not come exactly as others came. It had been the tradition of our older panics that, under the tightening strain on credit, breakdown of some over-expanded business enterprise would give the signal. In the early summer of 1907, the Westinghouse Electric suspended payments; in March 1893 the Reading

29 Galbraith (1954), p. 79.

30 Ibid., p. 80.

31 *SEP*, p. 1010.

> railway went into receivers' hands; there were large bank and commercial failures in the summer or spring of 1873. Those failures occurred, in each of the three earlier panic years, four to six months before the Stock Exchange crisis. They stopped the fury of speculation instantly, the effort of speculators thenceforward was to extricate themselves, but the...progressive disorder of the credit market made the effort vain.
>
> In 1929, there was no such preliminary warning. No banking institution, no industrial company, had closed doors. On the contrary, incorporation of new investment trusts with large capital, formed for no purpose but to trade in stocks, proceeded without diminution of enthusiasm.[32]

The View from Industry in 1929

Charles Persons, whom we featured in Chapter 7, studied trade magazines and drew many of his statistics and conclusions about credit sales from publications such as *Radio Retailing, Electrical Merchandising, and Automobile Trade Journal and Motor Age.*

Table 8.2, (following page) is a reproduction of Persons' published table about monthly car and trucks production in 1928 and 1929 and highlights the timing and impact with respect to the October Crash. There was a whopping 76% year-to-year growth in vehicles produced, from 240,191 in January 1928 to 422,538 in January 1929. Thereafter, even though there was one year-to-year monthly gain in March, the percentage gain shrank month by month. By August, gains all but evaporated, replaced by losses beginning in September, the month of the stock market high, and the Crash

32 Noyes (1938), pp. 325-6.

month of October. Following the Crash, production dropped dramatically below 1928 levels.

In considering the bellwether industries of automobiles and radios, Persons described worrisome market conditions that prevailed in the year of the Crash:

> The parallelism between developments in 1929 in the

Table 8.2 **Cars and Trucks Produced** (In Thousands)			
Month	1928	1929	Percent gain or loss
Jan.	240.2	422.5	+ 75.9
Feb.	336.3	497.6	+ 48.0
Mar.	430.8	625.8	+ 45.3
Apr.	434.3	663.2	+ 52.7
May	459.7	635.6	+ 38.3
June	425.2	566.8	+33.3
July	417.3	517.9	+ 24.1
Aug.	492.5	512.6	+ 4.1
Sept.	436.5	429.5	- 1.6
Oct.	415.8	394.5	- 5.1
Nov.	268.9	226.9	- 15.6
Dec.	243.5	131.9	- 45.9
Totals	4,601.1	5,625.0	+ 22.3

(Data differs from Table Prologue. 2 due to source difference)

Source: *Automobile Trade Journal and Motor Age, Feb. 1930*, pp.56-57 and Charles E. Persons, "Credit Expansion, 1920-1929, and its Lessons," *The Quarterly Journal of Economics, Nov. 1930*, p. 124.

> automobile and radio industries could hardly be more exact. In each case an expanded volume of goods was offered to a public highly desirous of purchasing them. In each industry a highly trained salesforce exhausted every device known to high pressure salesmanship to sell the accumulating stocks. And in each case they found it impossible to move the goods, primarily because the buyers (sic) resources in cash and credit had been expended. The effect of the great bulge in credit during the decade had been exploited. For the future, the automobile industry, and all others, must be content with a normal annual volume of sales.[33]

The Stock Market Drop Begins

While later chapters will show the extent of our research into the demographics and activities of speculators and long-term investors who bought and sold in the stock market in 1929, we offer a preview. In doing this fact-finding, we formed the opinion that long-term investors who had developed sell disciplines over the years were liquidating at least some of their stock portfolios as the market approached its high and began to drop and parking the proceeds of their stock sales in the call money market. This accounted for the rising supply of loans in the call money market despite the fall in call money loan rates at the time. Of course there had to be a rising demand for such loans in order for the market to clear. And there was. Addressing this aspect of 1929, Noyes wrote:

> On September 19, stock market averages, as computed by the daily newspapers, reached the high point of the period. It was a dizzy height. The average price of $311.90 per $100 share, by the New York Times's computation, compared

33 Persons (1930), p. 124.

> with $230.53 at the end of 1928, with $181 at the end of 1927, and with $139.33 at the end of 1926.
>
> Then, suddenly, the great decline began. At first the army of speculators did not take it seriously....The familiar comment, in an exchange of ideas in the customers' room, was that the market's ability to pay such [high] rates and go on rising was proof that the speculation was impregnable.[34]

As journalist and cultural critic Gilbert Seldes wrote in *The Years of the Locust (America, 1929-1932)*, the final days before the Crash were the true time of panic:

> I have used the word "panic" in the accepted sense for the event of October 1929, but I consider it misleading. There was a panic in America, running from 1926 and becoming a rout in the six months *before* the market break....I put it that *the boom was our panic....*
>
> I call it panic to be afraid to sell at a profit, less an additional profit be lost.... (T)he panic which keeps people at roulette tables, the insidious propaganda against quitting a winner, the fear of being taunted by those who held on, all worked together. It became not only a point of pride, but a civic duty, not to sell, as if there were ever a buyer without a seller.[35] (italics in original)

Clearly, the speculators Seldes focused on never learned—or had forgotten—the aphorism, "One can never go wrong taking a profit."

Parsing the Fed's Language

---

34 Noyes (1938), pp. 328-9. Noyes writes here of "stock market averages," not "indexes" which usually record stocks' high, low and closing prices.

35 Seldes (1938), pp. 128-9.

In its *Annual Report* for 1929, the Fed reported that rates charged by banks to commercial customers were "on a 6 per cent level...higher than at any other time since 1921." The *Report* continued:

> Loans to brokers and dealers in securities in the New York market are increasing rapidly. In these circumstances the discount rate at the Federal Reserve Bank of New York was advanced from 5 to 6 per cent [on August 9], a level consistent with the rates prevailing in the open market and calculated to exercise a restraining influence at the center of speculative activity.[36]

The Fed reported that loans made in the call money market "were...supplied almost entirely by nonbanking lenders" and elaborated dispassionately:

> These loans for nonbanking lenders had remained at a fairly constant level in April, May, and June, but increased by about $1,000,000,000 in the following four months. It would appear that a large part of this increase was supplied by investment trusts and trading companies, which...having obtained funds from the public through sale of their own securities, used portions of these funds in the call-loan market. The continued growth of brokers' loans up to the beginning of October, when security prices were tending downward, reflected also the effect of sales by outright owners or holders on relatively large equities to purchasers on credit whose equities were considerably smaller."[37]

We interpret this explanation to mean that, in the Fed's view, the two main sources of the bloated supply of call loans to brokers were the result of newly launched investment trusts and trading companies and also security sales by "outright owners or holders."

36 *ARBG for 1929,* p. 8.
37 *ARBG for 1929,* p. 9.

Such "outright owners" certainly included wealthy individuals, and "holders" included custodians of established private trust funds. In either case, the "outright owners or holders" were, at this time, reducing their exposure to risk and taking profits by selling holdings, while speculators or "purchasers on credit" were still buying. In these circumstances, the Fed drew a further conclusion:

> In September and October [1929], therefore, recession in industry, reports of smaller corporate earnings, continued growth of brokers' loans, indicating a movement of securities from stronger to weaker hands, and many other factors were weakening the security market.[38]

In other words, the stock market was becoming softer and more vulnerable on the downside. The Fed's euphemistic description of "weaker hands" turned out to describe the most vulnerable casualties in that the downside.

The Last Days Before the Crash

Addressing the NYSE's performance on Monday, October 21, historian Klingaman wrote:

> Chaos reigned on the floor on the New York Stock Exchange. By 10:15...the avalanche of sell orders overwhelmed the beleaguered ticker; by noon the system was running an hour late in recording the shocking price declines.
>
> By the time the frantic shouting was over [that evening], 920 issues had been involved in the trading—the broadest market on record—and an aggregate volume of 6,091,870

38 Ibid., p. 9.

shares had changed hands, the second busiest day of the year (behind only the debacle of March 26).[39]

"Taken as a whole," reported *The New York Times*, "the character of the market [on Monday, October 21] left Wall Street both bewildered and frightened."[40]

Describing the "character" of the NYSE on Wednesday, October 23, Klingaman continued:

> Those who confidently expected Tuesday's halfhearted rally to continue were disappointed as the much touted "organized buying support" failed to appear. By noon it was obvious that the market was heading for another sharp fall. And this time even the strongest nerves cracked.
>
> Terror struck the exchange that afternoon. Selling orders deluged the market; prices plunged violently. It seemed as if everybody wanted to get out. In the last hour of trading between two and three o'clock, more than 2.6 million shares changed hands. Investors watched stunned, as their fortunes melted away....
>
> One banker endeavored to find a silver lining in the black cloud that hovered threateningly over Wall Street. "It will send back to work many people who have been sitting around brokerage offices for a year or so on the trail of easy money," he claimed, not joking at all. "I have heard thousands of reports of merchants, farmers, and men and women in all walks of life literally giving up their businesses to watch the

---

39 Klingaman (1989), pp. 256-7.

40 Ibid., p. 257 and *The New York Times,* Oct. 22, 1929.

> stock market. Most of them will, by necessity, have to go back to earning their living in normal ways."
>
> Perhaps. But everything had changed over the past few months. Now all the support underlying the inflated bull market price structure had been washed away. All that was left were the rotten beams. That evening...an "avalanche" of margin calls went out from Wall Street through the country."[41]

Reflecting on a woeful drop in productivity in this time of wild speculation, especially among people normally employed in managing businesses, Galbraith commented, "Only in the case of the rarest individuals can speculation be a part-time activity. Money for most people is far too important."[42]

How large was Noyes's "speculating public" who was investing their time, energy and resources in dreams of riches? Verifiable statistics on the number of speculators are elusive, and the perceptions vary widely. We have seen estimates ranging from the hyperbolic "everyone was in the market" to as low as half a million, as we will revisit later. Meanwhile, as Galbraith hypothesized, the end of the speculative boom was inevitable:

> [A] roaring boom was in progress in the stock market and, like all booms, it had to end... When prices stopped rising—when the supply of people who were buying for an increase was exhausted—then...everyone would want to sell. The market wouldn't level out; it would fall precipitately.[43]

We turn next to the inevitably feverish events that followed as the stock market declined and panic set in.

41 Ibid., pp. 260-1.

42 Galbraith (1954), p. 80.

43 Ibid., p. 24.

Of Note

Statistics of U.S. Economic Activity

Located at the end of a number of our chapters hereafter are tables of Statistics of U.S. Economic Activity. These tables offer key monthly U.S. statistics that show trends and directionality at work for he quarter covered within the chapter and the two prior months.

Table 8.3

Statistics of U.S. Economic Activity

($ billion)

	May '29	Jun. '29	Jul. '29	Aug. '29	Sep. '29
Annualized personal income	$84.5	$85.1	$86.3	$86.9	$86.4
Index of factory employment	106.6	107.0	108.1	108.4	107.3
Index of industrial production	112	113	114	114	112
Index of wholesale prices	94.7	95.2	96.5	96.3	96.1
Friedman & Schwartz demand deposits	$22.2	$22.3	$22.8	$22.6	$22.6
Fed member bank loans		$25.7			$26.2

Sources: *HSUS* 1789-1945, pp. 328-330, 344; *Monetary History*, p.712; *BMS*, p.72.

Tables that show economic activity covering different months of 1929—with the same six categories similar to Table 8.3—appear at the ends of chapters 9, 10, 11, and 12 as well as in *The Deflation of 1930*. The four above-the-line measurements present key statistics that were the center of attention of President Hoover, his cabinet, the

Chairman and members of the Federal Reserve Board, members of Congress, the press, and other Washington "influencers."

Below the line are the Friedman & Schwartz demand deposits estimates stipulated in their *Monetary History*. Fed member bank loans statistics were only available quarterly rather than monthly.

The NBER identified August of 1929 as the "peak" of the expansion that occurred in the boom years of the late 1920s. All above-the-line statistics in Table 8.3 were down in September from the August peak:

- Annualized personal income:
–down $500 million dollars (or 0.6%)
- Index of factory employment:
–down 1.0%
- Industrial production:
–down 1.8%
- Wholesale prices:
–down 0.2% (annualized rate of -2.5%)

CHAPTER 9

THE CRASH

ACCORDING TO THE ACCEPTED VIEW of events, by the autumn of 1929 the economy was well into a depression. In June the indexes of industrial and factory production both reached a peak and turned down. By October, the Federal Reserve index of industrial production stood at 117 as compared with 126 four months earlier. Steel production declined from June on; in October freight-car loadings fell. Homebuilding, a most mercurial industry, had been falling for several years, and it slumped further in 1929. Finally, down came the stock market. A penetrating student of the economic behavior of this period has said that the market slump, "reflected, in the main, the change which was already apparent in the industrial situation."[1]

Many would argue that no writer has captured the frenzy of the days around the Crash in context of the larger economic climate better than John Kenneth Galbraith. We respectfully offer selections from his gripping day-by-day narrative of events in *The Great Crash, 1929*, beginning with the infamous Black Thursday (and perhaps predict a rise in blood pressure as Galbraith so skillfully tells the tale):

---

1 Galbraith (1954), p. 88. Galbraith quoted Thomas Wilson from his 1942 book *Fluctuations in Income and Employment,* 1942, p. 143.

Black Thursday, October 24

Thursday, October 24, is the first of the days which history—such as it is on the subject—identifies with the panic of 1929. Measured by disorder, fright, and confusion, it deserves to be so regarded. That day 12,894,650 shares changed hands, many of them at prices which shattered the dreams and hopes of those who had owned them. Of all mysteries on the stock exchange there is none so impenetrable as why there should be a buyer for everyone who seeks to sell. October 24, 1929 showed that what is mysterious is not inevitable. Often there were no buyers, and only after wide vertical declines could anyone be induced to bid.

The panic did not last all day. It was a phenomenon of the morning hours. The market opening itself was unspectacular, and for a while prices were firm. Volume, however, was very large, and soon prices began to sag. Once again the ticker dropped behind. Prices fell farther and faster, and the ticker lagged more and more. By eleven o'clock the market had degenerated into a wild, mad scramble to sell. In the crowded boardrooms across the country the ticker told of a frightful collapse. But the selected quotations coming in over the bond ticker also showed that current prices were far below the ancient history of the tape. The uncertainty led more and more people to try to sell. Others, no longer able to respond to margin calls, were sold out. By eleven-thirty the market had surrendered to blind, relentless fear. This, indeed, was panic.... [2]

2 Galbraith (1954), pp. 98-99.

The Fear of Closed Margin Accounts with Open Losses

The freefall of stock prices that occurred during the morning of October 24, was a phenomenon that was beyond the imaginings of all but the most experienced stock-market professionals of that time. The precipitous fall of stock prices really began late in the day, Wednesday, October 23, when the Index of 50 stocks tracked by *The New York Times* closed at 261.97, down -6.5% or -18.24 from its close of 280.21 on Tuesday, 22 October. On the morning of Black Thursday, *The New York Times* reported:

> What Wall Street described as an avalanche of margin calls went out of the financial district last night.... Few brokers expect a good response....[3]

Many, if not all, speculators, who had margin accounts that required maintenance on deposit of a minimum of 10% of the value of the stocks they held, received one of those margin calls.

It was the practice then to expect margin call recipients to "top-up" their accounts by 11:00 AM EST the next day. Soon after 11:00 AM EST on Black Thursday, the Index of 50 stocks tracked by the *Times* reached its low for the day—238.19—and continued to trade at about that value for some time. Thus, by the hour the top-up was due, the Index had fallen a further -15.0% from its value on 22 October. This meant that by the 11:00 deadline the morning of Black Thursday, all speculators with 10% margin accounts, who had received margin calls by telegram the night before *and* failed to top up their accounts, soon thereafter almost certainly had their stocks sold at substantial losses. When

3 *The New York Times* (October 24, 1929), p. 43.

they received the month-end statements for their now-closed or open-but-empty accounts, they would learn *just how much more their losses actually totaled.*

How could this addition of insult to injury happen? We take an example of a speculator with a deposit of $10,000 and stocks worth $100,000 who had his 10% margin account at its top-up value at the market close of Tuesday, 22 October. By 11:00 am Black Thursday, given the market plunge of 15%, he would have experienced a loss in the value of somewhat less than $15,000 when his margined stock was sold that morning and his account closed. Not only would he have lost his $10,000 deposit and all his stocks, *his account would show an additional loss of nearly $5,000, owed to his broker,* whose firm, of course, had taken out a call money market loan in order to lend its customer the funds to finance his stock purchases. The speculating customer would have experienced what we are calling an *"unexpected residual loss."* It was an unexpected loss for both the speculator and the speculator's broker. The speculator, who thought he had limited his risk to $10,000, actually had *considerably more* at risk, and the loss remained a residual debt in the speculator's account, whether closed or still open, after all else had been settled. The speculator's brokerage who had borrowed in the call loan money market was still on the hook to repay the call loan lender and expected the customer to repay his debt.

A second speculator, also with a 10% margin account and a full deposit of $10,000 on the morning of Black Thursday, decided to "plunge" by betting all his funds on one, highly volatile stock—Radio Corporation of America, called informally "Radio." His margin account allowed him to invest $100,000, and he gave his broker an order to purchase Radio stock at the opening price of $68½. He acquired nearly 1,450 shares. Briefly the market was firm, and the price per share of Radio went up to $70 7/8, but then the market turned down as described earlier in this chapter. Between 11:00 AM EST and noon, his brokerage firm sold him out at a price of $45 per share—close to the $44 ½ per share low for the day. For his shares, his brokerage firm received nearly $67,000.

After his margined stock was sold the morning of Black Thursday, his account was closed. He had lost his $10,000 deposit, all his broker-financed stock *and his account showed he owed his broker just under $23,000, an even more painful "unexpected residual loss."* If he had regarded his risk as limited to $10,000, the statement he received at month-end confronted him with how much he more he had had at risk.

We can easily imagine the shock and fear speculators felt finding themselves with closed margin accounts that contained open losses. First, having a closed margin account meant a speculator had not only lost everything in the account (his deposit and all his stocks), he no longer even had an account to engage in further speculation. Unless he had other assets, he was wiped out, and his dreams of getting rich were crushed. Worse still, he had *a significant debt* that his broker expected him to pay! This unexpected residual loss, a potential liability he had never understood, hung like a millstone around his neck.

Galbraith's dramatic account continues:

In New York at least the panic was over by noon. At noon the organized support appeared. At twelve o'clock reporters learned that a meeting was convening at 23 Wall Street at the offices J.P. Morgan and Company.... According to legend, during the panic of 1907 the elder Morgan had brought to a halt the discussion of whether to save the tottering Trust Company of America by saying that the place to stop the panic was there. It was stopped. Now, twenty-two years later, that drama was being re-enacted. The elder Morgan was dead. His son was in Europe. But equally determined men were moving in.... The very news that they would act would release people from the fear to which they had surrendered.

It did. A decision was quickly reached to pool resources to support the market. The meeting broke up, and Thomas Lamont [a Morgan partner] met with reporters. His manner was described as serious, but his words were reassuring.... The bankers, let it be known, had decided to better things.

Word had already reached the floor of the Exchange that the bankers were meeting, and the news ticker had spread the magic word afield. Prices firmed at once and started to rise. Then at one-thirty Richard Whitney appeared on the floor and went to the post where steel was traded. Whitney was perhaps the best-known figure on the floor. He was one of the group of men of good background and appropriate education who, in that time, were expected to manage the affairs of the Exchange. Currently he was vice president of the Exchange, but in the absence of E. H. H. Simmons in Hawaii he was serving as acting president. What was much more important at the moment, he was known as floor trader for Morgan's and, indeed, his older brother was a Morgan partner.

As he made his way through the teaming crowd, Whitney appeared debonair and self-confident.... At the Steel post he bid 205 for 10,000 shares. This was the price of the last sale, and the current bids were several points lower. In an

> operation that was totally devoid of normal commercial reticence, he got 200 shares and then left the rest of the order with the specialist. He continued on his way placing similar orders for fifteen or twenty other stocks.
>
> This was it. The bankers, obviously, had moved in. The effect was electric. Fear vanished and gave way to concern lest the new advance be missed. Prices boomed upward....
>
> In the closing hour, selling orders continuing to come in from across the country turned the market soft once more. Still, in its own way, the recovery on Black Thursday was as remarkable as the selling that made it so black. The *Times* industrials were off only 12 points, or a little more than a third of the loss of the previous day.... Many had good reason to be grateful to the financial leaders of Wall Street.[4]

October 25th Through 27th: Had Organized Support Prevailed?

There ensued three days—Friday the 25th through Sunday the 27th—during which market participants could reflect on this question of the impact of so-called organized support. We return to Galbraith's diurnal account:

> On Friday and Saturday trading continued heavy—just under six million on Friday, over two million at the short session on Saturday. Prices, on the whole, were steady—the averages were a trifle up on Friday but slid off on Saturday....[5]

---

4 Galbraith (1954), pp. 100-03.

5 Ibid., p. 105.

In the midst of his chronological account, Galbraith took a detour to muse about what might have been going on in the minds of dismayed and uncertain speculators:

> A depression, serious or otherwise, could not be foreseen when the market fell. There is still the possibility that the downturn in the indexes frightened the speculators, led them to unload their stocks, and so punctured a bubble that had in any case to be punctured one day. This is more plausible. Some people who were watching the indexes may have been persuaded by this intelligence to sell, and others may then have been encouraged to follow. This is not very important, for it is in the nature of a speculative boom that almost anything can collapse it. Any serious shock to confidence can cause sales by those speculators who have always hoped to get out before the final collapse, but after all possible gains from rising prices have been reaped.[7]

Monday, October 28

The three-day trading hiatus offered nervous market participants enough time to reflect and to prepare for what Galbraith described as "another terrible day:"

> Monday, October 28, was the first day on which this process of climax and anticlimax *ad infinitum* began to reveal itself. It was another terrible day. Volume was huge, although below the previous Thursday—nine and a quarter million shares as compared with nearly thirteen. But the losses were far more severe.... Indeed, the decline on this one day was greater than that of all the preceding week of

6 Ibid., p. 90.

panic. Once again a late ticker left everyone in ignorance of what was happening, save that it was bad....

At four-thirty in the afternoon the bankers assembled once more at Morgan's, and they remained in session until six-thirty. They were described as taking a philosophical attitude, and they told the press that the situation "retained hopeful features," although these were not specified. But the statement they released after the meeting made clear what had been discussed for the two hours. It was no part of the bankers' purpose, the statement said, to maintain any particular level of prices or to protect anyone's profit. Rather the aim was to have an orderly market, one in which offers would be met by bids at some price. The bankers were only concerned that "air holes," as Mr. Lamont had dubbed them, did not appear.

Like many lesser men, Mr. Lamont and his colleagues had suddenly found themselves over-committed on a falling market. The time had come to go short on promises. *Support, organized or otherwise, could not contend with the overwhelming, pathological desire to sell.* The meeting had considered how to liquidate the commitment to support the market without adding to the public perturbation. (emphasis ours)

The formula that was found was a chilling one. On Thursday, Whitney had supported prices and protected profits—or stopped losses. This was what people wanted. To the man who held stock on margin, disaster had only one face and that was falling prices. But now prices were to be allowed to fall. The speculator's only comfort, henceforth, was that his ruin would be accomplished in an orderly and

> becoming manner.
>
> There were no recriminations at the time. Our political life favors the extremes of speech; the man who is gifted in the arts of abuse is bound to be notable, if not always a great figure. In business things are different. Here we are surprisingly gentle and forbearing. Even preposterous claims or excuses are normally taken, at least for all public purposes, at their face value. On the evening of the 28th no one any longer could feel "secure in the knowledge that the most powerful banks stood ready to prevent a recurrence" of panic. The market had reasserted itself as an impersonal force beyond the power of any person to control, and, while this is the way markets are supposed to be, it was horrible. But no one assailed the bankers for letting the people down. There was even some talk that on the next day the market might receive organized support.[8]

So if organized support was no longer available, what then? That was the question that dominated speculators' skittish minds.

Black Tuesday, October 29

It was inevitable that things would grow worse. What Galbraith called, "the most devastating day in the history" of the NYSE up to that point fell upon market players, from the newest of speculators to the most seasoned and sophisticated of investors. We return to Galbraith's wild-ride account:

> Tuesday, October 29, was the most devastating day in the history of the New York stock market, and it may have been the most devastating day in the history of markets. It combined all of the bad features of all of the bad days before.

8 Ibid., pp. 109-11.

Volume was immensely greater than on Black Thursday; the drop in prices was almost as great as on Monday. Uncertainty and alarm were as great as on either.

Selling began as soon as the market opened and in huge volume. Great blocks of stock were offered for what they would bring; in the first half hour sales were at a 33,000,000-a-day rate. The air holes, which the bankers were to close, opened wide. Repeatedly and in many issues there was a plethora of selling orders and no buyers at all.... During the day someone—according to Frederick Lewis Allen it was thought to have been a bright messenger boy for the Exchange—had the happy idea of entering a bid for a block of stock at a dollar a share. In the absence of any other bid he got it.... The *Times* industrial averages were down 43 points, canceling all of the gains of the twelve wonderful months preceding....

The worst day on Wall Street came eventually to an end. Once again the lights blazed all night. Members of the Exchange, their employees, and the employees of the Stock Exchange by now were reaching the breaking point from strain and fatigue. In this condition they faced the task of recording and handling the greatest volume of transactions ever. All of this was without the previous certainty that things might get better. They might go on getting worse. In one house an employee fainted from exhaustion, was revived and put back to work again.[9]

9 Ibid., pp. 111-3.

A Week That Shook Wall Street

Again, from the nimble mind and pen of Galbraith:

> On the Exchange itself, there was a strong feeling that courage and hope might best be restored by just closing up for a while. This feeling had, in fact, been gaining force for several days. Now it derived support from the simple circumstance that everyone was badly in need of sleep.... A number of firms needed some time to see if they were still solvent....
>
> Yet to close the Exchange was a serious matter. It might somehow signify that stocks had lost all their value, with consequences no one could foresee. In any case, securities would immediately become a badly frozen asset.... [10]
>
> The next day those forces were at work which on occasion bring salvation precisely when salvation seems impossible. Stocks rose wonderfully, miraculously, though still on enormous volume.... Why this recovery occurred no one will ever know. Organized support can have no credit. Organized reassurance has a somewhat better claim....
>
> The accepted Wall Street explanation of Wednesday's miracle was not the reassurance but the dividend news of the day before. This also, without much question, was somewhat organized. [11]
>
> At the short session of three hours on Thursday, October 31, well over seven million shares traded, and the market made another good gain. The *Times* industrials were up 21 points.... [T]he market closed down for Friday, Saturday

10 Ibid., pp. 115-6.

11 Ibid., pp. 118-9.

and Sunday. They were not days of rest. Brokerage offices were fully staffed, and the Exchange floor was open for completion of trades and also for straightening out innumerable misunderstandings and mistakes.[12]

The Week of Monday, November 4

Sparing no words, Galbraith's vivid, nail-biting account of events continued into the following week:

> The papers described the reaction of professional Wall Street to Monday's market as one of stunned surprise, disbelief, and shock. Volume was smaller than the week before, but still well above six million. The whole list was weak; individual issues made big losses; the *Times* industrials were down 22 points for the day. Compared with anything but the week before, this was very bad....
>
> By now it was also evident that the investment trusts, once considered a buttress of the high plateau and a built-in defense against collapse, were really a profound source of weakness. The leverage, of which people only a fortnight before had spoken so knowledgeably and even affectionately, was now fully in reverse. With remarkable celerity it removed all the value from the common stock of a trust....
>
> A representative portfolio of securities owned by such a trust would, in the early days of November, have declined in value by perhaps a half.... The new portfolio value, $5,000,000, would be only enough to cover the prior claim on assets of the bonds and preferred stock. The common

12 Ibid., p. 120.

stock would have nothing behind it. Apart from expectations, which were by no means bright, it was now worthless.

This geometrical ruthlessness was not exceptional. On the contrary, it was everywhere at work on the stock of the leverage trusts. By early November, the stock of most of them had become virtually unsalable.[13]

Tuesday, November 5, was election day, and the market was closed all day.... Wednesday the market reopened for the first of a new series of short sessions of three hours.... There was another sickening slide. The *Times* industrials were off 37 points for the day, or only 6 points less than on the terrible Tuesday eight days earlier....

There was also disturbing news from beyond the market. Fundamentals seemed to be turning sour....

On Thursday the stock market was steady to higher, but on Friday it took a small drop. People had another weekend of contemplation. This time there was no talk of an accumulation of buying orders; indeed, there was little good news of any kind. On Monday, November 11, came another drastic slump. For the next two days trading was heavy—the Exchange was still on short hours—and prices went down still more. In these three days, November 11, 12, and 13, the *Times* industrials lost another 50 points.[14]

"At Long, Long Last...At Least, for a While"

Finally, Galbraith summed up events so that we can catch

---

13 Ibid., pp. 122-3.

14 Ibid., pp. 125-6.

our collective breath:

> In mid-November 1929, at long, long last, the market stopped falling—at least, for a while. The low was on Wednesday, November 13. On that day the *Times* industrials closed at 224 down from 452, or by almost exactly one half since September 3.[15]

> When the market fell many Wall Street citizens immediately sensed the real danger, which was that income and employment—prosperity in general—would be adversely affected.[16]

> A common feature of...earlier troubles was that having happened they were over. The worst was reasonably recognizable as such. *The singular feature of the great crash of 1929 was that the worst continued to worsen....* The Coolidge bull market was a remarkable phenomenon. The ruthlessness of its liquidation was, in its own way, equally remarkable.[17] (emphasis ours)

None of this boded well going forward, certainly on either the macro level for the economy as a whole or on a micro level for individual stock market participants, whether they were experienced investors who were old hands or virtually any speculators including deluded novices. A pall began to cover Wall Street and to spread outward to Main Street. In the following chapter, we move behind the scenes to begin examining how the various financial players were reacting.

---

15 Ibid., p. 135.

16 Ibid., p. 89.

17 Ibid., pp. 108-9.

How Did Margin Accounts Fare in the Crash?

One objective of our sidebar (page 221) was to use examples to introduce our concept of "unexpected residual losses" to make it clear that the amounts lost by speculators in the precipitous drops that resulted from the virtual disappearance of buy orders exceeded the collateral on deposit in their accounts. Thus, these margin accounts, although closed to any further speculation, came to contain newly created, and, in many cases, substantial debt obligations that speculators owed their brokers, labeled by us "unexpected residual losses."

After Black Thursday the freefall continued throughout October 28 and October 29, "Black Tuesday." As we quoted above in his account of October 28, Galbraith stated:

> The decline on this one day was greater than that of all the preceding week of panic. Once again a late ticker left everyone in ignorance of what was happening, save that it was bad.[18]

Of Black Tuesday, Galbraith wrote:

> The air holes, which the bankers were to close, opened wide. Repeatedly and in many issues there was a plethora of selling orders and no buyers at all.[19]

Given that brokers' own credit was obviously threatened in the call money market after Black Thursday, it is likely that customers whose accounts were clearly near or beyond their credit limits were ordered sold out immediately as soon as identified. On October 28, the low of 232.57 was 20.6% below the October 22 close, and it is also likely that most accounts below 25% margin—or, quite probably for virtually *all margin accounts*—received margin calls because on Black Tuesday the low of 183.50 was 34.5% below the

18 Galbraith (1954), p. 109.

19 Ibid., p. 111.

October 22 close.[20]

Can We Measure Total Unexpected Residual Losses as the Crash Ended?

Having established that unexpected residual losses certainly occurred in open margin accounts as well as those that were closed, what did these losses total? As we have conducted our research for *The Great Deleverage Series,* we have kept our eyes open for answers to this question, but we have found neither relevant commentary nor statistics. However, we consider this a sufficiently important question to venture an order of magnitude guestimate. We begin by looking at the big picture to find how many margin accounts there were in 1929.

The Senate Committee on Banking and Currency hearings led by Ferdinand Pecora, summarized in the Committee's report *Stock Exchange Practices* (*SEP*), revealed that for the period between January 1, 1928, and August 31, 1933, the New York Stock Exchange (NYSE) and the 28 other exchanges that existed in the U.S. earned commissions totaling $1,640 million and interest income totaling $325 million, with the NYSE earning 95.2% of these commissions and 98.5% of the interest income.[21] Further, we learned that during 1929, the NYSE reported that member firms had 1,371,920 customers, of whose transactions were 59.2% of a cash character and 40.8% of a margin character.[22]

As to the total losses on the NYSE from October 23 to the end of the month, the *Times* Index of 50 Stocks closed September 30 at

20 In the chaos of the time and with stock prices dropping precipitously, we couldn't help but wonder when the barrage of ordered margin account closings actually finished and took full effect.

21 *SEP,* p. 6.

22 Ibid., p. 9. We are certain that among the customers of brokerage firms in 1929 were many who speculated using conventional accounts "of a cash character" because they neither needed to borrow in order to speculate nor wanted to pay margin account interest expenses (which were valuable sources of interest income for brokers). This means that we can provide an estimate only for speculators using margin accounts.

290.21, October 22 at 280.21, and October 31 at 230.00 indicating that 16.6% of the losses happened before October 23 and 83.4% afterwards in the month.

Table 10.1 (page 246) shows that the market value of all listed stocks was $87,074 million on 1 October 1929 and $71,753 million on 1 November, a decline of $15,321 million in October 1929. With 83.4% of the drop occurring from October 23 onwards, the amount of money lost in the Crash period was $12,778 million.

How much of this amount was due to speculation? If 40.8% of the accounts of NYSE brokers were margin accounts as the Pecora hearings revealed, then $5,213 million, 40.8% of the $12,778 million, is one plausible guesstimate of losses from speculation on credit from margin accounts.

We consider this to be a significant sum because its repayment involves two players in terms of credit and creditworthiness. Most obvious includes brokers' speculating customers who place the buy/sell orders (and may sit or stand in the brokers' customers rooms). But the most immediate credit consideration for the brokerage firm is its own credit because its *modus operandi* requires it to repay the firm's call money market loans as fast as possible as its customers *lose money.*

Our Estimate of Unexpected Residual Losses of Margin Account Speculators in the Crash Period

While *SEP* revealed that the Pecora hearings looked into some specific aspects of loans made for the purpose of short selling, we have found nothing in *SEP* devoted to practices associated with brokers' loan accounts.

Our first example in the sidebar above is of a speculator with

$10,000 on deposit in 10% margin accounts. The speculator (and presumably his broker) made the assumption that he had $10,000 at risk, but in point of fact actual losses totaled nearly $15,000, as we described, when his account was closed by his broker. The unexpected residual losses of nearly $5,000, was nearly 50% greater than the amount he assumed was at risk. Or, looked at another way, one third of the speculator's loss of nearly $15,000, was an unexpected residual loss. Using this example, we regard it as reasonable to estimate that one third of total losses in margin accounts in the Crash period were unexpected residual losses. With the total speculative losses from margin account stock purchases of $5,213 million, unexpected residual losses would, therefore, total $1,737 million for the Crash period.

Another approach to guesstimating is to suppose that $1,737 million loss lies in the middle of a range from low to high. After thoughtful consideration, we suggest a reasonable low value of 25% of the $5,213 million loss and a reasonable high value of 42%, thus leading to our estimate of unexpected residual losses over and above speculators' basic margin account collateral—i.e., their margin deposits and broker-financed stock—of $1.3 billion to $2.2 billion.

In summary, we understand that $5,213 million was lost by holders of margin accounts in the immediate period of the Crash and guestimate that somewhere between 25% to 42% of this amount consisted of unexpected residual losses which margin speculators remained obligated to pay. When brokers rendered their account statements to their margin account customers at the end of October 1929—which they no doubt sent as expeditiously as possible—we contend that the margin speculators—whether their accounts were closed or still active—had obligations to pay enormous sums to their brokers following the Crash period because the brokers were clearly "on the hook" to repay the amounts they had borrowed in the call money market that enabled their customers' speculations.

From *The New York Times* of October 30, 1929:

TOPICS IN WALL STREET

So great was the confusion in Wall Street yesterday [Black Tuesday, Oct. 29, 1929] that the wide-open break on the Stock Exchange was generally accepted as an episode of a week-old debacle.... The speculative element was in that mood which blinded it to everything but the most unpleasant sensations.

The Use of Discretion

Members of the Stock Exchange, and particularly the specialists on the floor, had free rein yesterday in the use of discretion, and it was this, more than anything else, that prevented more calamitous happenings.... Many customers do not know what they received or paid for stocks.

Ringing the Knell

The closing gong of the Stock Exchange took on a new significance.... When its reverberations had ceased, one of the few spectators admitted to the visitors' gallery remarked: "There's the knell for many a bank account." ... The market situation was so desperate ... that it overshadowed all other considerations, and the prices at which stocks were sold were of more importance to those who watched the market than any sort of outside news.

Trying to Stem Niagara

Any attempt to support the market by buying stocks yesterday was like trying to stem the falls of Niagara.... It represented ... a desperate anxiety to get entirely out of the stock market on the part of thousands of persons in all parts of the country....[T]hose who stood on the sidelines and witnessed it were literally awe-struck by the violence of the shrinkage in values and the tremendous losses established by individuals and institutions.[23]

23 *The* New York Times (10/30/1929), p. 32.

Table 9.1					
Statistics of U.S. Economic Activity ($ billion)					
	Jun. '29	Jul. '29	Aug. '29	Sep. '29	Oct. '29
Annualized personal income	$85.1	$86.3	$86.9	$86.4	$86.3
Index of factory employment	107.0	108.1	108.4	107.3	106.6
Index of industrial production	113	114	114	112	110
Index of wholesale prices	95.2	96.5	96.3	96.1	95.1
Friedman & Schwartz demand deposits	$22.3	$22.8	$22.6	$22.6	$24.4
Fed member bank loans	$25.7			$26.2	

Sources: *HSUS* 1789-1945, pp. 328-330, 344; *Monetary History*, p.712; *BMS*, p.72.

All above-the-line statistics were down in October from September and the August peak:

- Annualized personal income:
    - –down $100 million from September
    - –down 0.7% or $600 million from August
- Index of factory employment:
    - –down 0.7% from September
    - –down 1.7% from August
- Industrial production:
    - –down 1.8% from September
    - –down 3.5% from August
- Wholesale price index:
    - –down 1.0% from September
    - –down 1.2% from August (annualized rate of -7.5%)

CHAPTER 10

Deleveraging Begins With a Drastic Liquidation of Security Loans

(October 24 to November 30, 1929)

THE DRAMATIC DAYS of the Crash reverberated throughout the financial community, across the nation and overseas, as individual speculators—and even bystanders—felt the shock waves and assessed the impact on their lives. To set the stage for what was happening in financial markets in particular during the Crash period, we cite the telling, matter-of-fact summation from the beginning of the *Annual Report of the Federal Reserve Board for 1929* from which our chapter title comes:

> At the end of October the drop in security prices was accompanied by a subsidence in the demand for credit from the stock exchange; a drastic liquidation of security loans; outflow of gold; and an easing of credit policy by the Federal Reserve System.[1]

Our data-rich narrative now delves into statistics that provide evidence and clues as to what led to the Crash and describes the economic climate that followed. The statistics on security loans, to use the Fed's description of the relevant market segment, tell a vitally important part of this story. First, though, we need to address the rather complex issue of nomenclature. Briefly, whereas the Federal Reserve often used the term security loans, as they did in the above

---

1 *ARBG for 1929*, p. 1.

quote, in its reports and tables they used the term "Brokers' Loans." The NYSE, in contrast, referred to security loans as "call loans" and the market for them on the trading floor as the call loan market. In this work, we have chosen to use "call loans" as the term that describes the transactions in the call loan market on the NYSE in which brokerage houses borrow funds. We use "brokers' loans" for brokerage transactions specifically made, using those call loan borrowings from the call loan market, to their customers who were speculating by purchasing stock on margin.

Statistics related to call loans highlight what took place during and after the Crash. This chapter will explore, through the data, the various players in the call loan market and how the Crash altered their behaviors such that they put the entire U.S. (and, eventually, global) economy at risk. As we will see, banks, corporations and wealthy individuals, in their search for return, had eagerly lent an abundance of funds in order to earn attractive returns via the NYSE call loan market. These call loans enabled brokers in turn to make almost limitless margin loans to their speculating clients. But indeed, there was a limit. The Crash resulted in a rapid decline in call loan volumes as speculators met margin calls or were sold out and brokerages repaid call loans to the various call loan lenders. With rates on call loans quickly dropping, many lenders exited the call loan market and made new cash management decisions as to how best to deploy their returned cash.

A survey of year-end banking statistics enabled us to consider what decisions exiting call loan lenders made. Did these lenders leave their newly liquidated call loan cash in their banks as demand and time deposits? Did they reinvest in short-term open-market financial instruments? Or, as we contend, did these former call loan lenders use the proceeds to repay their own existing bank borrowings, thereby reducing outstanding bank loans overall, which consequentially caused the money supply to shrink, as well as interest rates to decline? This complex interconnection between markets and players provided the scaffolding for the challenging times ahead.

The Volume of Call Market Loans Drops Like a Stone

As stock prices fell during the Crash, brokers widely issued margin calls requiring their customers to come up with additional cash to maintain their agreed-upon margins. Speculators, in order not to lose their investments, met their margin calls if possible. However, particularly as stock prices continued to fall, many were able only to maintain their holdings by going deeper into debt. This might mean, for example, pledging other assets as security or mortgaging previously wholly-owned homes. Comedian Groucho Marx was one of those speculators, as his son Arthur's memoir of Groucho's tragic experience in the Crash conveys in chilling detail.

From *Life with Groucho*
by Arthur Marx

The next day—it wasn't really the next day, but it makes a better story—the stock market began its historic collapse. [Authors' note: the date this refers to is unclear from the book.]

At nine in the morning Father was wakened from a sound sleep by an urgent call from his broker.

"There's been slight break in the market, Mr. Marx. You'd better get down here with some cash to cover your margin."

"I thought I was covered."

"Not enough for the way things are going. We'll need more. And you'd better hurry!"

All was bedlam at Newman Brothers & Worms when Father arrived there. Ticker tape was knee-deep on the floor, people were shouting orders to sell, and others were frantically scribbling checks in vain efforts to save their original investments.

Father joined the latter group, but it was hopeless. He was in much too deep. He quickly went through his cash that wasn't already tied up in stocks, and then he left to borrow more.

In the next two days he borrowed money from the bank, he borrowed money on his insurance, and he even mortgaged the house. But soon all that was gone, too.

Three days after that first call from his broker, he knew the worst. Not only was he penniless, but he was in debt, besides.

Returning home after writing his last check and seeing it go down the drain along with the others, he walked through the front door just as the phone was ringing. Wearily he picked up the receiver, to find that it was Max Gordon, phoning from New York.

"Marx," said Gordon solemnly, "the jig is up!"

The jig was up, and there was nothing Father or anybody else could do about it.[2]

For those speculators who could not meet margin calls with cash or had no assets to pledge, their brokers liquidated enough of the customers' margined stocks to maintain the agreed-to margins. At the outside limit, this may have meant a full liquidation of a customer's portfolio. Regardless of the impact on the customer, the brokers almost simultaneously used those proceeds to repay corresponding portions of their own outstanding call market loans. Thus, as the value of stocks continued to fall and margin account offerings dwindled, the volume of call market loans taken out by brokerages dropped precipitously. Brokerage firms collected cash from their speculating clients who could top up their margin accounts or, for clients who were unable to do so, obtained the cash by selling their shares. The firms then used the cash to repay their own debts to call market lenders. This two-fold loan repayment procedure resulted

2 Arthur Marx, *Life with Groucho*, Simon & Schuster, 1954, pp. 124-5.

in what the *Federal Reserve Annual Report for 1929* referred to as "a drastic liquidation of security loans." Table 10.1, next page, shows the implications of this process in connection with stock prices.

As to the implications facing speculators, many of those whose accounts allowed 10% margin were wiped out in the Crash period. Speculators who maintained 25% margin accounts were definitely teetering on the edge. Even those with 50% margin accounts could face losing everything. From the Dow Industrials high of 381 on September 3 to the closing low of 198 on November 13,[3] the Dow dropped 52%. This meant that if the holder of a 50% margin account invested in the Dow Industrials (as Exchange-Traded Funds can be today) had instructed his broker to meet margin calls by selling stocks in his portfolio from September 3 onwards, he very likely would have been wiped out.

Table 10.1, following page, shows the relationship between "Call Market Loans" and the "Market Value All Listed Stocks" on the NYSE on a monthly basis for 1929 and 1930. The volume of call market loans grew aggressively up to October 1 when they reached their peak of $8,549 million. Then suddenly a true and dramatic reversal—indeed, an inversion—took place. One month later on November 1, as the table shows, call market loans had dropped 28.5%, or $2,440 million to $6,109 million, as speculators' demand for new borrowed money to acquire or carry shares of stock plummeted—right along with brokers' demand for call loans.

The Volume of Short-Term Borrowing in 1929-1930

Shortly, we will look at the supply of lenders' money for investment in the call loan market and the terms on which brokers lent to their margined customers, but first we consider the open-market volumes for all short-term financial instruments as they existed in 1929-1931.

3 *ARGB for 1929*, pp. 3, 24.

Table 10.1			
Percent of New York Stock Exchange Loans to Total Market Values of Listed Shares			
The appended table shows the ratio of total Stock Exchange member borrowings on security collateral to total listed share values ($ million)			
1929	Call market loans	Market value all listed stocks	Ratio %
1-Jan	6,440	67,472	9.54
1-Feb	6,735	71,060	9.48
1-Mar	6,679	71,872	9.29
1-Apr	6,805	69,770	9.75
1-May	6,775	73,719	9.19
1-Jun	6,665	70,921	9.39
1-Jul	7,071	77,264	9.15
*1-Aug	7,474	81,569	9.16
1-Sep	7,882	89,668	8.79
1-Oct	8,549	87,074	9.82
1-Nov	6,109	71,753	8.51
1-Dec	4,017	63,589	6.32
1930			
1-Jan	3,990	64,708	6.16
1-Feb	3,985	69,009	5.77
1-Mar	4,168	70,807	5.89
1-Apr	4,656	76,075	6.12
1-May	5,063	75,305	6.72
1-Jun	4,748	75,019	6.33
1-Jul	3,728	63,892	5.83
1-Aug	3,690	67,221	5.49
1-Sep	3,599	67,721	5.31
1-Oct	3,482	60,143	5.79
1-Nov	2,556	55,026	4.65
1-Dec	2,162	53,312	4.06

*Corrected total

Source: NYSE, New York Stock Exchange Year Book, 1929-30, p.111.

Broadly speaking, from 1929-1930, corporate treasurers or wealthy individuals who wanted to put idle cash to work profitably could choose among five different short-term investment categories. Table 10.2 shows these categories and the volumes outstanding semi-annually from December 1928 to December 1931. Commercial paper, bankers' acceptances and U.S. bills and certificates were usually readily saleable in New York City to bankers, brokers and dealers who acted as "market makers." Held to maturity, these instruments were automatically repaid, typically in 90 days or less (so long as the borrower didn't become insolvent before the end of the period). One instrument—call market loans — was mostly callable by lenders on one day's notice or repayable on one day's notice by borrowers. Besides loans callable daily, lenders could also make 90-day loans in the NYSE call money market.)

Table 10.2

Volume of Short-Term Borrowing

($ million)

Date	Commercial paper	Bankers' acceptances	Call market loans	US bills & certificates	Loans by all commercial banks
Dec. 1928	383	1,254	6,440	n/a	35,123
Jun. 1929	274	1,113	7,070	1,640	35,738
Dec. 1929	334	1,732	4,110	n/a	35,966
Jun. 1930	527	1,305	3,795	1,420	34,539
Dec. 1930	358	1,556	2,105	n/a	32,034
Jun. 1931	298	1,368	1,600	2,246	29,166
Dec. 1931	120	974	715	n/a	25,226

Source: *BMS*, pp.19, 465-66, 494, 511.

Bank loans, the fifth category, were different. Only banks could make bank loans—there was no secondary market—and banks controlled their purse strings by setting lending standards. Corporate treasurers and wealthy individuals with bank loans outstanding in 1929-1933 could, of course, use idle cash to pay down those bank loans. Doing so had benefits and risks at both the micro and macro levels. Since bank borrowing rates were usually appreciably higher than other short-term borrowing rates, borrowers, by reducing their outstanding bank loans, saved more in interest expense than they could earn by investing their idle cash in an alternative, short-term interest-bearing financial instruments. This strategy had risks, however. First was the risk that using their idle cash to repay a bank loan meant they no longer had the cash. The second risk was that, however committed the bank credit might have been during better times, borrowers couldn't count on the ability—or willingness—of their banks to continue honoring their line of credit commitments in a time of panic.

At a macro level, loan repayments, while saving interest expense for borrowers, directly impacted the country's total money supply—M2, to use the preferred money supply measure of Friedman and Schwartz. Indeed, when borrowers repaid bank loans *en masse* the money supply shrank via the reverse of the bank credit multiplier effect. (In forward gear, the bank credit multiplier explains how the money supply grows.) When borrowers write checks against deposits to their banks to repay some or all of a bank loan, the effect is simultaneously to reduce the bank's loan assets and deposit liabilities by the amount of those repayment checks. All else being the same, the money supply falls by the amount of each check/repayment: the bank credit multiplier in reverse gear.[4]

Table 10.2 shows the drastic fall in the volume of call market loans, in particular, around the time of the Crash and after. Lenders who pulled out of the call loan market at that time then had to decide what to do with the liquidated funds. As we discussed, they had options. Before we can determine to what extent this newly liquidated cash might have been used to repay outstanding bank

4 Shrinkage of the money supply creates deflationary pressure. At least one important traditional monetarist, Irving Fisher, whose ideas we will discuss in Chapter 1 of *The Deflation of 1930*, regarded the reduction in the money supply brought about by bank loan repayments in 1929-33 as a key to the onset, duration and severity of the Depression.

loans rather than reinvested in short-term open market instruments, we must consider the conditions that prevailed in the short-term open market in the closing months of 1929.

It is pertinent to observe at this point that Friedman and Schwartz argued that bank depositors who held idle cash balances should invest their "redundant balances" in the asset categories shown in Table 10.2 in order to earn income. (See the Endnote to this chapter, "Friedman and Schwartz Sub-Optimize," on p. 266.) What Friedman and Schwartz overlooked is the possibility that holders of idle cash might find it more profitable to save interest expense by repaying bank borrowings than to earn interest income by investing in marketable securities, particularly as the stock market was tanking and U.S. markets, in general, were experiencing liquidity panic. Table 10.1 (p. 239) shows that call market loans declined $4,559 million from October 1, 1929, to January 1, 1930. Table 10.2 shows that call market loans declined $2,960 million in the second half of 1929. Of course, Table 10.2 also shows that the volume of bank loans actually went up in the second half of 1929 by $228 million. In fact, of all the asset classes of short-term marketable securities, the volumes of commercial paper and of bankers' acceptances both rose, but only by $679 million in total. In other words, the increase in the rise in the volume of short-term marketable securities was far from enough to absorb the multi-billion dollar in-flow of liquidated funds from the call market in the final months of 1929. We will spend the remainder of this chapter looking very carefully at what actually happened in U.S. financial markets to accommodate the vast inflow of funds from "drastically" liquidated security loans

Of particular significance are, first, the volume of short-term borrowing in the main U.S. money markets; second, the timing and size of the cash in-flows into the lenders' demand deposit accounts resulting from the liquidation of call loans; and third, the interest rates prevailing in those main U.S. money markets week by week in that period. We use three additional tables to discuss each of these factors.

Funds Flows Measuring Change in the Volume of Call Market Loans

Having examined the decreasing volume of short-term borrowing in Table 10.2 as call market loans fell precipitously, we now turn to how the composition of call loan market lending changed in the lead-up to the Crash and in the months that followed in terms of both quantity and the sources of these bellwether loans. To show the flow of funds into and then out of the call loan market during that time, we have had to gather statistics from different sources that used different time intervals. While there are some gaps in existing data making certitude impossible,[5] the trend lines are clear and unambiguous. Table 10.3, below, shows three different measures of the

Table 10.3

Funds Flows That Result From Changes In Call Market Loan Volumes

($ million)

Date	NYSE	Federal Reserve Statistics				
	Change in call market loans	From Quarterly Reports		From Weekly Reports		
		Member banks	Non-bank others	N.Y. City banks	Out-of-town banks	Non-bank others
1929						
July	+402.6			+167	+160	+89
Aug	+407.8	-140	+1,595	-213	+60	+410
Sep	+667.8			+32	+120	+392
Oct	-2,440.6			+1,045	-871	-1,396
Nov	-2,092.2	-225	-4,190	-1,238	-367	-482
Dec	-27.1			+336	+71	-434
1930						
Jan	-4.7			-344	+166	+100
Feb	+182.8	+680	-240	+130	-92	-92
Mar	+488.7			+471	+138	-278

Sources: NYSE: *New York Stock Exchange Year Book*, 1929-30, p.111.
BMS, pp.494 & 498.

5 The principal gap is in U.S. Bills and Certificates. One reason is that the Fed only recorded the volume of this short-term borrowing vehicle annually. Another reason is that, whereas the volumes of all other borrowing vehicles declined in 1929-33, this vehicle grew. The reason for the growth was that the federal government was operating at a loss from mid-year 1930 onwards, and the deficit was growing.

changes in the volume of call market loans made by the dominant call loan market lenders: Fed member banks (system-wide), New York City banks, "Out-of-town banks" and "Non-bank others."[6] In each case, positive numbers denote funds paid into the call loan market by lenders and negative numbers denote funds paid out of the call loan market to lenders. In other words, positive numbers signify increases in call loans and negative numbers signify decreases in call loans as such loans are repaid. The three measures and their sources are as follows:

• The first measure, as reported in *New York Stock Exchange Year Book* 1929-1930, shows *monthly* changes in the aggregate volume of call market loans made by all types of lenders. [7]

---

6 We looked carefully for any evidence that nonmember banks were lending in the call loan market, but found it only in the Weekly Report statistics. *BMS* Table 141, page 498, provided its statistics under three column headings: "For own account," "For out-of-town banks," and "For others." (We have kept the *BMS* capitalization style in this case.) The middle column carried a telling footnote that read in its entirety, "Member and nonmember banks outside New York City (domestic banks only); includes unknown amount for customers of these banks." For the period July-December 1929, adding "For own account" plus "For out-of-town banks" begins with the total $1,900 million for October 3, and ends with $1,660 million for December 31. *BMS* Table 19 for All Member Banks on their page 76, shows Loans "To brokers and dealers In New York City" beginning with $1,899 million for October 3, and ending with $1,660 million for December 31. While the numbers in the two columns are not identical, we feel confident concluding that Table 141 must include numbers *just for Member Banks*. What were nonmember banks doing? We have included the NYC and out-of-town banks together in the column in Table 10.3, page 243, headed "In NYC Banks." The column headed "For Non-Bank Others" shows the "For others" statistics in *BMS* Table 141. While we sought diligently to find out what nonmember banks were doing, we have not yet found an answer. This, too, is a data gap.

7 The "Call Market Loans" in Table 10.3 are labeled "Brokers' Loans" in the sources cited.

• The second measure, taken from Table 139 of *BMS 1914-1941*, uses *quarterly* statistics of changes in call loan volume divided between all member banks and non-bank others. [8]

• The third measure, also from the Fed (Table 141 of *BMS 1914-1941*), provides *monthly* numbers lent into the call loan market or received as repayments from the call loan market based on the *weekly* reported statistics on the call market loan volumes provided in the accounts of New York banks and non-bank others. [9]

During the pre-Crash third quarter of 1929, lending by non-bank others dominated the increase in lending in the call loan market. The data from our two Fed sources confirm this conclusion. Our NYSE statistics show that call market loans grew by a total of $1,478.2 million in the third quarter, and almost all (98.4%) of this increase was accounted for by the Fed's quarterly statistics, broken down into member banks and non-bank others.[10] As for the Fed's weekly statistics for New York City and out-of-town banks and non-bank others, we see that these statistics accounted for $1,217 million or 82.3% of the total rise with non-bank others providing 60.3% of the total increase.

In the fourth quarter of 1929, the volume of NYSE call market loans plunged $4,559.9 million, with the Fed's quarterly statistics accounting for $4,415 million or 96.8% of that drop. Notably, the quarterly statistics for non-bank others accounted for an astounding 91.9% of the drop. Meanwhile, the Fed's weekly New York City banks' statistics for the fourth quarter (the third measure), were down $3,380 million or 73.2% of the total fall in call market loans,

---

8 See page 494.

9 See pages 497-8.

10 We suggest that the small, unaccounted-for amount could well have been funds lent in the call loan market by brokers themselves representing their own clients and was immaterial except that the funds had to be returned to the lenders.

with non-bank others accounting, in the weekly statistics, for 50.7% of the decline.

As we indicated earlier, in attempting to identify fully who was participating in the call loan market pre-Crash, it became clear, that no single data source provided all the relevant statistics we sought. For example, our primary source from the NYSE presented clearly the most accurate and comprehensive month-end numbers on the volume of total call loans but not broken down by type of lender. The type of lender in the call loan market, however, appeared in quarterly Fed reports, and the Fed statistics accounted for nearly all lenders in the call loan market, though presumably (and herein lies a data gap) excluding non-member banks. The third measure—again from the Fed—used weekly statistics originated by member banks in New York City. While these Fed statistics also included those member and nonmember banks outside of NYC who were represented in the call loan market by the reporting NYC member banks, these weekly statistics did not account for any activity in the call loan market by member or non-member banks that were not represented by the NYC weekly reporting member banks. This gap was unfortunate, as this was a group of call loan market participants that belonged here. To complete the picture and assess this group's impact, we must accept the data gaps.

Regardless, among the three different sources we found and compiled in Table 10.3 there was sufficient evidence of the importance of the various non-bank entities—namely, the newly funded corporations and the individuals bloating the call market with stock gain proceeds—in fueling the frenzy of speculation in the lead-up to the Crash.

Furthermore, the sources we combed indicated where the cash went that was returned to call loan lenders when they withdrew, enabling us to answer that critical question. Did those exiting call loan lenders simply leave the cash as bank deposit accounts? Did they invest the returned cash in other short-term open market instruments? Or, as we suspect, did they, instead, repay bank loans?

Those are options we examined in order to fill in what we believe to be the critical missing piece that explains one long-standing mystery of the times.

To summarize that mystery, in the fourth quarter of 1929, call market lenders were repaid $4,559.9 million (see Table 10.3, p. 243). This returned *an enormous sum of money* back into the hands of lenders/recipients who then, autonomously, decided how to redeploy that cash to avoid its being idle. What happened to that money? In the End Note to this chapter we discuss how Friedman and Schwartz hypothesized theoretically about this very situation in which lenders cease holding interest bearing instruments and must do something with the cash they receive in exchange to avoid holding what they called "redundant balances." Now, we look back at the data on short-term borrowing in Table 10.2. With the first four columns of the table covering four market-driven investment opportunities, the table might have been titled "Volume of Short-Term Investing," instead of borrowing. Yet the data in Table 10.2 gives hardly any hint at what withdrawing call market lenders, again, all operating autonomously, actually did with the $4.6 billion in loan repayments they received in the last quarter of 1929.

As to the disposition of the money, recognizing that a critical piece was missing from the data in Table 10.2, we looked through our forensic financial management and historians' lens(es) and turned to the statistics in order to light the way and identify what happened.

Investible Funds and Interest Rates

In the weeks before, during and after the Crash, three ingredients stirred together made for a volatile, even explosive, stew: falling stock prices, diminished speculative activity and the rapid exit of non-bank lenders from the call loan market. Table 10.4, following page, offers insights into the implications of the third ingredient, specifically how the rapid contraction in call loans as non-bank call loan lenders pulled their funds and how the resulting return of investible cash to those lenders led to a reduction in short-term interest rates. Table 10.4 offers relevant statistics from two sources: the Fed and the NYSE. The Fed's weekly reports on loan volumes (see Table 10.3) enabled us to compare changes in "Investible Funds"—the measure of the net cash repaid to withdrawing call loan market lenders week-by-week during this period of what the Fed called the "drastic liquidation"—with "Short-Term Open-Market Rates in New York City."[11]

Table 10.4								
Investible Funds			**Short-Term Open-Market Rates in New York City** (Per cent per annum)					
As the result of the liquidation of brokers' loans ($ million)			Week ended	Prevailing rate on—			Average rate on Stock Exchange call loans	
Week ended	Banks' accounts	Non-bank "Others"		Prime commercial paper 4 to 6 months	Prime bankers' acceptances, 90 days	Stock Exchange time loans, 90 days	New	Renewal
1929			1929					
Sept. 4	-139	+1	Sept. 7	6.13	5.13	8.88	8.65	9.00
Sept. 11	+29	-149	Sept. 14	6.25	5.13	8.88	8.09	8.20
Sept. 18	-85	-10	Sept. 21	6.25	5.13	9.00	8.48	8.40
Sept. 25	+43	-234	Sept. 28	6.25	5.13	9.13	9.03	8.40
Oct. 2	+3	-47	Oct. 5	6.25	5.13	9.13	8.08	8.20
Oct. 9	+125	-34	Oct. 12	6.25	5.13	8.63	5.63	6.20
Oct. 16	-154	+66	Oct. 19	6.25	5.13	7.75	6.28	6.40
Oct. 23	+116	+52	Oct. 26	6.25	4.94	7.25	5.35	6.00
Oct. 30	-224	+1,359						
Nov. 6	+591	+65	Nov. 2	6.13	4.63	6.00	5.94	5.80
Nov. 13	+515	+195	Nov. 9	5.88	4.63	6.00	6.00	6.00
Nov. 20	+411	+173	Nov. 16	5.88	4.38	5.75	5.90	5.90
Nov. 27	+88	+49	Nov. 23	5.63	3.81	5.25	4.86	5.00
Dec. 4	-3	+61						
Dec. 11	-44	+12	Dec. 7	5.13	3.81	4.63	4.50	4.50
Dec. 18	-66	+105	Dec. 14	5.00	3.88	4.88	4.50	4.50
Dec. 24	+21	+37	Dec. 21	5.00	3.88	4.88	4.56	4.50
Dec. 31	-315	+219	Dec. 28	5.00	4.00	4.88	5.66	5.50
1930			1930					
Jan. 8	+166	-94	Jan. 4	5.00	3.94	4.88	5.86	6.00
Jan. 15	-20	+6	Jan. 11	5.00	3.88	4.75	4.25	4.60
Jan. 22	-42	-17	Jan. 18	4.88	4.00	4.69	4.24	4.50
Jan. 29	-10	+5	Jan. 25	4.88	4.00	4.75	4.06	4.50

Source: *BMS*, pp.456 & 498.

We should observe that we use positive and negative numbers differently in Table 10.4 from our practice in Table 10.3 where our focus was on the volume of call loan lending. In Table 10.3, positive numbers signify increases in call loan market volumes, and negative

11 Minus signs indicate further lending of cash to the call loan market, such as occurred in September and early October.

numbers signify decreases in call loan market volumes as such loans were repaid rather than rolled over. In contrast, Table 10.4 focuses on funds that were repaid to call loan lenders which those lenders then had to put to work profitably once more in order to avoid having the returned funds become idle cash or redundant balances, per Friedman and Schwartz. Thus, in Table 10.4 positive numbers represent funds repaid from the call loan market to lenders, and negative numbers represent funds put into the call loan market by lenders.

To explain the changing structure of rates, Table 10.4 shows what various short-term rates were available in financial markets over a five-month period beginning with the week ended September 7 when the call market renewal rate—9.0%— was the highest short-term rate, and the commercial paper rate averaged 6.13%.[12] To take one example, a highly credit-worthy company such as the General Motors Acceptance Corporation could sell short-term financial obligations at roughly 6.13% at a time when long-term General Motors debt instruments were yielding approximately 4.8%.[13] The week following September 7, the rate on call market time loans was 8.88%, still highest and remaining highest until the week ended October 26 when it fell to 7.25%. The following week, ending November 2, which included the principal days of the Crash, the commercial paper rate was highest at 6.13%. The next two weeks, call market rates were highest again, first at 6.00% during the week of November 9 then at 5.90% during the week of November 16. Then, for five weeks, from the week ended November 23 until the week ended December 21, commercial paper rates were highest even as rates fell from 5.63% to 5.00%. Briefly around the New Year, call money rates were highest. Then from the week ended January 11, 1930, the rate on commercial paper was highest for the remainder of January.

While we could sum up the prior paragraph by saying that this is what happens to short-term asset rates as financial markets pass from a period of credit stringency to whatever follows, this is only part

---

12 The table does not show long-term rates so as to indicate whether the yield curve was upward sloping, level or inverted, which is something we will look into presently.

13 *BMS*, p. 469.

of the story we want to convey. Nevertheless, we pause here, because this is the narrative Milton Friedman and Anna Schwartz—either together or independently—focused their readers and followers on generally. In so doing, they persuaded their "school" to sub-optimize theoretically as is explained in this chapter's Endnote, "Friedman and Schwartz Sub-optimize".

In order to avoid sub-optimizing, we realized we needed to focus on more than assets alone. We needed to focus on assets and liabilities together. Doing so revealed that it was almost always the case that a bank borrower found it more profitable to use idle cash to repay bank loans than to invest in short-term marketable securities. Understanding this strategy proved pivotal.

Payment Transactions During the Week of the Crash

Of particular note in Table 10.4 is the payment of $1,359 million to non-bank others during the week ended October 30. Before delving into that payment, however, we first point out that the numbers reported in the other two call loan market participant categories that week showed an inflow to call money loans of $992 million "For own account" of the New York City banks and an outflow of $728 million "For out-of-town banks."[14] (Table 10.4 shows the sum of these two numbers as -992 +728 = -264.) These figures were the result of a complex set of transactions that took place during the dismal week ending Wednesday, October 30, which included the core days of the Crash. On Black Thursday, October 24, prices plummeted in the morning, organized support appeared at mid-day and the market clawed its way back up almost to its opening prices. Day five was Black Monday and day six was Black Tuesday, October 29. Table 10.4 shows a cash in-flow of investible funds during that week of $1,359 million to non-bank others and

14 *BMS*, p. 498.

a cash outflow from banks' accounts (i.e., a net payment into the call loan market) of -$264 million as these non-bank others exited the call loan market. The weekly-reporting Fed member banks in New York City reported that out-of-town banks had called and withdrawn $728 million from call loans.[15]

What these statistics in Table 10.4 also indicate is the strong actions taken by member banks in New York City in their own form of organized support. They stepped in—for their own account—to replace $992 million in funds pulled by their customers or out-of-town bank correspondents from the call loan market. By looking closely at the statistics for the week ending October 30, we can see this taking place. Responding to a large number of requests from customers withdrawing, or calling, next-day amounts that these clients had been lending in the call loan market, the banks withdrew those customers' funds from the call loan market and credited their customers' accounts. Consulting daily with the Federal Reserve Bank of New York as they did this, the NYC member banks then replaced the $992 million withdrawn by their customers from the call loan market with funds *lent for their own account*.

As we see in Table 10.3, member banks in New York City reported their statistics weekly in three categories in 1929: for own account, for out-of-town banks and for others (specifically, non-bank others.) We turn to Barrie Wigmore for his description of a large component of these non-bank others:

> Major corporations in the auto, petroleum, and steel industries, investment trusts, and utilities built up large portfolios of call loans. U.S. Steel, General Motors, AT&T, and Standard Oil Co. of New Jersey had hundreds of millions of dollars in the call loan market, a disproportionate share of their short-term investments, which they normally would never have countenanced.[16]

---

15 Adding to the intricate nature of all these transactions was the fact that they had to be effected in "same-day" funds.

16 Wigmore (1985), p. 94.

The statistics are clear: non-bank others were playing a substantial role in the call loan market leading up to the Crash. These non-bank entities accounted for 57.4% ($3,907 million) of the $6,804 million in funds lent to the call loan market on October 2 according to statistics from the group of member banks in New York City that reported weekly.[17] More significantly, and as commented on above, evidence appeared in the October 4 quarterly report of all member banks (NYC and elsewhere) and showed that the "by others" group accounted for 77.9% ($6,640 million) of the $8,525[18] million funds lent to the call loan market by all member banks.[19]

Reducing Interest Expense Proves More Profitable than Investing for Income

Clearly, at this particularly vulnerable time, non-bank "others" were the predominant force in the NYSE call market, comprising 77.9% ($6,640 million) of call market lending. Though their ongoing participation was uncertain, especially as borrowing rates fell in the fall of 1929, it seems likely that these sophisticated non-bank others who were likely also bank borrowers, came to see the potential to achieve greater profitability by reducing borrowing costs than by increasing investment for income in instruments in a declining rate environment.

We now turn to this other short-term option for putting idle cash to work—repaying bank loans. Bank-borrowing rates on commercial loans represent the rates at which bank borrowers reduce

17 *BMS,* p. 498.

18 Ibid, p. 494.

19 Wigmore claims, "(C)orporations, investment trusts, individuals, governments, and foreigners...accounted for over 60% of the call loan market by October 1929." p. 94.

Table 10.5

Rates Charged on Commercial Loans by Banks in Principal Cities

(Weighted averages. Per cent per annum)

($ million)

Year and month	Total 19 cities	New York City	7 Northern and Eastern cities	11 Southern and Western cities
1929				
January	5.64	5.50	5.70	5.73
February	5.62	5.48	5.64	5.77
March	5.69	5.57	5.71	5.80
April	5.77	5.72	5.75	5.86
May	5.81	5.76	5.79	5.88
June	5.87	5.79	5.85	5.97
July	5.85	5.80	5.80	5.98
August	5.99	6.03	5.92	6.03
September	6.05	6.09	6.01	6.04
October	6.06	6.11	5.99	6.08
November	5.89	5.70	5.93	6.07
December	5.74	5.54	5.78	5.93
1930				
January	5.67	5.43	5.72	5.90
February	5.47	5.10	5.55	5.80
March	5.29	4.91	5.3	5.73
April	5.02	4.61	4.98	5.56
May	4.90	4.44	4.93	5.42
June	4.82	4.28	4.89	5.36
July	4.66	4.22	4.53	5.31
August	4.59	4.14	4.47	5.25
September	4.50	4.00	4.44	5.15
October	4.50	3.92	4.49	5.18
November	4.41	3.79	4.38	5.17
December	4.37	3.82	4.38	5.01

Source: *BMS*, p.464.

their costs when they use idle cash to repay bank loans. Table 10.5, above, offers these important rates.

As the data show, bank-borrowing rates differed across the United States. Except from August through October 1929, rates in New York City were consistently lowest, but nationwide all rates fell significantly in a stair-step fashion in the short period of time from September 1929 to January 1930.

However, these commercial bank loan rates are only one component of the total cost borrowers pay for the borrowed money they withdraw and spend. The cost of money that borrowers withdraw and spend is actually higher (and was so in 1929). What we are calling the "Effective Bank Rate" is what is important here. That is the rate at which borrowers decide to reduce their borrowing costs—i.e., save—by repaying bank loans.

What is the Effective Cost of Bank Borrowing?

In our experience, it is virtually unknown for a bank borrower to borrow at what is today called "the Prime Rate" and get to spend 100% of the borrowed funds. This is because banks require borrowers to maintain some of the funds they borrow on deposit. Today these funds on deposit are known as "compensating balances." This was the practice followed in the 1920s and in our period of focus as we saw in a June 1925 paper by banking expert Ray B. Westerfield. At the end of his introduction, Westerfield wrote:

> [T]he bargaining advantage being in his favor, the banker is then in a position to levy terms upon his borrowing customers which promote his profits or security, as well as the permanence of his customers' accounts....One such requirement from borrowers is that they maintain a fair "balance" of account, in amount varying as among the banks from 10 to 25 per cent of the borrowings, the most common proportion probably being 20 per cent. ... [O]ccasionally some such percentage as 10 per cent of the full line plus 20 per cent of the used line is asked. Among the larger banks, particularly in reserve cities, the practice is nearly universal."[20]

20 Ray B. Westerfield, "The Balance Required by Borrowers, " *The Journal of Political Economy*, Vol. 33, No. 3, June 1925, pp.257-8.

To calculate the "N.Y. City Effective Bank Rate 10%" shown in the fifth column of Table 10.6, below, we chose to use 10% because it was the lowest figure cited by Westerfield in the above passage. This percentage, which would apply to a very highly creditworthy borrower, meant that the borrower could withdraw and spend 90% of any borrowed money and that the effective rate would be the bank prime rate divided by 0.9 (P/0.9). In short, the borrower could spend ninety cents of every dollar borrowed.

Table 10.6

Average Yields on Short-Term Financial Instruments and Average Bank Borrowing Rates

(Per cent per annum)

Week ended	Call market loan renewals	Commercial paper	Bankers' acceptances	N.Y. City bank prime rate	N.Y. City effective bank rate 10%*	N.Y. City effective bank rate 20%*
1929						
5-Oct	8.20	6.25	5.13	6.11	6.79	7.64
12-Oct	6.20	6.25	5.13	6.11	6.79	7.64
19-Oct	6.40	6.25	5.13	6.11	6.79	7.64
26-Oct	6.00	6.25	4.94	6.11	6.79	7.64
2-Nov	5.80	6.13	4.63	5.70	6.33	7.13
9-Nov	6.00	5.88	4.63	5.70	6.33	7.13
16-Nov	5.90	5.88	4.38	5.70	6.33	7.13
23-Nov	5.00	5.63	3.81	5.70	6.33	7.13
30-Nov	4.50	5.38	3.81	5.70	6.33	7.13
7-Dec	4.50	5.13	3.81	5.54	6.12	6.93
14-Dec	4.50	5.00	3.88	5.54	6.12	6.93
21-Dec	4.50	5.00	3.88	5.54	6.12	6.93
28-Dec	5.50	5.00	4.00	5.54	6.12	6.93

Bond Yields By Type of Security

(Per cent per annum)

Year and month	U.S. government	Municipal (high-grade)	Corporate (Moody's) By ratings: Aaa	Aa	A	Baa
1929						
Oct.	3.61	4.29	4.77	5.01	5.38	6.11
Nov	3.35	4.25	4.76	4.94	5.33	6.03
Dec.	3.36	4.22	4.67	4.84	5.21	5.95

*Adjusted for compensating balances to show proportion of any loan to be on deposit
Source: *BMS*, pp.456, 464, & 469.

In the sixth column, to calculate the "N.Y. City Effective Bank Rate," we used 20%, which Westerfield described as "the most common proportion." This means that the borrower could withdraw and spend 80% of the borrowed money and that the effective rate would be the bank prime rate divided by 0.8 (P/0.8), reflecting that the borrower could spend eighty cents of every dollar borrowed.

In our quest to find the highest weekly borrowing rate, we find that during the week ended October 5, the call market loan renewal rate was still the highest at 8.20%. But beginning in the week ended October 12, the New York City effective bank rate of 10% in the fifth column became the highest and continued to be highest throughout the remainder of the table. What this means is that the very highly creditworthy borrower could have made money before and up to October 5 by borrowing funds from his bank and lending the funds to brokers in the call loan market. But after October 5 this was no longer the most profitable move. We hasten to add that, if the banker were to discover that this is what the borrower was doing, the borrower would almost certainly have lost "that warm relationship that exists between the banker and his borrowing depositor" that Westerfield referred to in the conclusion of his paper.[21] If we include the sixth column of Table 10.6, it became the highest rate in the week ended October 12 and remained so.

The fundamental point is that the most profitable move for virtually all bank borrowers whenever they had idle cash come into their hands after October 5 was to use the cash to pay down their bank loans.

Is There Evidence That Investible Funds Were Used to Repay Bank Loans?

Before we produce the evidence, there is a good reason why this strategy has gone so long unobserved and unremarked on. It

21 Ibid., p. 277.

was an unfortunate impediment to our deep research that there were no records published by the Federal Reserve System that account for bank loans more frequently than quarterly during the 1920s or 1930s. Thus, while we know that all member banks reported loans totaling $26,165 million on October 4 and $26,150 million (down $15 million) on December 30, lamentably, there is neither a record nor even estimates of the ebb and flow of monthly loan volumes for the critical months of October and November.

There were other missing components than more frequent reporting of bank loan statistics. As a workaround to this information gap as it related to deposits, Friedman and Schwartz resorted to scrutinizing laboriously bank deposit records and then formulated month-by-month estimates of the components of their money supply series. But it appears no one has given even remotely similar attention to the implications of bank loan volumes or searched for any record of loan volumes more frequently than quarterly. After careful evaluation, we will shortly offer our own insights to explain the downside of Friedman and Schwartz's "sharp wiggle in the money series." (See Chart 10.1, following page).

Stated best in their own words, a portion of which we provided earlier, Friedman and Schwartz offered their own explanation:

> The stock market crash is reflected in the sharp wiggle in the money series, *entirely a result of a corresponding wiggle in demand deposits,* which in turn reflects *primarily* an increase in loans to brokers and dealers in securities by New York City banks in response to drastic reduction of these loans by others. The adjustment was orderly, thanks largely to prompt and effective action by the New York Federal Reserve Bank in providing additional reserves to the New York banks through open market purchases.... In particular, the crash left no mark on currency held by the public. Its direct financial effect was confined to the stock market and

Chart 10.1

Money Stock, Currency, and Commercial Bank Deposits, Monthly, 1929–March 1933

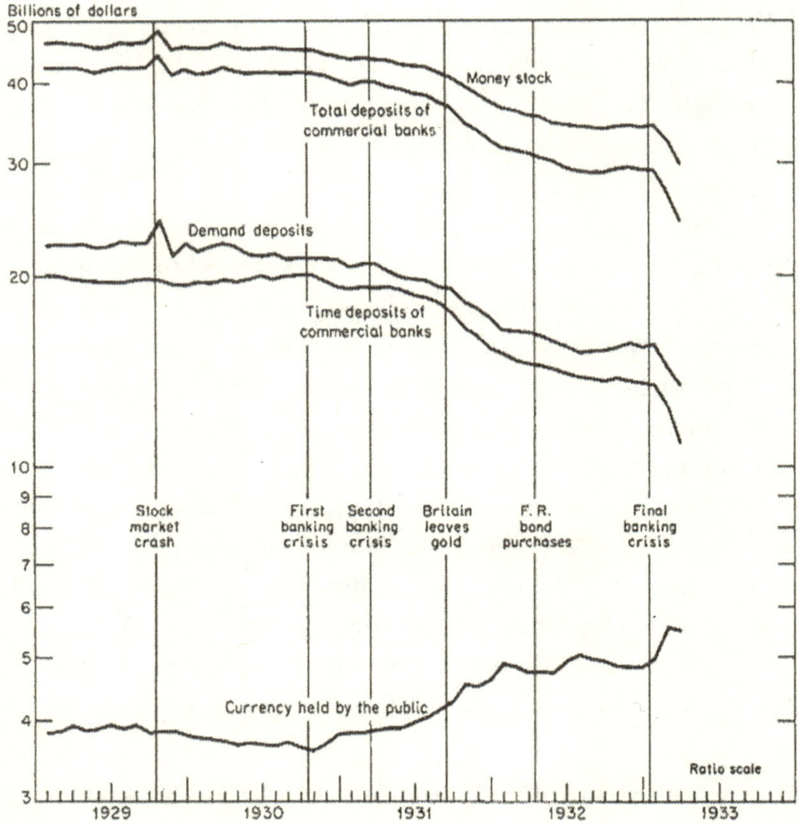

did not arouse any distrust of banks by their depositors.[22] (emphasis ours)

We see Friedman and Schwartz focused "primarily" on explaining the October upside of the wiggle during which New York money center banks, actively conferring with the New York Fed, lent money from their own accounts in the call loan market to brokers to replace funds withdrawn during the week of the Crash by out-of-

22 Friedman and Schwartz (1963a), pp. 305-6. Chart appears on p. 302.

town banks and non-bank others. But the November downside is a different phenomenon demanding its own, and different, explanation.

To explain both the upside and the downside of the "wiggle," it is fruitful to delve into the data they represented more deeply. We set the stage to do that by observing how that turbulent final week of October was, both in plain sight to the public at large, but also more privately in the back offices of New York City banks, brokers and dealers. Thousands of margin calls required fast action by all participants in the call loan market. Among those back-office actions, New York City banks made loans to brokers and dealers to enable them to repay the large volume of withdrawing call loan lenders. The banks did this by crediting funds to the brokers and dealers' demand deposit accounts—probably on a daily basis—thus increasing the stock of demand deposits and M2. Using Friedman and Schwartz's own month-end estimates of the stock of demand deposits of $22,593 million in September, up 7.5% to $24,432 million in October, we see that increase in demand deposits at the end of October—*thereby explaining the upside of the wiggle.*

Explaining the Downside of the Sharp Wiggle

What about the downside of the wiggle that then registered in November when, by Friedman and Schwartz's own estimate, the stock of demand deposits went down 11.4% or $2,781 million to $21,651 million in one month? It takes no more than a glance at demand deposits in their Chart 27 (our Chart 10.1) to see that the downside of the wiggle from the end of October to the end of November was actually more dramatic than the October's upside from September. But what explanation is there? Money appeared simply to vanish. Where did it go? We focused carefully on this large one-month drop and what could have explained it.

Evidence from the Fed and from Friedman and Schwartz

To gain more evidence on what happened, we examined the reports of the Federal Reserve and the views of Friedman and Schwartz for more detailed accounts of what they thought took place in November and up to the end of 1929.

We begin with the Fed. In the *Federal Reserve Bulletin* of December, the "Review of the Month" opened with the following explanation:

> In November changes in the banking position were largely in the nature of readjustment accompanying and following the drop in security [i.e., stock] prices. Since it was chiefly at the member banks in New York City that the changes occurred, the course of events can best be described by a reference to the figures for these banks alone. During the week ending October 30 loans and investments of these banks had increased by $1,400,000,000, largely because they had taken over a large part of the loans in the call loan market which had previously been made by out-of-town banks and non-banking lenders, as these lenders withdrew funds from the market.[23]

The *Bulletin* further commented on various increases, including "also a considerable growth in...loans for commercial purposes" and "outside New York City...an increased demand...for other loans." The *Bulletin* appeared to draw a tentative conclusion, stating:

> Too little time has elapsed yet since the end of October to make possible a comprehensive appraisal of the effects of the drop in security prices on the banking situation. The diminution in the demand for credit from the security market has resulted in a decline of money rates.[24]

---

23 *Federal Reserve Bulletin,* Vol. 15, No. 12, 1929, p. 755.

24 Ibid., p. 756.

In their *Annual Report* for 1929, the Fed Board of Governors offered additional explanations:

> Liquidation of bank credit in the last two months of 1929 and the easing policy of the reserve system were reflected in a decline of money rates in the United States, and particularly of the open-market rates on call and short-term money. The decline of money rates and the diminished attractiveness of the security market as a field of investment caused the withdrawal of foreign funds, which had flowed to the United States in large volume during the period of high money and rising stock prices.... Open-market rates abroad also became easier. It was apparent at the close of 1929, therefore, that the liquidation of security loans, which took place in the last two months of the year and resulted in an improvement in the credit situation in the United States, had also exerted an important favorable influence on the world-credit conditions.[25]

All this is to say that we looked carefully to see if Fed sources explained the $2,781 million drop in the stock of demand deposits that Friedman and Schwartz estimated to have occurred in November but found neither an explanation nor, in fact, much focus on November at all.[26]

We turned next to Friedman and Schwartz's account of "Factors Accounting for Changes in the Stock of Money" in their Monetary History. Friedman and Schwartz explained the October upside of the wiggle by saying, "Indeed, the [sharp increase in demand deposits]

---

25 *ARBG 1929*, p. 12.

26 It should be noted that while the Fed did accumulate *weekly* statistics on the stock of call loans from Fed member banks in NYC, the Fed likely had no concrete statistics on aggregate amounts of demand deposits and time deposits at Fed member banks at the ends of October and November. While such data might have offered further clues as to what was happening, it is impossible to say whether the Fed would have acted differently if they had this month-end data.

in our estimates understates the magnitude of the action of the New York banks."[27] They further commented:

> The actions taken by the New York Reserve Bank were timely and effective. Despite the stock market crash, there were no panic increases in money market rates such as those in past market crises, and no effects on confidence in banks which might have arisen if there had been any sizable defaults on security loans.[28]

About the November downside of the wiggle, Friedman and Schwartz had much less to say:

> In the month following the crash, there was a reversal. Deposits declined, as more lasting arrangements for the transfer and reduction of stock market loans replaced the temporary shift of money of those loans to New York banks.... At the end of November 1929, the stock of money was $1.3 billion, or 3 per cent, less than it had been at the end of September. By the end of December, most of the loss had been made up; the stock of money was about $0.5 billion, or 1 per cent, less than in September. These changes were concentrated in demand deposits.[29]

With all due respect to Friedman and Schwartz, while they assert the stock of money declined from the end of September—and $1.3 billion was a big number for the time—they did not explain what happened to the $2.8 billion ($2,781 million) that seemingly disappeared from the demand deposit portion of the money supply that their own estimates indicate took place in November and that

---

27 Friedman and Schwartz (1963a), p. 337.

28 Ibid., p. 339.

29 Ibid., pp. 339-40.

their Chart 27 (our Chart 10.1) shows as the downward side of the wiggle.

Despite the intervening years since the Crash and its immediate aftermath, by 1963 Friedman and Schwartz still failed to estimate their money series numbers more confidently. We suggest the following alternative explanation for November's precipitous plunge in the money stock.

The November Fall in the Stock of Borrowed Money: Post-Crash Money Management Moves

With the public reeling and back offices overwhelmed with paperwork, what were money managers doing? Before turning to those actions, we take a look at general money management practices not just at the time, but even now. Particularly in times of high short-term interest rates, as they were in the late 1920s,[30] corporate financial managers and the money managers of the cash flows of many individuals or families tried to minimize idle cash and maximize the profitability of cash-flow operations with a vigilant eye on opportunities and costs. Businesses, then as now, typically employ a cash manager while many individuals or families likely engage accountants and financial advisors at least in part for this purpose. Both rely heavily on banking relationships, including commitments for lines of credit. For example, a so-called "revolving credit" enables a cash manager to draw down (i.e., borrow) or pay back (i.e., repay) bank credit virtually at will without notice up to the maximum loan commitment. While the most creditworthy bank borrowers officially borrow at the "prime rate" (shown in Table 10.4 (p. 248), skilled cash managers know what the effects of compensating balances are, as we discussed earlier in the chapter.

30 Call loan rates reached 9.03% in the week ending September 25; 90-day NYSE time loan rates reached 9.13% that same week, continuing into the following week.

Returning to our time period in October and November, as interest rates fell, participation in the call loan market by lenders became less and less attractive. We have already seen how, from October 5 onwards, a lender could save more by using idle cash to repay bank loans than by lending in the call loan market. By late November, for attentive cash managers anywhere, it was unmistakable that it was wiser to save money by repaying bank loans that cost effectively 6.33% (or the 5.70% prime rate itself) than it was to lend in the call loan market at 4.50% for both new money and renewals.

Friedman and Schwartz explained the upside of the "sharp wiggle" that resulted in the quantity of demand deposits at commercial banks in late October (and early November) being $24,432 million.[31] Table 10.4 shows that both "Banks' Accounts" and "Non-Bank 'Others'" received cash totaling $2,177 million throughout November as a consequence of the liquidation of call loans. As always happens, the great majority of demand deposit check transactions passed from non-bank payers to non-bank payees and did not result in the quantity of demand deposits shrinking. We also know that Friedman and Schwartz estimated that the quantity of demand deposits closed that month at $21,651 million, a drop of $2,781 million in November.[32] We offer the view that this decline occurred because holders of demand deposits, after weighing their options, repaid autonomously in November a quantity of their U.S. bank loans that equaled $2,781 million. This repayment process eliminated—simultaneously—the repaid portions of those bank loans and the demand deposit quantities used to make the repayments from the national stock of bank loans and demand deposits respectively, thus causing the downside of the "wiggle." While the lack of data prevents us from estimating the maximum quantity of bank loans that may have been repaid at any given time *within* the month of November, we are confident that $2,781 million had been

31 Friedman and Schwartz (1963a), p. 712.

32 Ibid.

repaid by the end of November—thus explaining the downside of Friedman and Schwartz's "wiggle."

Then in December, creditworthy borrowers could draw down their still-committed lines of credit once again as dictated by business conditions and in order for businesses and the well-to-do to make the year-end look healthy and the holidays bright as President Hoover urged.

A Shifting Demand Curve or Supply Curve?

It is seldom easy to determine whether economic events show an unambiguously shifting demand or supply curve. Only when quantity and price are moving in the same direction, either up together up or down together, can one argue that a demand curve or a supply curve is shifting unambiguously.

In early October, for example, the volume of call loan lending and of brokers' loans to their margined clients reached their recorded peak in statistical values, and these peak values remained the records for decades. The NYSE recorded the peak as $8,549 million as Table 10.1 shows, and *BMS* shows it as $8,525 million on October 4. But we could not attribute this to an upward shifting supply curve because the rate of interest paid for call loan renewals was falling. It had averaged 9.25% in July, fell to 6.70% in October and further to 4.75% in December when the NYSE recorded the December 1 volume of call loans as $4,017 million. A year later, the average rate had fallen to 2.08% at a time when the volume of call loans was $2,162 million.[33] In fact, we think these statistics, rather than documenting an upward shifting supply curve do a much better job of

33 *NYSE Yearbook*, p. 111; Wigmore (1985) pp. 648-9; *BMS*, pp. 455-6 & 494-5.

documenting a *downward shifting demand curve* for borrowed funds that enabled margined purchasing of stocks.

Our principal task has been to explain how American bank borrowers came to repay $2,781 million in bank loans in November 1929. This was an enormous sum of money. *BMS* shows the total amount of bank loans held by *All Commercial Banks* in the U.S. on December 31, 1929 as equaling $35,966 million and on December 31, 1927, as equaling $33,196 million. The difference between the year-end 1927 figure and the year-end 1929 figure, was $2,770 million—the total growth of bank loans at all commercial banks in the U.S. during the two most vibrant boom years of the 1920s—1928 and 1929. By comparison, the sum of bank loans paid back in November 1929, was slightly *larger* than the total growth of bank loans in these two years. Furthermore, the sum of bank loans repaid in November, according to the unofficial estimates of Friedman and Schwartz, dwarfed the officially recorded "growth of bank loans in 1929," which was $843 million. In the chapters that follow, we will be looking at copious statistical evidence showing not only how bank loans, generally speaking, continued to drop through the Great Depression but beyond this, how borrowing volumes, broadly speaking, also fell.

Corporate Borrowing Falls

Table 8.1 showed a succession of yield curves beginning with December 1927 and ending with October 1929, covering corporate borrowing rates. The first yield curve ended 1927 with a moderate range of rates and an upward-sloping dispersion. Then, with call loan rates rising, the yield curve rose and flattened in mid-1928 and ended the year inverted. Next, yield curves were shown for 1929. By May 1929, the call loan renewal rate had reached its high for the year and thereafter tended to decline, while the corporate rate had risen to 6.0% in May and continued to rise to 6.25% in October, though not as rapidly.

Table 10.7							
Yield Curves **Oct. 1929 - June 1930** (% Percent)							
	Call market loan renewals	Commercial paper	Corporate bonds (Moody's) By ratings				
			Aaa	Aa	A	Baa
1929						
Oct	6.70	6.25	4.77	5.01	5.38	6.11
Nov	5.44	5.78	4.76	4.94	5.33	6.03
Dec	4.75	5.03	4.67	4.84	5.21	5.95
1930						
Jan	4.90	4.94	4.66	4.86	5.23	5.92
Feb	4.30	4.76	4.69	4.89	5.25	5.89
Mar	3.82	4.33	4.62	4.80	5.15	5.73
Apr	4.00	3.88	4.60	4.78	5.12	5.70
May	3.22	3.80	4.60	4.77	5.07	5.72
June	2.65	3.57	4.57	4.76	5.08	5.78

Source: *BMS*, pp. 456 & 469-70.

From October 1929 on, market rates on corporate debt instruments fell, and we consider it fitting to show this.

Table 10.7, above, shows a succession of yield curves beginning with October 1929, and ending with June 1930, covering corporate borrowing rates. As a benchmark, the New York Fed, alone among regional Federal Reserve Banks, raised its discount rate in August 1929 to 6% in an attempt to curb speculation. That month the call loan renewal rate was already above 6% as was Moody's average rate on Baa rated bonds. By October, all of these rates but two had risen. As Table 8.1 shows, the average rates on Aaa Bonds had fallen 2 basis points and on A rated bonds had fallen 5 basis points. Thus, the yield curve in October was significantly inverted. In November 1929, every interest rate was below the October high. In January 1930, the call market loan renewal rate was below the commercial paper rate, and the inversion of rates was diminishing. In March, the yield curve resumed its normal upward-sloping posture. By June, every rate was down very significantly. The call market loan rate had nearly fallen more than in half. The commercial paper rate was only 57% of what it had been the prior October. The Aaa bond rate had lost 20 basis points. The Aa rate was down 25 basis points. The A rate was down 30 basis points. The Baa rate was down 33 basis points.

Investors turned to fixed income markets after the Crash causing new bond issues, which had been at the lowest level since 1924, to rise, but that upswing lasted only into the summer of 1930.

In closing, we express deep respect for the work of Milton Friedman and Anna Schwartz and appreciate all their years of efforts in achieving their money series estimates, most particularly their statistics on the sharp wiggle in bank loan volumes in November 1929. If we have seen something in the downside of that dramatic wiggle that differs from what they saw, we find ourselves recalling Keynes's comment regarding the importance of staying open to new insights: "The composition of this book has been for the author a long struggle of escape…from habitual modes of thought and expression."[34] We, too, have found ourselves there.

In this chapter, we took an in-depth look at call loan lenders and the impact of their behavior, as reflected in critical balance sheet line items and in sources and uses of funds statements compared over various time periods surrounding the Crash. We now turn to a different reality of American life at the time that added the determinative and decidedly toxic ingredient to the U.S. economy that shifted it from depression to Depression with a capital D.

34 Keynes (1936), p. xxiii.

Table 10.8					
Statistics of U.S. Economic Activity ($ billion)					
	Jul. '29	Aug. '29	Sep. '29	Oct. '29	Nov. '29
Annualized personal income	$86.3	$86.9	$86.4	$86.3	$83.6
Index of factory employment	108.1	108.4	107.3	106.6	104.4
Index of industrial production	114	114	112	110	105
Index of wholesale prices	96.5	96.3	96.1	95.1	93.5
Friedman & Schwartz demand deposits	$22.8	$22.6	$22.6	$24.4	$21.7
Fed member bank loans			$26.2		

Sources: *HSUS* 1789-1945, pp. 328-330, 344; *Monetary History*, p.712; *BMS*, p.72.

All above-the-line statistics were down in October from September and the August peak:

- Annualized personal income:
  - –down$2.7 billion from October
  - –down $3.3 billion from August (-3.8%)
- Index of factory employment:
  - –down 2.1% from October
  - –down 3.7% from August
- Industrial production:
  - –down 4.5% from October
  - –down 7.9% from August
- Wholesale prices:
  - –down 1.7% from October
  - –down 2.9% from August (annualized rate of -11.1%)

Endnote

Friedman and Schwartz Sub-Optimize

In a paper published in the Review of Economics and Statistics in 1963, the same year as their opus *Monetary History*, Friedman and Schwartz sought to describe in careful detail, albeit deeming their efforts as "sketching very broadly," how the practical implementation of monetary policy succeeds in achieving real economic stimulus. Their theory captured the attention of many economists and important policy-makers in the decades that followed to the extent that monetary policy came to dominate policy very broadly indeed.

However, from the perspective of what actually happened in 1929-30, a period they covered in *Monetary History*, their theoretical framework left out important economic realities. Looking, as we are, at Friedman and Schwartz's broad sketch through the lens of financial management tools and history leads us to conclude that their theory resulted in sub-optimized economic results.[35]

We offer extended, curated quotes from their paper, entitled "Money and Business Policy," before weighing in on which assumptions they made that we contend led to sub-optimized economic results. In a section titled "A Tentative Sketch of the Mechanism Transmitting Monetary Changes," Friedman and Schwartz explained:

> However consistent may be the relation between monetary change and economic change, and however strong the evidence for the autonomy of the monetary changes, we shall not be persuaded that the monetary changes are the source of the economic changes unless we can specify in some detail

35 "Sub-optimization is a reduced level of output that results from an inefficient or ineffective process or system. Sub-optimization can also arise from a focus on optimizing a unit of a business rather the results of the entire business," from AccountingTools.com.

the mechanism that connects the one with the other. Though our knowledge is at the moment too meager to enable us to do this at all precisely, it may be worth sketching very broadly some of the possible lines of connection, first, in order to provide a possible rationalization of our empirical findings; second, to show the monetary theory of cyclical fluctuations can accommodate a wide variety of other empirical findings about cyclical regularities; and third, to stimulate others to elaborate the theory and render it more specific.

Let us start by defining an Elysian state of moving equilibrium in which real income per capita, the stock of money, and the price level are all changing at constant annual rates. The relation between these rates depends on whether real income is rising or falling, whether wealth is remaining constant as a ratio to income or is rising or falling relative to income, on the behavior of the relative rates of return on different forms of wealth, and on the wealth elasticity of demand for money....

Let us now suppose that an unexpected rise to a new level occurs in the rate of change in the money stock, and it remains there indefinitely—a single shot, as it were, displacing the time path of the money stock.... To be definite...let us suppose it comes from an increased rate of open market purchases by a central bank.

Although the initial sellers of the securities purchased by the central bank were willing sellers, this does not mean that they want to hold the proceeds in money indefinitely....

It seems plausible that both non-bank and bank holders of redundant balances will turn first to securities comparable to those they have sold, say, fixed-interest coupon, low risk obligations. But as they seek to purchase these they will tend to build up the prices of those issues. Hence they, and also other holders not involved in the central bank open-market transactions, will look further afield: the banks, to their loans; the non-bank holders to other categories of securities—higher-risk fixed-coupon obligations, equities, real property, and so forth.

As the process continues, the initial impacts are diffused in several respects: first, the range of assets affected widens; second, potential creators of assets now more in demand are induced to react to the better terms on which they can be sold, including business enterprises wishing to engage in capital expansion, house builders or prospective homeowners, consumers who are potential purchasers of durable consumer goods—and so on and on; third, the initially redundant money balances concentrated in the hands of those first affected by the open market purchases spread throughout the economy.

As the prices of financial assets are bid up, they become expensive relative to non-financial assets, so there is an incentive for individuals and enterprises to seek to bring their actual portfolios into accord with desired portfolios by acquiring non-financial assets. This, in turn, tends to make existing non-financial assets expensive relative to the newly constructed non-financial assets. At the same time, the general rise in the price level of non-financial assets tends to raise wealth relative to income, and to make the direct acquisition of current services cheaper relative to the purchase of the sources of services. These effects raised demand curves for current productive services, both for producing new capital goods and for purchasing current services. The monetary

> stimulus is, in this way, spread from financial markets to the markets for goods and services.[36]

When they talked about the impact on the money stock of central bank OMO, we see that Friedman and Schwartz considered a policy change of the very sort they rebuked the Fed for not making in 1930-33. They discussed how such an increase in open market purchases leads to effects that spread *from* financial markets outward *to* markets for goods and services and thus cause an upward shift in the "demand curves for current productive services, both for producing new capital goods and for purchasing current services."

How Is This Approach Sub-optimal?

Before turning to this question, we repeat what we regard as an ill-considered assumption Friedman and Schwartz advanced as to the "plausible" actions holders of idle cash would take with, what they called, "redundant" funds. Their assumption was that they would use that idle cash to purchase interest-bearing assets. In our view, however, the focus of the entire referenced passage was sub-optimal because it focused only on assets and failed to take the idle cash-holder's liabilities into consideration. Plausibility opens the door for alternative and additional explanations, and therefore, it seems logical to explore liabilities—assets' counterpart on any entity's balance sheet—for equally tenable explanations or actions.

Debt is just such a liability Friedman and Schwartz failed to include in their discussion of plausible assumptions. Chapter 10 discussed that carrying debt incurs interest expense, while short-term marketable investments earn interest. The spread between interest expense and interest earned is key in deciding what to do with idle

36 Milton Friedman and Anna J. Schwartz, "Money and Business Cycles," *The Review of Economics and Statistics*, Vol. 45, No. 1, Part 2, Supplement, February 1963, pp. 59-61. Hereafter referred to as Friedman and Schwartz (1963b).

cash. As we learned in Table 10.6 (p. 255), the additional cost to borrowers of banks' compensating balance requirements on loans may make the effective bank-borrowing rate higher than available returns on short-term marketable instruments. If indeed rates on short-term marketable instruments are lower than the effective bank borrowing rate, borrowers have a sound and usually easily exercised option for employing their idle cash. They can use idle cash to pay down bank borrowings. In so doing, rather than earning interest, they reduce the amount of interest they are obligated to pay.

Using redundant balances to pay down bank borrowings does *not* in fact "build up the prices of [fixed-interest coupon, low risk obligations]," as Friedman and Schwartz asserted. Rather, done in any volume, repaying bank borrowings softens the demand for bank loans, thus tending to encourage a *falling* prime rate in order to stimulate loan demand.[37]

Writing from the vantage of 1976 in *Did Monetary Forces*, when Peter Temin pondered why the money supply fell, he made use of this same passage. Following what he called the "money hypothesis," Temin explored other ways people used their idle cash, again focusing on using it to acquire other assets, "This reaction to a change in the supply of money is known as the liquidity or portfolio effect. There is general agreement among all economists that a process like this takes place."[38] Unlike Friedman and Schwartz, however, Temin soundly raised an explanation the likely relevance of the what he called the "spending hypothesis" stating, "A decrease in spending decreased the demand for money instead. Interest rates fell as a result."[39] Temin recognized what was missing from Friedman and Schwartz's analysis, but he lacked the supporting data to test his argument.

By the 1960s and 1970s, at a time when our economy was experiencing stagflation and the quantity of money held as demand

37 The reduction in the money supply that results from loan repayments is a topic for elsewhere.

38 Temin (1976), pp. 97-8.

39 Ibid., pp. 102-3.

deposits was growing faster than the real economy indicated the, "general agreement among all economists" Temin spoke of regarding the money supply might have existed in support of the process presented by Friedman and Schwartz. However, in the early 1930s, not all economists took the same position. Much consideration of this subject lies ahead in this volume. For the time being, we conclude with thoughts from monetarist economist Irving Fisher, who wrote in 1932:

> A man-to-man debt may be paid without affecting the volume of outstanding currency; for whatever currency is paid by one, whether it be legal tender or deposit currency transferred by check, is received by the other, and is still outstanding. But when a debt to a commercial bank is paid by check *out of a deposit balance*, that amount of deposit currency simply disappears.
>
> Thus to pay a debt at the bank tends to contract the circulating medium. But this tendency is, in normal times, neutralized by a counter-tendency. For generally, as fast as some bank debtors pay off their debts, the extinguished currency is replaced by new depositors who obtain new credits. When, however, by reason of a general state of over-indebtedness, there is a stampede of liquidation, then the new borrowings will by no means suffice to restore the balance, and there must follow a net shrinkage of deposits, or "credit currency."[40]

It is this "stampede of liquidation," in Fisher's vivid description that further explains our departure from Friedman and Schwartz's singular focus on uses of idle cash with regards to assets and their failure to address liabilities.

---

40 Irving Fisher, *Booms and Depressions*, Adelphi Company, 1932, p. 15.

CHAPTER 11

Market Events Reveal Major Over-Indebtedness

(October 24 to November 30, 1929)

THE NATION'S FIRST ERA of blasé borrowing, enabled by actively-marketed, ready credit, had ballooned to a level never seen before. With the Crash, this unconstrained practice—some would even call it folly—came to an abrupt end. Americans, individually and with Crash-heightened awareness, suddenly awoke to the heavy weight of debt they realized they bore. These individuals included both naïve speculators of ordinary means and experienced investors with wealth materially reduced by the Crash. Especially for speculators—including speculating investors—whose debts ballooned as they met margin calls, their priorities, and even their expectations, changed overnight.

Indebted Americans also included householders who had succumbed to newly minted marketing and advertising techniques and taken advantage of the increasing availability of financing to purchase all manner of consumer durables, including houses. Now they feared they had been living way beyond their means. Indeed, they had been. Home mortgages as they were then offered added greatly to the woes debtors faced. The 1920s had created a great many new American homeowners carrying debt in the form of the touted, yet very limited, mortgages of the period that required interest-only payments for three or four years. Then in the last year the homeowner had to pay off the loan, usually by refinancing the mortgage, or face foreclosure. When the prices of houses fell (as they did), lenders were increasingly unwilling to extend new mortgage loans sufficient to pay off the old mortgages, and homeowners confronted the very real prospect of losing those homes.

Whether wiped out financially due to speculation, unemployed, facing uncertainty of continued employment or apparently comfortable but uncomfortably leveraged, each individual saw the Crash as casting a glaring spotlight on his or her own personal debts. Repaying those debts became an urgent priority, and many debtors realized—and feared—that the need to tighten belts in order to pay off debts would seriously impact their standard of living.

The experience of economist Irving Fisher illustrated that even some of the wisest suffered. In the autumn of 1929, Fisher was a well-known and respected professor of economics when he voiced the heartfelt but unfortunate prediction that history has not forgotten: "Stock prices have reached what looks like a permanently high plateau."[1] About this "immortal estimate," as Galbraith called

1 James P. Warburg and Irving Fisher, "Reply to Senator Elmer Thomas and Professor Irving Fisher," *The Annals of the American Academy of Political and Social Science*, Vol. 171, Jan. 1934, p. 151. In a response Fisher gave in November 1933, to a talk by Mr. Warburg—and with the benefit of four years of reflection—he gave an explanation of his statement: "In regard to Governor Strong, we owe to him, to a very large extent, the prosperity which this country enjoyed between 1921 and 1929; because he...was really stabilizing our dollar. It was his open market operations to which we owe the stable price level in that period....It is true that he left a tradition behind him in his own bank, but what I feared [about what would happen after Strong died] came to be true. I did not at the time fear it so much. I took comfort from what he said, and it was on that basis that I believed that the price level which we then had and the prosperity that went with it and the high price of stocks would be continued....The quotations from me are not altogether correct. In particular, I did predict that there would be a recession, and I think I was the only man that publicly 'called the turn.' It is true, however, that I underestimated this fall enormously. I do humbly confess it. But it was partly because I believed that the policy that Governor Strong had initiated and the policy which Governor Rooth is now successfully carrying out would be continued. Governor Strong died in 1928. I thoroughly believe that if he had lived and his policies had been continued, we might have had the stock market crash

it, and its impact on Fisher's standing, Galbraith was moved in his 1954 *The Great Crash, 1929* to write an apologia of Fisher:

> Irving Fisher was the most original of American economists. Happily there are better things—his contributions to index numbers, technical economic theory, and monetary theory—for which he is remembered.[2]

In 1967, Paul Samuelson added an enthusiastic defense of Fisher's place in the pantheon of American economists:

> [E]ach generation must rewrite its history books. Starting out today, we would not find ourselves studying the history of *doctrines*....Instead, in the spirit of Schumpeter's classic *History of Economic Analysis,* we would give greatest weight to *analytical* contributions. And from this standpoint, Irving

---

in a milder form, but after the crash there would not have been the great industrial depression. I believe some of the crash was inevitable because of over-indebtedness, but that the depression was not inevitable. The reason is that the deflation that went with over-indebtedness was not necessary. We can always control the price level....When Governor Strong was ill...he found that his colleagues were not raising the rate of rediscount in order to prevent the crash that he saw coming. If his open market operations had been properly continued, I believe the crash would have been greatly reduced, the open market operations would have been reversed in time, and the industrial depression would have been prevented. I apologize for not having foreseen clearly what was going to happen. But I believe that I was justified, in view of what Governor Strong told me, in thinking that we would continue to have a one-hundred-cent dollar, and that it was not going to be a one hundred-and-eighty-one-cent dollar. Incidentally, I hope you will not forget that my opinion in 1929, whether justifiable or not, was then shared by the great majority of observers, from the President and the Secretary of the Treasury [Andrew Mellon] down—including the chief bankers of New York City."

2 Galbraith (1954), pp. 70-71.

> Fisher would emerge perhaps as the greatest single name in the history of American economics.[3]

Although the repercussions of believing in his immortal estimate and acting on it personally impacted both his reputation and his finances, Fisher turned from his tragedy to scholarship to try to explain what had happened to him and so many others. As Samuelson's observation suggested, he did so with profound success. In the process of writing *The Stock Market Crash and After* (1930) and *Booms and Depressions: Some First Principles* (1932) among other works, Fisher coined the term "over-indebtedness" and conceived and articulated what we call, "The Debt Factor Approach" (see Chapter 1 of *The Deflation of 1930*). Over-indebtedness, a concept Fisher and millions of other Crash-clobbered Americans experienced first-hand, is the important theme explored in this chapter.

The Vanishing of Financial Cushions

In the 1920s and 1930s, the New York Stock Exchange was responsible for the great majority of equity trading that occurred in the United States, making their records an important source of data. Those records stated the total market value of all stocks listed on the NYSE as of the first of each month. The statistics for the last quarter of 1929—even while recognizing the huge disparity in scale between then and now—were shocking. The high value of the Dow Industrials for 1929—381.17—occurred on September 3; the NYSE recorded the value of all the stocks listed on the NYSE merely two days earlier as $89.67 billion. By October 23 the Dow Industrials had already fallen 19.8% to 305.85. Then the Crash occurred.

By November 1, the value of all stocks listed on the NYSE had fallen to $71.76 billion—a drop of 20% or $17.91 billion from the September 1 high. But things got worse. Stock prices continued

3 W. J. Fellner, et al., *Ten Economic Studies in the Tradition of Irving Fisher*, Wiley, 1967, p. 17. Samuelson's emphasis.

dropping until November 13 when the Dow Industrials closed at 198.69—down 47.9% from the September 3 valuation. On Monday, December 2, the Dow Industrials closed at 241.70, down 36.6% from the September high and up 21.6% from the November 13 low. On December 1 the value of all the stocks listed on the NYSE had fallen to $63.59 billion—a drop of 29% or $26.08 billion from the high a mere three months earlier.[4]

It had been a wild, mostly downhill ride from the beginning of September to early December. By then, many speculators were wiped out completely. Even many affluent investors, whether speculating or not, suffered tumbles awful enough to lead to a change in their spending habits.

Even in market favorites, the losses could be great. One such stock, Radio Corporation of America (RCA), was especially volatile. The 1929 price of RCA stock ranged between a high of $115 per share to a low of $26 per share.[5] According to Barrie Wigmore:

> RCA was the darling of the 1929 stock market with the biggest trading volume on the NYSE....[I]n the Crash RCA suffered drastically as its valuation was brought into line, and it became more evident that RCA's net income for stockholders was going to be only $10.4 million, as opposed

---

4 These sums need to be "grossed up" for the trading on other U.S. stock exchanges as well as in other U.S. markets—most obviously bond markets and commodity exchanges—where trading also was occurring. Unfortunately, it isn't clear what number or numbers to use to perform this exercise in grossing up. For example, *Stock Exchange Practices* (p. 8) stated that 61% in total *shares* of U.S. equities were traded on the NYSE in 1929 and 76% were traded in 1932. But there were high-priced shares and low-priced shares. On the other hand, *SEP* (p. 6) also reported that $1,649.7 million in commissions were received by all 29 stock exchanges in the U.S. between Jan. 1, 1928, and Aug. 31, 1933. Of this amount, 94.7% was paid to the NYSE, 2.8% was paid to the NY Curb Exchange, and 2.5% was paid to the other 27 stock exchanges (p. 6).

5 For an account of the Radio Corporation of America and the wild ride of "Radio," its bellwether stock, see Robert Sobel's 1986 book *RCA*.

> to $18.5 million in 1928.... The stock broke to only 23% of its highest 1929 price, compared with the average of 48%.[6]

The ride had also been bumpy for entire industries. Wigmore cited auto stocks, for example, which fell to an average of 34% of their 1929 high prices, compared with 48% for all stocks.[7] Wigmore also pointed out that the Crash ended the high valuations of financial stocks and that the holding company and investment trust stocks declined approximately 70%, compared to the average decline of 52%.[8]

For speculators, the Crash and the need to meet margin calls must have been truly stomach-churning experiences. Many speculators, disbelieving the severity of the downward trend, sought frantically during the Crash to borrow more and more money to meet their margin calls and stay in the market. As their stock holdings became far less valuable, and the collateral with which to maintain the margin level required by their broker became increasingly inadequate, speculators lost even greater sums. We can only surmise that the internal dialogue by speculators led to more than a few ulcers as they pondered how much longer they could hold on and when the much-hyped turnaround would take place. They may not have known those answers, but they knew if they sold out their positions, all hope was lost.

Tragically, by scrambling to respond repeatedly to margin calls, they incurred debt obligations that were far greater and longer-term than any debts they had just days and weeks earlier. Had they been throwing good money after bad? For many, the process appeared

---

6 Wigmore (1985), pp. 85-86. On p. 3 in his Introduction, Wigmore stated, "The sample group of stocks which is the data base for much of this study averaged a decline from 1929 high to low prices of 52%." Obviously, the high prices occurred on different calendar days from each other, and the same held true for the low prices (although one might guess that the lows tended to cluster around the day—Nov. 3—when the market touched its low).

7 Ibid., p. 68.

8 Ibid., p. 87.

to end with the one-two punch of falling significantly deeper into debt to meet margin calls and then, in what looked like the final blow, getting wiped out. Yet for many speculators, a third gut-punch was still to come when they saw their October 1929 margin account statements from their brokerage firms and discovered that a sink-hole of indebtedness appeared to have opened up. Although they had no collateral left, their brokers had charged to their accounts large sums of unexpected residual losses and were demanding payment of onerous fees and interest expenses until the speculators had paid off all they owed.

What About Borrowing by Ordinary Americans?

How were the many Americans doing who weren't in a financial position to speculate in the stock market in the late 1920s, and what were their concerns? Statistics in the NBER's *Recent Economic Changes (REC)* from the period enabled us to reach reasonable conclusions about earnings and indebtedness in this large group.

Statistics regarding weekly wage earnings in manufacturing jobs indicated that it was unlikely that many workers were speculating in the stock market. In the late 1920s much of American industry was engaged in manufacturing, so weekly earnings in manufacturing provided reasonable support for this supposition. Based on a full-time week of 51 hours which *REC* used for "1923 and thereafter," the full-time weekly earnings of workers in one grouping of twelve industries were $27.09, and in a larger grouping of forty-two industries, weekly earnings were $27.74.[9]

Given that the price of *one share* of RCA stock at its high equaled over four weeks of earnings for these earners and at its low

9 *Recent Economic Changes (REC),* p. 432-3. Earnings changed very little over the four years from 1923, when average weekly earnings were $27.58 and $27.67, respectively. For reference, a full-time workweek was 56 hours in 1917 and 53 hours in 1920.

to one week of earnings[10], it is doubtful that more than a handful speculated in the stock market—despite the often-told stories about speculating elevator operators, shoeshine men and the odd taxi driver. In reality, however, though not speculating in the stock market, many wage earners were doing a different form of speculating: incurring installment debt as they enthusiastically responded to new and increasingly persuasive advertising and marketing techniques and purchased consumer durables on time. As we saw in the Prologue, consumer debt reached deep into the wage-earning sector with automobile financing leading the way down the road to indebtedness at levels that jeopardized workers' financial health, just as speculating jeopardized shareholders. Of the rapid growth in automobile time purchases, the NBER's *REC* offered the following report on consumers and their purchases:[11]

> Production of cars and trucks in...1928 exceeded 4,000,000 units.... [T]he purchase and use of automobiles is participated in by all classes of the population....[A] sample study was made from the records for deliveries at retail by a large automobile distributor...for the period from April 6, 1928, through June 15, 1929.... The make of car to which the figures pertain is a popular one, selling...in price roughly from about $1,000 to about $1,600.... It is clear that a large proportion of the current purchasers for passenger automobiles is made by the members of the wage earning and lower salaried groups.... For all the groups together it is seen that 38.6 per cent of the total sales were made for cash and 61.4 per cent on time.... It should be noted in this connection that while, in the groups of manufacturers, merchants, professionals, and sub-executives, the number of installment sales was almost matched by the number of cash sales, the ratio of installments to cash sales in the groups of

10 Given that weekly earnings changed very little in the 1920s, 1925 weekly earnings figures stand in for 1929 weekly earnings in these calculations.

11 According to Persons (1930), 4.6 million cars and trucks were produced in 1928, p. 124.

> salesmen, clerks, firemen and policeman, and laborers and artisans is more than two to one.[12]

Added to installment debt burdens, the limited terms of mortgage debt at the time carried special risks, as we discussed earlier. Suburban communities sprouted up nationwide in the 1920s. Aggressively pitched by developers with rapidly growing housing inventory, urban buyers embraced home ownership, persuaded it was almost a civic duty to own a home. The essential strategic partners of developers in this seismic population shift were an increasing variety of willing corporate mortgage lenders offering ample credit, but with limited mortgage terms which went on to threaten many borrowers in the post-Crash environment of declining home values with foreclosure and a painful loss of hopes and dreams. Again, according to *REC*:

> Of the [$5.0 billion] worth of private construction carried on annually, probably a greater proportion than formerly [of the financing] is now handled by means of building and loan associations, life insurance companies, savings banks, and other banking institutions, and less by personal transactions between the building owner and the lender. The increased rate of growth in building and loan associations and the passage of the McFadden Act in 1927, which permitted national banks to invest as much as one-half of their savings deposits in realty loans for periods of up to five years, have been notable.[13]

The impact that debts had on household budgeting for a wide swath of Americans, from the wealthy to the hourly worker, and the serious risks associated with nonpayment of debt, such as repossession, have been widely discussed by others. Nonetheless, as reported in the Prologue, studies have shown that people were highly conscientious about repaying debt. They took those debts seriously

12 *REC,* Volume I, pp. 59-61.

13 Ibid., p. 227.

and *prioritized debt obligations over other expenditures.* [14] Following the Crash, individuals, regardless of income, were answering the same question, "What do I do now?" and assessing based on their own values, how to handle their debt burdens. Shared by all was the motivation to get out of debt as quickly as possible.

The Significance of Over-Indebtedness

Stimulated by his own painful experience of the Crash, Irving Fisher was the first economist to look at the risks of having too much debt, giving it a name that resonates to this day. Describing what he called succinctly "over-indebtedness," Irving Fisher wrote in his 1932 volume *Booms and Depressions: Some First Principles*:

> Chance is inseparable from life. Every transaction is a taking of chances, and over-indebtedness is whatever degree of indebtedness multiplies *unduly* the chances of becoming insolvent. [15] Everyone who is not a gambler provides himself with a margin of safety. He puts a buffer between his debts and the collector. This buffer is the difference between assets and liabilities. Corporations call it "capital plus surplus." But the sufficiency of the buffer is not solely a matter of quantity. It must be varied according to the quality of the assets. It must be varied according to the quality of the liabilities. Slow assets [16] and quick liabilities [17] (such as call loans) require

---

14 According to Martha Olney, "Despite the layoffs, the wage cuts, and the unprecedented prevalence of installment credit use, families with installment debt were avoiding default. ... Families were keeping up with their installment payments." See "Avoiding Default: The Role of Credit in the Consumption Collapse of 1930," *The Quarterly Journal of Economics,* February 1999, pp. 325-6.

15 A person or corporation becomes insolvent when unable to pay debts.

16 *Slowness* here is a question of the length of time it takes to convert an asset into cash at a reasonable price. An example of a slow asset is a house. Selling a house, especially in an unfavorable market, can take months or even years.

17 *Quickness* here is a question of how soon a liability comes due.

> a larger buffer than quick assets and slow liabilities. The quickest asset, and therefore *the safest* when pressure comes, is cash. The quickest liability and therefore *the most unsafe* in times of pressure, is the call-loan. *Over-indebtedness is largely a question of dates of maturity*.... A balance sheet is the result of anxious efforts to weigh correctly these and many other considerations.[18] (emphasis ours)

Fisher's insightful breakdown of debt risks by timing of debt maturity and debt liquidity, likely the fruitful wisdom of personal hindsight, highlighted the urgent issues of personal indebtedness given the instability of the times. In fact, in *The Emotional Life of the Great Depression* published in 2019, Professor John Marsh describes how debt continued to cast gloom on the Fishers' lives:

> Irving Fisher...never managed to climb out of the hole he dug in the early years of the Great Depression. By the end of the 1930s, he remained well over $1 million in debt, which, adjusted for inflation, is a little over $17 million today. He could not make the mortgage payments on his house and sold it to his former employer, Yale University, which agreed to let Fisher and his wife stay in the house so long as they pay rent. Soon, they could not manage even that, and the Fishers moved into a small apartment off campus.[19]

Measures of Total Debt

The exhaustive work of Raymond Goldsmith steps in once again to give us a sense of the considerable amount of debt individuals were carrying in 1929. Using the IRS framework and extrapolating from certain IRS data, though without interpreting that data, Goldsmith

18 Fisher (1932), p. 9.

19 John Marsh, *The Emotional Life of the Great Depression,* Oxford University Press, 2019, p. 191.

estimated that total 1929 liabilities of Non-farm Households were $41.8 billion, of Non-farm Unincorporated Business were $16.8 billion and of Agriculture were $14.6 billion.[20] Goldsmith estimated the total liabilities of individual U.S. taxpayers as $73.3 billion, confirmation that individual tax-filers had a lot of debt obligations in 1929. Goldsmith's mission was to present data, however, not to offer analyses or the implications of this unfamiliar situation.

Aggregate debt, of course, is not the measure of U.S. individuals' and corporations' abilities to meet their debt obligations; income is. There is no better place to look at the income statistics of Americans than in the IRS treasure trove of data.

American Income Tax Filers—The General Picture in 1929

In order to offer a more detailed look at who was speculating, we first take a top-down approach to the U.S. population as a whole at the end of the 1920s. In 1929, the population of the United States was 121.8 million people.[21] This number, of course, included everyone—men, women, children, income earners and non-earners alike. Of this grand total, the IRS only required some to file income tax returns (about 3.3% of the total population).[22] Fewer still paid taxes (2% of the population). Income was the determining factor.

Roughly speaking, the requirement to file a return was determined by two income-based tests. The first income-based test required U.S. citizens and residents who were married and living together to file if household *net* income was $3,500 or more, or, in the case of "single" households, if the household had a *net* income of

20 Individual farmers owned their farms as a rule in 1929; very few farms were corporations then.

21 Est. U.S. population on January 1, 2023: 334.2 million.

22 Per IRS data (www.irs.gov/statistics/soi-tax-stats-historical-data-tables), in 2020, approximately 155.1 million individuals filed tax returns—47% of the population.

$1,500 or more. The second income-based test required filing if the filing party had a 1929 *gross* income of $5,000 or more.[23] There was also a source-based filing requirement that included all Americans who had "incomes, regardless of amount, from business, profession, rents, or sale of property."[24] There is a lot we can learn about the demographics and behavior of this more-or-less affluent group of Americans who filed tax returns in 1929-1933.

While the numbers may appear shockingly low to today's taxfiler, we present the actual statistics for our period to show the actualities of those times, including how few citizens filed tax returns, the small amount of taxes actually paid by taxpayers (their tax liability) and average tax rates. In summary, according to *SOI for 1929:*

> The number of tax returns for 1929, filed by individuals, was 4,044,327, of which 2,458,049 were taxable and 1,586,278 nontaxable. The aggregate net income was $24,800,735,564, the net income on taxable returns was $20,493,491,443, on which the tax liability was $1,001,938,147. The average amount of tax liability was $247.74 for all returns and $407.62 for taxable returns; and the average tax rate was 4.04 per cent for all returns and 4.89 per cent for taxable returns.[25]

While net income on all individual tax returns filed in 1929 totaled $24.8 billion, *SOI for 1929* gave the figure for aggregate *gross* income of all individual tax returns filed in 1929 as $29.9 billion.[26] These are very big numbers, relatively speaking. The National Income and Product Accounts (NIPA) of the Commerce Department estimated that the Gross National Product of the U.S. in 1929 in current dollars was $103.4 billion. Since the IRS numbers are also

23 *SOI for 1929*, pp. 396-7. We are not adjusting the data to current values in our analyses, but a 1929 dollar translates to roughly $17.59 in 2023.

24 Ibid., p. 411.

25 Ibid., p. 4.

26 Ibid., p. 8.

in current dollars, this suggests that the gross income of the 4.0 million individuals who filed income tax returns in 1929 accounted for 28.9% of GNP that year.

Corresponding data from *SOI for 1928* showed that while the numbers of tax return filers and taxpayers were similar to the 1929 figures, not surprisingly, taxpayers' net income was significantly higher in 1928 than for the year of the Crash:

> The returns for 1928 filed by individuals number 4,070,851, of which 2,523,063 were taxable and 1,547,788 nontaxable. The aggregate net income was $25,226,326,912 and the tax liability $1,164,254,037.[27]

Regardless of how few Americans filed and paid taxes then, these few mattered. IRS statistics from actual individual U.S. tax returns during this eventful period provided a rich assortment of data about economically significant Americans from which we learned a great deal that proved essential, even pivotal, to our research. The IRS archives conveyed highly revealing details about how taxfilers did in the Crash and after, why and even what they did, and moreover made it clear who the speculators were and who was encouraging that speculation by lending in the call loan market.

One key marker for speculation activity on the part of taxfilers, for instance, shows up in the difference reported between gross income and net income—what the IRS called "General deductions." A total deduction was allowed for losses on the sale of capital assets, including stock, but the IRS taxed those losses based on how long stocks had been held by the taxfiler. The tax laws of 1929-33 allowed the total deduction of a loss on the sale of a capital asset (e.g., shares of a stock) only if the asset had been held for at least two years. Speculators, who bought and sold quickly, could deduct only 12.5% of their losses. IRS regulations clearly favored longer-term investors, not speculators, making speculation losses

27 *SOI for 1928*, p. 3.

especially painful for taxfilers. Considering the disastrous fourth quarter of 1929, a key deduction to note for taxfilers in 1929 was losses on the sale of capital assets—including shares of stock held either short or long-term, as we will see.

Taxpayers as Brokerage House Customers

Anecdotes about stock tips from the aforementioned elevator operators, cabbies and bootblacks, though graphic, are mostly apocryphal, though there were certainly speculators at every income level who purchased stock based on all manner of information, credible or dubious. It is, however, highly likely that the great majority of active speculators were U.S. taxpayers in 1929, or at least among those individuals required to file. The IRS data we explore in great detail in Chapter 3 of *The Deflation of 1930* confirm this likelihood and far more about speculative behavior.

In order to connect the dots between taxpayers and their speculating behavior, it is useful to compare the IRS statistics pertaining to deductions taken for capital losses with information on brokerage house customers, especially margin customers. To help us do this we turned to data collected by the U.S. Senate Committee on Banking and Currency in the course of the Pecora Hearings in 1933 and summarized in the Committee's 1934 publication *Stock Exchange Practices* (*SEP*):

> During the year 1929 the total number of customers of member firms of 29 [U.S. stock] exchanges was 1,548,707. The transactions of 949,470, or 61.31 percent of the total number of customers, were of a cash character and the transactions of 599,237, or 38.69 percent, were of a margin character.
>
> The member firms of the New York Stock Exchange had 1,371,920 customers out of the total. The New York Stock

> Exchange member firms reported that the transactions of 811,986, or 59.19 percent, of their customers were of a cash character and the transactions of 559,934, or 40.81 percent, of their customers were of a margin character.[28]

To counter the widely perceived but highly inaccurate notion that everyone was speculating, we searched for creditable estimates. In January of 1930, Julius Klein, an economist serving as President Hoover's Assistant Secretary of Commerce, pronounced the palliative post-Crash position that, "The stock market crash affected approximately only 1,000,000 persons, the speculative element."[29] Even this number was probably overstated. John T. Flynn, described as "the shrewdest and most aggressive of Pecora's investigators," provided one estimate that we regard as plausible:

> The game of speculation is one played by some three or four thousand insiders and some half a million outsiders on terms of complete inequality.[30]

Where Flynn got his statistics is unknown. But according to *SEP*, in 1929 almost 600,000 people nationwide were purchasing stock on margin at brokerage houses, in the same ballpark as Flynn's "some half a million." This figure hardly includes "everyone." If we take 20% of the 2,458,049 U.S. taxpayers in 1929, we arrive at a figure of 491,610. Whether among the few thousand sophisticated insiders or among the more plentiful, disadvantaged outsiders, these 20% or so were likely among the same active speculators experiencing the Crash.

Also included in this group were the, at first, eager, then increasingly anxious shareholders who spent hours at brokerage houses either watching the ticker or, due to the crowds, hearing

---

28 *SEP*, p. 9.

29 Edward J. Angly, *Oh Yeah?*, 1932, p. 52.

30 Brooks (1969), p. 68. Brooks description of Flynn is p. 198.

others who were closer to the ticker call out what was happening. These people, instead of being engaged in normal work endeavors, were the precursors to today's day traders glued to their computer screens while believing they are making money the best possible way. Whether or not they eschewed work, the point is that this group of some hundreds of thousands of taxpaying Americans is worthy of attention, and not just in loss of productivity before the Crash and broken dreams afterwards. Even if behaving autonomously and keeping their financial decision-making utterly private, as taxpayers tend to do, their collective actions in 1929-33, as future chapters will describe in detail, redirected their spending away from consumption toward repayment of their debts. This had a major impact on the economy. And because debt repayment was such a normal and expected practice, market observers from businessmen, journalists, politicians and economists to Fed officials at the time failed to focus on the dramatic impact this collective individual debt repayment was having on the economy.

How Much Did Debtors Owe and How Soon?

Is there a way for us to determine how much debt U.S. taxpayers were in and how much pressure they felt to repay? In the spirit of Irving Fisher and the influence of dates of maturity on the condition he called over-indebtedness, we would be inclined to assume that what sharply focused the mind of each debtor was not only the total amount of indebtedness, but the amount that was due and payable *now.*

Key to measuring over-indebtedness is to observe short-term debt levels. To approach this unknown, we shifted our attention to other important statistics, again from the IRS treasure trove, to help us assess the extent of the most pressing debt burdens requiring taxpayers' attention. Because, in general, borrowers owed money to an entity such as a corporation or a bank, all of which filed tax returns, we turned from individual taxpayer data to corporate filing data to arrive at a supportable estimate of the amount of short-term debt around the time of the Crash. Since the schedule the IRS sent to corporate filers asked specifically for "Notes payable (less than one year),"[31] we found the relevant data in the IRS Aggregate U.S. Corporate Balance Sheet for 1929 as shown in Table 6.1 (p. 140.)

The Aggregate U.S. Corporate Balance Sheet for 1929 showed "Notes and accounts payable (less than one year)" of $29.45 billion. While this figure did not, in and of itself, indicate impending danger, the aggregate balance sheet also enabled us to determine to whom this aggregate sum was owed. We concluded that these short-term payables were owed to other corporations (including banks).

How was it apparent that aggregate payables were in fact owed to other corporations (including banks) on the 1929 Aggregate U.S. Corporate Balance Sheet? To answer this, we must turn from liabilities to assets, specifically receivables. Notes and accounts receivable of all these corporations (including banks) totaled $66.8 billion, more than double corporate payables— $37.4 billion more to be exact. This was a very large number that demanded attention. It was, in fact, 43.3% larger than the total amount that was lost on the NYSE in the entire Crash period (i.e., the time from September 1 to December 1, 1929).[32]

The bottom-line assumption is that entities other than U.S. corporations owed a lot of money to U.S. corporations, and, glaringly, this money was due and payable within a year. As Fisher noted, over-indebtedness, as a state of mind, depends on how much debt is owed *soon*. "Due and payable within a year" is soon. Debt owed soon weighs most heavily on the debtor. In Chapter 5 in *The Deflation of 1930*, we consider who these "entities other than U.S.

31 *SOI for 1934,* Part 2, p. 219.

32 The sum lost in the Crash was $26.08 billion.

corporations" were and conclude that *U.S. individuals owed more than 90% of the debt.*

Individual debtors, of course, were unaware of these huge aggregate numbers. However, whether speculators, investors, householders paying off mortgages or wage earners using consumer finance to purchase automobiles, radios or living room furniture, each individual knew well what his or her short-term debt obligations were, when they were due, and what was at risk if they weren't paid. Payment schedules were included in the signed legal documents that had created the debt obligations. Those signed papers were also reminders that the lenders held their assets as security and kept those assets if the debtor failed to pay. Monthly account statements and, if necessary, past due bills regularly reminded each individual of his or her debt obligations.

We contend that U.S. individuals who owed, collectively, more than 90% of $37.4 billion in debt due and payable in one year found their minds sharply focused on their portion of this number. For those with secure incomes or resources, it may not have mattered. But 1929 and beyond were increasingly insecure years—indeed, for many, hugely insecure years. What these individual debtors saw—and foresaw—concerned them to the core and led them to make drastic changes in their lives.

Those individual changes in how people with debt were living their lives, when aggregated, created the depression conditions in the U.S. that grew worse by the month.

Table 11.1					
Statistics of U.S. Economic Activity ($ billion)					
	Jul. '29	Aug. '29	Sep. '29	Oct. '29	Nov. '29
Annualized personal income	$86.3	$86.9	$86.4	$86.3	$83.6
Index of factory employment	108.1	108.4	107.3	106.6	104.4
Index of industrial production	114	114	112	110	105
Index of wholesale prices	96.5	96.3	96.1	95.1	93.5
Friedman & Schwartz demand deposits	$22.8	$22.6	$22.6	$24.4	$21.7
Fed member bank loans			$26.2		

Sources: *HSUS* 1789-1945, pp. 328-330, 344; *Monetary History*, p.712; *BMS*, p.72.

CHAPTER 12

A Sudden Reversal of Mood Leads to a Pivot in Behavior

(November to December, 1929)

REACTION IS ALWAYS a matter of perspective. Some events cause a macro-reaction for a nation as a whole, even while, on a micro level, each individual's response to that event filters through his or her own life's experiences. The October Crash was an event that elicited reaction on all levels. History recognizes October 29—Black Tuesday—as the last day of the Crash. It is likely that as Wednesday, October 30 dawned, almost every investor, speculator, business leader or even bystander wanted to hide his or her head in denial at the seismic shock waves that had just hit the country.

One astute observer of the day was Alexander Dana Noyes from his long-time perch as financial editor of *The New York Times.* Early in his wise, now out-of-print 1938 memoir, *The Market Place*, he outlined the admirable principles that he had followed as a reporter from the beginning of his career in the distant 1880s. One principle was to "abstain altogether from personal speculation, which is the only way for preserving an unbiased mind." Another was to "judge every rumor by the source from which it comes, but until the rumor, from whatever source, had been investigated, to receive it with cool skepticism."[1]

Later in his memoir, Noyes recalled the alarming shift brought on by the "panic of 1929," as he called the Crash:

1 Noyes (1938), p. 51.

> So far as concerned the great stock speculation, the panic of 1929 brought sudden recognition of the economic realities. It punctured, almost overnight, the ill-fated Stock Exchange illusions. No more was heard of the New Economic Era, in which there was to be nothing but increasing earnings and rising [stock] prices. Wall Street began to hear, as it had not heard for at least two years, that old-fashioned precedent has value, that exorbitantly high money rates mean over-strain on credit, that speculative valuations which were utterly out of line with anything except the imagination of the buyers of stocks had made violent downward readjustment inevitable. But the crushing severity of the business reaction which ensued, during the next two years, was not predicted.[2]

Clearly, Noyes saw sentiment change "almost overnight." As we shall see, numerous prominent authors wrote about the state of mind or "mood" of the times. We would call the mood of the speculation that preceded the Crash one of almost heedless abandon. Suddenly, with the Crash, illusions were "punctured," to use Noyes's word, and the state of mind pivoted to one of exercising strong financial caution, requiring what Noyes delicately called "downward readjustment."

Before we examine the implications of this reversal in mood, however, we want to offer our take on Noyes's comment about "the crushing severity of the business reaction which ensued." Data confirm that businesses certainly did reduce their investment in property, plant and equipment over the multi-year post-Crash period. As we shall see in Chapter 12 in *The Deflation of 1930*, gross revenue for virtually all American industry, as reported to the IRS, dropped precipitously in 1930. It is our view, however, that the "crushing severity" of the American business reaction of cutting production and laying off workers was due to declines in demand for their products by customers, some of whom were businesses who were also experiencing a reduction of demand for their products. For example,

2 Ibid., p. 337.

the manufacturers of spark plugs had fewer orders from automobile manufacturers as demand for automobiles declined.

Our focus in this chapter, though, is on the crucial influence of American consumers, who began exercising strong financial caution post-Crash and making what Noyes called "downward readjustment." We will see how that behavior rapidly impacted key American industries by examining, in particular, radio and automobile dealers, given their prominence in the economy and the culture, as well as other major retail segments. We have focused on radios already and do so again ahead. Scrutinizing automobile installment sales statistics for 1928 through 1933—for which we drew heavily on an NBER study published in 1940—we arrived at another clear set of cause-and-effect relationships linking the 1929 Crash to the Great Depression. In a series of downward steps precipitated by the Crash, these automobile credit sales statistics show that the nation had demonstrably descended fully into depression—later known as the "Great Depression"—in the second quarter of 1930. May 1930 was, in our view, the likeliest month by which this outcome had taken full effect.

Consumer "Wants" Pivot in their Effect from Expansion to Contraction

Before the Crash, it seems safe to say that Americans, in general, expected prosperity—as they had come to understand and desire it—to continue unaltered into the future, perhaps even indefinitely. It was the shock of the Crash that led both consumers and businesses alike to assume more vigilant and certainly more cautious postures. The result was almost immediate. Sometime between the run up to the Crash and early 1930, ordinary Americans, in aggregate, shifted away from pursuing that debt-driven prosperity and began prioritizing debt repayment over consumption month-by-month.

We have discussed finding and utilizing tabulated aggregated annual balance sheets of nearly all operating business corporations in the U.S. from 1927 through 1933. We explored how these "top down" statistics revealed an overall picture of this large and important sector of the U.S. economy as well as offered inferences about the actions of individual Americans. But in order to show linkages between the Crash and the Great Depression, we needed a different kind of data to do a different kind of analysis that would provide more than just inferences. We needed hard data about individuals—especially ordinary Americans or consumers—to take a "bottom up" approach to what they did and why. Installment sales statistics for radios, automobiles and other retail segments proved to be the bottom up, hard data we needed to scrutinize in order to reach sound conclusions. More than one source proved critical.

What Radio Sales Tell Us about Consumer Behavior Post-Crash

In Chapters 7 and 8, we discussed Charles E. Persons who, in his November 1930 paper on credit expansion and what he called "credit sales," addressed conditions in the radio industry in November and December 1929 and drew attention to the fall in radio sales:

> We are told that *after the stock market break* the retail [radio] dealer "practically stopped buying." Despite this disastrous close to the year, the total sales reached the enormous total stated above [4 million sets].[3] (emphasis ours)

After months of strong sales, Persons noted that from November on, retail radio dealers weren't buying additional radio sets. The reason, we suggest, was because the brisk growth in sales radio dealers had become accustomed to had certainly slowed if not ended, and they had plenty of radio sets in their inventories already.

Speaking more generally about the radio industry, Persons

3 Persons (1930), p. 121.

recognized that serious over-production had occurred in the industry in 1929. He wrote:

> The radio industry at the end of [1929] was in sharp distress. Factories closed or went on part-time. The surplus of sets in stock were sold at bargain prices. Thereafter production was resumed at a sober rate.... The industry had enjoyed ten years of unbroken and very rapid progress and prosperity. Yet in full career it met a decisive check. With all its attractiveness and despite its liberal terms of sale, *it had exhausted its credit line.* Producers, financial backers, dealers, purchasers, and would be purchasers had expanded their debt burden to the full amounts they were either able *or willing* to assume.[4] (emphasis ours)

In fact, given the rapid easing of credit by the Fed after the Crash (see pp. 256-7), we contend that the radio industry had *not* "exhausted its credit line." The industry's bankers and other financing sources would still have extended credit. The problem was, again, on the demand side. In our view, potential radio buyers simply no longer wanted to go deeper into debt.

To reinforce our understanding of this situation, we consulted two primary industry sources Persons turned to. *Radio Retailing,* in its December 1929 issue, confirmed that over-production took place in 1929, and radio consultant Edgar Felix wrote in the January 1930 issue of *Electrical Merchandising* that "when the [stock] market break took place, [radio dealers] virtually stopped buying," though he softened that fact for his readers by adding that "the retail situation [in the radio industry], while unusual, is not alarming."[5] However, neither trade magazine Persons referenced suggested that any part of the radio industry had reached a credit limit, nor did they imply that dealers no longer regarded retail radio customers as creditworthy.

---

4 Ibid., p. 122.

5 Edgar Felix, *Electrical Merchandising,* January 1930, p. 69.

We offer a second reason radio dealers "virtually stopped buying." The dealers themselves were well aware of the over-production that had occurred in 1929 and didn't want to purchase radio sets they would either be stuck with or forced to sell at bargain prices. Further reinforcing our bottom up focus, Persons's hinted that potential radio purchasers were *unwilling* to take on more debt obligations.

Financing Sales of Automobiles at the Time of the Crash

After covering conditions in the radio industry, Persons turned his attention to the automobile industry where half of all consumer installment sales took place. In his discussion, unlike with radio sales, Persons did call automobile buyers' credit worthiness into question:

> In each industry a highly trained sales force exhausted every device known to high pressure salesmanship to sell the accumulating stocks. And in each case they found it impossible to move the goods, primarily because the buyers [sic] resources in cash and credit had been expended.[6]

Persons positioned automobile customers as arguably having exhausted their personal credit limit from the dealers' point of view. However, we again contend that the industry, its bankers and other financing sources would have offered credit. For example, lenders considered extending installment sales payment terms of new cars from 12 months to as long as 17 months to attract buyers. The problem was that potential automobile consumers, having become much more financially cautious, reduced their demand for automobiles and, thus, for automobile financing.

With Persons as the starting point, we delved further into the financing of automobile sales as illustrative, even emblematic,

6 Persons (1930), p. 124.

of general consumer behavior in the late 1920s and following the Crash. Fortunately, we found important statistics to help us. Our findings led us to data from the January 1931 issue of the *Survey of Current Business* prepared by the Commerce Department's Bureau of Economic Analysis (BEA). As evident in the *Survey* data, Tables 12.1 and 12.2, address the issue of consumer retreat.

Table 12.1

Analysis of Automobile Financing

($ million)

New cars			Used cars		
1930		% change from 1929	1930		% change from 1929
Jan	$45.2	-7.2	Jan	$25.6	12.3
Feb	53.0	-14.5	Feb	29.2	18.4
Mar	77.3	-20.2	Mar	42.5	12.1
Apr	94.1	-19.5	Apr	48.9	3.5
May	94.2	-24.8	May	42.8	-16.2
Jun	91.3	-25.2	Jun	43.1	-14.5
Jul	73.6	-41.0	Jul	42.8	-12.9
Aug	63.1	-43.3	Aug	37.2	-18.8
Sep	53.0	-43.6	Sep	35.3	-10.8
Oct	45.8	-43.1	Oct	33.9	-18.9
Total	$690.6	-29.7%		$381.1	-7.1%

Source: Survey of Current Business; "The Volume of Consumer Instalment Credit 1929-38," Feb. 1940, Appendix A & author's calculations.

Table 12.1 (opposite page) considers the new and used car statistics presented in Table 12.2 for 1930 and 1929 (January through October only), then calculates the change between the two years by dividing the financing amounts of the monthly statistics for 1930 by the financing amounts that occurred in 1929. [7]

Table 12.2 (next page) lays out in detail what was happening specifically in 1929 through October 1930 in terms of monthly new and used automobiles purchased on credit (not by buyers with cash) including the number of cars, the volume of financing and the per car average financing.[8] Scanning the passing months on the table shows how quickly dealers felt impact from the Crash, but the data merits a closer look.

On their own, the new car financing numbers for 1930 tell a straightforward and not unexpected story. Month-by-month the volume of new car financings fell when compared with the prior year. For example, in January 1930, the drop was -7.2% from January 1929. By the final three months, August to October 1930, the declines all exceeded -43%.

The used car financing statistics for 1930, however, tell a different story. From January to April the financing amounts spent buying *used* cars rose rather than fell. The January sales volume shown in Table 12.1 was $25.6 million, which was 12.3% higher than the January 1929 volume of $22.8 million. This rise from the prior year continued through April 1930, as Table 12.1 shows. Then from May to October, while the financing amounts spent buying used cars fell, they fell more slowly than new car financing numbers. This tells us that from January to April 1930 frugal buyers chose less expensive used cars, a trend that continued throughout the remainder of the time period covered by Table 12.1.

However, since this chapter covers November and December

7 The *Survey of Current Business* offered no corresponding statistics for the periods before January 1929 or after October 1930.

8 The table also includes "Unclassified" entities which table footnote #1 explains as submitted by "smaller organizations that "found it impossible to segregate their operations."

Table 12.2

AUTOMOBILE FINANCING[1]

	WHOLESALE FINANCING	RETAIL FINANCING										
		TOTAL			NEW CARS			USED CARS			UNCLASSIFIED		
(thousands) (except "Per car")	Volume in dollars	Number of cars	Volume and average		Number of cars	Volume and average		Number of cars	Volume and average		Number of cars	Volume and average	
			Total amount	Per car		Total amount	Per car		Total amount	Per car		Total amount	Per car
1929													
January	$36,900	157	$75,692	$481	79	$48,766	$620	69	$22,784	$330	9.6	$4,142	$431
February	47,963	191	91,242	478	104	61,979	598	77	24,663	321	10.7	4,600	431
March	61,171	306	142,117	465	166	96,881	582	122	37,907	312	17.9	7,329	410
April	74,885	412	172,811	420	206	116,938	569	185	47,222	255	20.8	8,651	416
May	72,292	403	184,939	459	213	125,284	588	169	51,104	302	20.7	8,551	414
June	63,412	387	180,098	465	204	122,038	598	164	50,380	306	18.6	7,681	413
July	61,839	391	180,845	462	212	124,762	589	163	49,105	302	17.0	6,979	410
August	69,959	350	163,896	468	184	111,299	604	150	45,850	306	16.3	6,747	415
September	60,195	301	129,447	430	158	93,951	593	128	29,558[3]	231	14.6	5,938	407
October	63,641	278	126,590	455	132	80,373	607	135	41,725	309	10.7	4,493	418
Total (10 mths)	612,256	3,177	1,447,679	456	1,659	982,271	592	1,362	400,297	294	156.9	65,110	415
November	(2)	211	95,001	451	96	58,246	604	104	32,260	310	10.2	4,495	439
December	(2)	172	80,089	466	74	48,061	647	90	28,674	319	7.6	3,353	440
Total (year)	---	3,560	1,622,768	456	1,829	1,088,578	595	1,556	461,232	296	174.7	72,958	418
1930													
January	52,447	166	73,619	443	79	45,245	575	81	25,596	316	6.4	2,778	433
February	61,245	200	85,770	429	96	53,011	555	96	29,206	305	8.6	3,552	415
March	77,548	316	123,786	392	139	77,332	555	167	42,478	255	9.7	3,976	408
April	85,346	346	146,987	425	171	94,086	549	164	48,854	297	10.4	4,047	390
May	83,660	349	141,307	405	170	94,236	554	168	42,805	254	10.6	4,266	401
June	53,802	341	138,520	406	160	91,278	571	171	43,074	252	10.7	4,168	388
July	55,430	287	119,044	414	131	73,596	562	150	42,780	285	6.4	2,668	418
August	45,411	248	102,530	414	111	63,144	567	130	37,222	286	6.2	2,165	347
September	45,387	220	90,466	412	92	52,962	573	122	35,266	289	5.5	2,238	410
October	35,962	201	81,504	405	79	45,751	582	119	33,852	286	4.3	1,901	440
Total (10 mths)	596,238	2,675	1,103,533	413	1,228	690,639	562	1,368	381,134	279	78.9	31,761	403

[1]Compiled by the U.S. Department of Commerce, Bureau of the Census, from reports of 492 financing organizations. Some of the smaller organizations found it impossible to segregate their operations, their totals being shown in the unclassified group. This summary revises previous tables shown in the survey due to the addition of 27 organizations.

[2]Data not available

[3]Cross references with other SCB monthly reports indicate the September 1929 used car "total amount" figure is a misprint. The correct number would be approximately $39.3 million.

Source: Department of Commerce, Survey of Current Business, Jan. 1931.

1929 in particular, we also needed monthly 1928 data for comparison and had to search more widely for additional automobile financing and installment sales statistics. As has occurred frequently throughout our research, luck was on our side.

Drawing Conclusions About November and December of 1929

Using reliable data—as we do throughout *How the Crash Caused*—is an obvious, acknowledged and respected method to draw and validate conclusions. Our wider search for the relevant monthly automobile financing data turned up a study published in 1940 by NBER entitled *The Volume of Consumer Installment Credit, 1929-38*. It proved invaluable.[9]

Analyzing the statistics presented in this NBER study led us to pursue two logical, albeit tentative, propositions. The first proposition was that sometime between the lead-up to the Crash and early 1930, ordinary Americans, in aggregate, shifted away from adding more each month to the retail installment debts they owed and began repaying those debts month-by-month. Our second proposition was that while the U.S. was heading into recession in the autumn of 1929, it was the shock and magnitude of the Crash that caused this shift to propel the country into the Great Depression. Both entail bottom up analysis.

Others have also suggested propositions closely related to ours, though focused slightly differently. As the 1940 NBER study, for instance, summarized one of its findings:

> Consumer installment credit [totals outstanding] fall off rapidly during periods of severe business recession, owing to *the excess of* repayments over new credits granted.[10]

It is often said that what occurred in the Great Depression was a downwardly spiraling process. This NBER passage presents an essential element of this process that is important for understanding

9 Duncan M. Holthausen, Malcolm L. Merriam and Rolf Nugent, *The Volume of Consumer Installment Credit, 1929-38,* NBER, 1940. We sourced the book from FRASER, the digital archive maintained by the Federal Reserve Bank of St. Louis. The data in this study provided aggregated figures, but did not separate new and used cars financing.

10 NBER (1940), Summary of Findings, second page, unnumbered.

Table 12.3A

Monthly Totals of Installment Credit Sought and Granted, Repayments, Net Credit Change, and Total Outstanding for Dealers in New and Used Automobiles[1], 1928-30

($ million)

Month	Credit sought/granted	Repayments	Net credit change[2]	Total outstanding[3]
1928				
Jan	$84.2	$120.9	-$36.7	$684.4
Feb	102.7	119.7	-17.0	667.4
Mar	151.2	119.9	31.3	698.7
Apr	180.9	120.3	60.6	759.3
May	211.6	120.0	91.6	850.9
Jun	206.1	122.7	83.4	934.3
Jul	195.1	127.2	67.9	1,002.2
Aug	194.7	131.8	62.9	1,065.1
Sep	163.9	136.4	27.5	1,092.6
Oct	168.1	141.1	27.0	1,119.6
Nov	138.1	146.4	-8.3	1,111.3
Dec	118.6	151.5	-32.9	1,078.4
1929				
Jan	110.7	157.1	-46.4	1,032.0
Feb	132.5	159.3	-26.8	1,005.2
Mar	205.9	161.8	44.1	1,049.3
Apr	251.7	166.4	85.3	1,134.6
May	270.3	172.4	97.9	1,232.5
Jun	264.6	177.3	87.3	1,319.8
Jul	265.9	182.2	83.7	1,403.5
Aug	240.9	188.2	52.7	1,456.2
Sep	185.7	192.1	-6.4	1,449.8
Oct	190.7	194.0	-3.3	1,446.5
Nov	142.2	196.0	-53.8	1,392.7
Dec	121.2	196.4	-75.2	1,317.5
1930				
Jan	103.5	196.8	-93.3	1,224.2
Feb	120.0	196.2	-76.2	1,148.0
Mar	175.0	195.3	-20.3	1,127.7
Apr	207.3	192.8	14.5	1,142.2
May	164.2	189.3	-25.1	1,117.1
Jun	193.6	180.8	12.8	1,129.9
Jul	170.2	175.2	-5.0	1,124.9
Aug	146.8	167.6	-20.8	1,104.1
Sep	130.7	160.0	-29.3	1,074.8
Oct	118.7	155.5	-36.8	1,038.0
Nov	88.8	149.8	-61.0	977.0
Dec	96.8	145.5	-48.7	928.3

[1]Passenger cars only.

[2]Minus sign indicates decrease in net credit; otherwise an increase to be understood.

[3]End of month.

Source: "The Volume of Consumer Instalment Credit, 1929-1938," NBER, Feb 1940, Appendix A, pp. 9 & 10.

the dynamics of the 1929-33 period. We contend that the true impact of the plunge in credit use in favor of debt repayment in the auto

Table 12.3B

Monthly Totals of Installment Credit Sought and Granted, Repayments, Net Credit Change, and Total Outstanding for Dealers in New and Used Automobiles[1], 1931-33

($ million)

Month	Credit sought/granted	Repayments	Net credit change[2]	Total outstanding[3]
1931				
Jan	$76.4	$143.5	-$67.1	$861.2
Feb	81.9	141.3	-59.4	801.8
Mar	112.9	138.1	-25.2	776.6
Apr	138.2	132.9	5.3	781.9
May	133.5	127.1	6.4	788.3
Jun	127.6	124.3	3.3	791.6
Jul	117.3	118.8	-1.5	790.1
Aug	97.6	114.2	-16.6	773.5
Sep	83.6	110.0	-26.4	747.1
Oct	75.0	106.0	-31.0	716.1
Nov	60.2	102.3	-42.1	674.0
Dec	62.5	99.8	-37.3	636.7
1932				
Jan	48.1	96.9	-48.8	587.9
Feb	48.3	94.7	-46.4	541.5
Mar	55.2	92.1	-36.9	504.6
Apr	60.9	87.5	-26.6	478.0
May	63.1	81.2	-18.1	459.9
Jun	68.6	75.7	-7.1	452.8
Jul	48.2	71.0	-22.8	430.0
Aug	48.0	65.5	-17.5	412.5
Sep	41.6	61.6	-20.0	392.5
Oct	36.3	58.2	-21.9	370.6
Nov	29.8	55.1	-25.3	345.3
Dec	29.1	52.7	-23.6	321.7
1933				
Jan	39.4	50.0	-10.6	311.1
Feb	37.0	49.1	-12.1	299.0
Mar	42.5	48.2	-5.7	293.3
Apr	56.9	46.9	10.0	303.3
May	72.8	46.3	26.5	329.8
Jun	81.8	46.8	35.0	364.8
Jul	81.3	47.5	33.8	398.6
Aug	88.6	49.9	38.7	437.3
Sep	78.3	52.9	25.4	462.7
Oct	72.2	55.5	16.7	479.4
Nov	55.6	58.3	-2.7	476.7
Dec	42.2	60.2	-18.0	458.7

[1]Passenger cars only.

[2]Minus sign indicates decrease in net credit; otherwise an increase to be understood.

[3]End of month.

Source: "The Volume of Consumer Instalment Credit, 1929-1938," NBER, Feb 1940, Appendix A, pp. 9 & 10.

industry as well as elsewhere is what, in Noyes's words, "made violent downward readjustment inevitable." What a lawyer might call "the totality of the evidence" shows that what happened resulted from consumer reluctance to borrow rather than dealer reluctance to lend. Tables 12.3A, prior page, shows that as November and December 1929 sales of automobiles fell, repayment of monthly installment debt grew, and, as the months went by, the situation worsened.

Tables 12.3A and 12.3B (prior pages) present January 1928 through December 1933 statistics found in the NBER study's Appendix A (Table A-8) entitled "Monthly Totals of Installment Credit Granted, Repayments, Net Credit Change and Outstandings for Dealers in New and Used Automobiles, 1926-38."[11] The table's first data column presents new credit granted, the aggregate quantity lent by automobile dealers to finance new and used car sales in a particular month, followed by the monthly repayments of debt obligations that purchasers had incurred over the prior ten to twelve months—the lengths of the typical installment sale contracts. The third data column shows the net credit change, the difference between repayments made that month and new credit granted. Positive net credit change indicates that total outstanding credit grew. If net credit change was negative, repayments exceeded the credit granted, thus showing a drop in total credit outstanding. The final column of monthly total outstanding credit figures easily shows the downward directionality over the six-year period.

One of the ongoing missions of NBER is to designate the peaks and troughs of U.S. business cycles. Sometime after analyzing statistics of the period, NBER declared August 1929 as the peak of the expansion (really of the boom) that began in the late 1920s. Tables 12.3A and 12.3B confirms that the total outstanding automobile installment credit of $1,456 million for August 1929 was indeed the highest amount. Thereafter contraction ensued, throughout what we know of as the Great Depression. NBER declared March 1933 as the trough, or the end of the Great Depression, the same month

11 For clarity in Tables 12.3A and 12.3B, "outstanding" is substituted for "outstandings," as in "monthly totals outstandings" "average outstandings," etc. In addition, we have chosen to use the current spelling of installment with two l's, not one as appears in the 1940 tables.

Franklin Roosevelt was sworn in as President of the United States.

Tables 12.3A and 12.3B shows two periods of expansion. The first was the twenty months prior to the end of August 1929 of which fourteen showed positive net credit change, while six months were negative. During this first period, total credit outstanding rose 101.9% from $721.1 million at the end of 1927 to $1,456.2 million at August peak.[12] Clearly this was a boom period. The second period of expansion shown in Table 12.3B ran nine months from April through December 1933, when seven of the nine months showed positive net credit change. During this second period total credit outstanding rose 56.4% from $293.3 million at the end of March 1933 to $458.7 million at year end.

Automobile sales, then, as now, were a strongly seasonal business. Sales were strongest from March to August and slowest in the winter. Even in the prosperous full year 1928, there were four months with a combined negative net credit change of -$94.9 million: January, February, November and December. Anticipated seasonality aside, the total outstanding at the end of 1928 was $1,078.4 million, up 49.5% or $357.3 million from $721.1 million at the end of the recession year of 1927.[13] The strongest sales in 1928 were recorded in the combined spring months of April, May and June, an aggregate net credit gain of $235.6 million. In 1929, the same three months accounted for a positive net credit change of $270.5 million.

We can readily see in Tables 12.3A and 12.3B that the period from the end of August 1929 to the end of March 1933—43 months from peak to trough—was *strongly contractionary.* During that period, total credit outstanding dropped 79.9% or $1,162.9 million, from $1,456.2 million at the end of August 1929 to $293.3 million at the end of March 1933. Only five months in this entire period showed positive net credit change, all of which were during normally strong sales periods: April, May and June in both 1930 and 1931. Notably, while the three combined spring months of 1929 produced that positive net credit change of $270.5 million, net

12 NBER (1940), p. 9 of Appendix A.

13 Ibid.

credit change was only \$2.2 million in the combined three spring months of 1930 and went up to \$15.0 million in 1931 but then dipped -\$51.8 million in 1932.

Credit granted to buy automobiles in the peak month of August 1929 was \$240.9 million. Following that peak month, contraction developed and began to worsen, with credit granted falling to \$185.7 million in September and \$190.7 million in October. Meanwhile, contractual repayment requirements, which had been established in the twelve earlier months of boom, grew through January 1930, then turned downwards and dropped consistently month-by-month until March 1933. Repayment requirements were \$192.1 million in September 1929 and \$194.0 million in October. This meant that and net credit changes became negative to the tune of -\$6.4 million in September and -\$3.3 million in October. We consider these small negative numbers as harbingers of the Crash which we add to the list of other hints and forewarnings and cautionary signs.

The above provides a template for performing a bottom up analysis. In Tables 12.3A and 12.3B, for each month, the only new column of data was the monthly amount of credit granted. To arrive at repayments in any month, we looked at the credit terms (including, obviously, interest) entered into by automobile buyers *in earlier months*. Net credit change, as we described, was that month's repayments of prior contracts deducted from new credit granted. (Total credit granted, of course, was a direct function of how many potential customers walked into dealers' showrooms and decided to buy on credit.)[14]

After 1929, however, this trend—diminishing new credit granted paired with repayments that were larger than the credit granted—was obvious, and we considered the statistics in Tables 12.3A and 12.3B to validate our first proposition that sometime between the lead-up to the Crash and early 1930, ordinary Amer-

14 We saw no evidence in the trade press of the time that dealers or their sales staffs were turning customers away for any reason, certainly not for lack of creditworthiness, as we mentioned earlier. But we also see no suggestion that those who were wiped out in the Crash or were seriously damaged were visiting showrooms.

icans, in aggregate, shifted from adding more each month to the retail installment debts they owed to repaying those debts month-by-month. Along with the negative net credit changes in September and October 1929 as omens of a crash, the 80% drop in total credit outstanding from the end of August 1929 to the end of March 1933 is more than an adequate validation of indebted car owners' financial behavior after the Crash.

As to our second proposition of the direct effects of the Crash, we sought to validate that, while the U.S. was heading into recession in the autumn of 1929, it was the shock and magnitude of the Crash that propelled the country into the Great Depression. As Noyes observed, "the panic of 1929 brought sudden recognition of the economic realities." Here, too, the statistics supported our assumption. While the net credit change statistics totaled -$9.7 million in September and October, the net credit change statistics plummeted after the Crash to a total -$129.0 million in November and December, and, as we will see shortly, this began our nation's descent into the Great Depression.

It is critical to understand the broader implications of the data in Tables 12.3A and 12.3B. Repayment of debt occurred. Fewer and fewer automobiles were sold. As a result, fewer and fewer automobiles were assembled. Employment declined all along the automobile production chain (e.g., fewer spark plugs ordered). Worker income declined along with consumption. And this contractionary process did not end until March 1933 when, as mentioned above, nearly 80% of the automotive installment debt outstanding at the August 1929 peak had been repaid.

When Did the Great Depression Begin?

To answer this question, we first looked for harbingers of the Crash beyond the ongoing growth in speculation. We saw those small negative automobile dealer net credit change numbers shown in Table 12.3A totaling -$9.7 million for September and October 1929 as just such harbingers. And then, too, there was what was going on in the stock market.

History records the Crash as beginning shortly after the opening bell of Black Thursday, October 24, as waves of sell orders engulfed the NYSE. Most of those waves were thought to result from unfulfilled margin calls sent out by brokers the previous evening. On the 24th, the ticker tape was quickly overwhelmed and fell further behind what was actually happening. Chaos and panic ensued as customers' rooms around the country learned that stock prices on the Exchange floor, reported periodically on the bond tape, were far below the prices shown on the ticker tape. The fearful, shocked reactions led to significant distressed selling which spread to other markets such as those for commodities and foreign exchange. Ruthless liquidation gripped markets—and everyone involved in them—all across the U.S. History records the Crash as ending on Black Tuesday, October 29 when the NYSE closed in mid-afternoon, but the lagging ticker continued reporting stock transactions until early evening. The shock of the Crash, reported as front-page news by newspapers throughout the nation and the world, was pervasive. Stock prices continued to fall until November 13.

As to the financial magnitude of the Crash, the NYSE reported the total dollar value of all listed stocks as of the first of each month as seen in Table 10.1. The value of all listed NYSE stocks in 1929 fell in the following amounts:

- September 1 to October 1 -$2.5 billion
- October 1 to November 1 -$15.3 billion
- November 1 to December 1 -$8.2 billion

Thus, between September 1—the NYSE high was on September 3—and December 1, the value of all listed stocks fell $-26.1 billion. For perspective, this represented 25.2% of the 1929 GNP of $103.4 billion. However, this only measured the fall in the value of stocks listed on the NYSE. To estimate the total magnitude of the Crash, we need to take into account the decline in the value of stocks traded on other exchanges and in the value of commodities, as well as the loss in the value of properties, such as houses sold or mortgaged to meet margin calls.

Reflecting on the immediate impact once Crash week had passed in late October, American historians, including Noyes, Galbraith, Frederick Lewis Allen and others, observed that stock market illusions were punctured, and reality appeared suddenly to have begun breaking through. Indeed, the statistics certainly suggest that reality had broken through to automobile buyers. It became evident to us that the shock and magnitude of the Crash propelled the U.S. into the Great Depression when, in November and December 1929, the net credit change statistics for automobile dealers fell a total of -$129.0 million, and total credit outstanding extended by automobile dealers to their customers declined -8.9%. Clearly in the immediate wake of the Crash, fewer Americans bought automobiles on credit, and debt repayments came to exceed credit granted, a condition that prevailed. No longer was the country headed for just a recession. These drops *established the nation's path of descent into the Great Depression.*

At the end of February 1930, a mere two months later, the net credit change in automobile credit sales statistics were down an additional -$169.5 million from the December 1929 decline of -$129.0 million. Clearly downward momentum was accelerating. This brought total credit outstanding down -20.8% or -$298.5 million in the four months from just after the Crash (i.e., the end of the day, October 30, 1929). By that time, *the nation was firmly committed to that descent.*

Thus, it is our view that the nation was *fully into the Great Depression by the second quarter of 1930* when the net credit change in automobile installment sales was only $2.2 million in contrast with the second quarter of 1929 when the net credit change was a robust $270.5 million. On the basis of these automobile installment sales statistics, we consider that the U.S. was thoroughly engaged in the Great Depression by May 1930—a month of normally brisk sales—when the net credit change was -$25.1 million.

Longer term, averaging the monthly statistics in Tables 12.3A and 12.3B for 1930 to the end of 1932 confirms the ongoing monthly declines in outstanding automotive credit:

- 1930: -$32.4 million (-2.5% of total outstanding at the end of 1929)

- 1931: -$31.4 million (- 3.4% of total outstanding at the end of 1930)

- 1932: -$26.3 million (-4.1% of total outstanding at the end of 1931)

Each year of the Great Depression, total outstanding aggregate installment credit for automobile financing fell by a greater percentage than the prior year, reflecting two Depression-era trends: 1) fall in consumption and 2) diligent repayment of consumer indebtedness.

One dramatic way of highlighting these conclusions is to contrast two key seven-month periods, seasonally including the strongest sales months of the year for automobiles. Tables 12.3A and 12.3B confirms that in the seven-month period of *contraction,* total credit outstanding *fell* 23.4% or -$339.1 million from $1,456.2 million at the end of August 1929 to $1,117.1 million at the end of May 1930. By contrast, in the year earlier seven-month period of expansion, total credit outstanding rose 13.4% or $167 million from $1,065.1 million at the end of August 1928 to $1,232.5 million at the end of May 1929. Measuring the same seven months (August of one year to May of the next) between these two extraordinarily different years, shows a definite shift from expansion to contraction. In fact, it was a disastrous -$0.5 billion decline— from a $167 million rise to a -$339 million drop—that caused a painful reversal for the automotive industry with much broader implications for the nation.

Expanded Statistics on Installment Sales Strengthen These Conclusions.

Other than the auto dealer segment, which as we said earlier comprised more than half of the total volume of installment credit sales, the 1940 NBER study also looked more broadly at retail establishments. Tables 12.4A and 12.4B that follow on the next two pagess (formatted like Tables 12.3A and 12.3B) add to the automobile statistics separate data for each of four different retailing groups: department stores, furniture stores, household appliance stores and jewelry stores. (Radio sets were included in the household appliance group.)

In the period of the Great Depression, the NBER study indicated that 60% of automobile sales, 40% to 50% of furniture and household appliance store sales, just under 20% of jewelry sales and just under 10% of department store sales were financed with installment loans.[15] The statistics in Tables 12.4A and 12.4B validated both our first proposition about Crash-induced debt repayment and our second proposition that it was the shock and magnitude of the Crash that propelled the country into the Great Depression.

Table 12.5 (on page 328) compares statistics for automobile dealers from Tables 12.3A and 12.3B with corresponding statistics for NBER's five retailing groups taken from Tables 12.4A and 12.4B. Our two propositions showed up in relation to the five retail groups as they did in the automobile dealers' statistics. Even given some holiday seasonality, the data reflected the shock and magnitude of the Crash. The net credit change numbers in November and December 1929 were both negative and totaled -$69.0 million. This sum indicates that installment credit borrowers within the five retail categories were reducing purchases and repaying their loans in both post-Crash months. Then the first two months in 1930 resulted in an additional -$247.5 million for those five categories that, combined with the reduction in automobile installment credit, committed the nation to

15 Seasonality affected several of the five retail groups. Jewelry, furniture and department stores all experienced high levels of sales each year in December.

Table 12.4A

Monthly Totals of Installment Credit Sought and Granted, Repayments, Net Credit Change, and Total Outstanding for Five Types of Retail Establishments Combined[1], 1929-1931

($ million)

Month	Credit sought/granted	Repayments	Net credit change[2]	Total outstanding[3]
1929				
Jan	$200.8	$280.7	-$79.9	$2,029.9
Feb	234.9	283.4	-48.5	1,981.4
Mar	331.2	286.5	44.7	2,026.1
Apr	402.0	292.0	110.0	2,136.1
May	426.2	298.8	127.4	2,263.5
Jun	410.9	304.5	106.4	2,369.9
Jul	387.5	310.1	77.4	2,447.3
Aug	374.4	316.8	57.6	2,504.9
Sep	319.5	321.3	-1.8	2,503.1
Oct	331.3	323.6	7.7	2,510.8
Nov	274.3	325.9	-51.6	2,459.2
Dec	308.8	326.2	-17.4	2,441.8
1930				
Jan	190.4	326.9	-136.5	2,305.3
Feb	214.9	325.9	-111.0	2,194.3
Mar	282.8	324.1	-41.3	2,153.0
Apr	339.5	320.2	19.3	2,172.3
May	296.0	315.1	-19.1	2,153.2
Jun	313.3	304.9	8.4	2,161.6
Jul	268.7	296.8	-28.1	2,133.5
Aug	255.2	287.4	-32.2	2,101.3
Sep	240.1	278.2	-38.1	2,063.2
Oct	233.0	271.9	-38.9	2,024.3
Nov	196.7	264.1	-67.4	1,956.9
Dec	247.3	258.0	-10.7	1,946.2
1931				
Jan	148.3	253.5	-105.2	1,841.0
Feb	160.2	250.2	-90.0	1,751.0
Mar	205.1	245.7	-40.6	1,710.4
Apr	243.1	239.6	3.5	1,713.9
May	237.8	232.1	5.7	1,719.6
Jun	222.0	227.4	-5.4	1,714.2
Jul	193.7	220.2	-26.5	1,687.7
Aug	181.0	214.2	-33.2	1,654.5
Sep	167.0	208.0	-41.0	1,613.5
Oct	161.9	202.2	-40.3	1,573.2
Nov	138.9	196.5	-57.6	1,515.6
Dec	175.0	191.7	-16.7	1,498.9

[1]Includes dealers in new and used (passenger) automobiles, department stores, furniture stores, household appliance stores and jewelry stores.

[2]Minus sign indicates decrease in net credit; otherwise an increase to be understood.

[3]End of month.

Source: "The Volume of Consumer Instalment Credit, 1929-38," NBER, Feb 1940, Appendix A, p. 2.

Table 12.4B

Monthly Totals of Installment Credit Sought and Granted, Repayments, Net Credit Change, and Total Outstanding for Five Types of Retail Establishments Combined[1], 1932-1934

($ million)

Month	Credit sought/granted	Repayments	Net credit change[2]	Total outstanding[3]
1932				
Jan	$90.2	$186.3	-$96.1	$1,402.8
Feb	95.9	181.9	-86.0	1,316.8
Mar	108.1	176.8	-68.7	1,248.1
Apr	124.3	169.7	-45.4	1,202.7
May	122.8	160.3	-37.5	1,165.2
Jun	124.4	151.9	-27.5	1,137.7
Jul	83.4	144.3	-60.9	1,076.8
Aug	95.9	136.1	-40.2	1,036.6
Sep	93.8	129.8	-36.0	1,000.6
Oct	93.7	123.9	-30.2	970.4
Nov	80.7	118.4	-37.7	932.7
Dec	96.8	113.8	-17.0	915.7
1933				
Jan	70.0	107.8	-37.8	877.9
Feb	69.6	106.0	-36.4	841.5
Mar	82.3	103.7	-21.4	820.1
Apr	113.1	101.4	11.7	831.8
May	140.8	100.4	40.4	872.2
Jun	147.1	101.2	45.9	918.1
Jul	130.9	102.1	28.8	946.9
Aug	157.1	105.3	51.8	998.7
Sep	141.5	109.5	32.0	1,030.7
Oct	135.4	112.7	22.7	1,053.4
Nov	113.3	115.6	-2.3	1,051.1
Dec	124.9	117.5	7.4	1,058.5
1934				
Jan	82.1	119.4	-37.3	1,021.2
Feb	105.5	119.7	-14.2	1,007.0
Mar	140.0	121.9	18.1	1,025.1
Apr	173.9	125.8	48.1	1,073.2
May	190.2	130.3	59.9	1,133.1
Jun	178.7	134.4	44.3	1,177.4
Jul	160.9	136.7	24.2	1,201.6
Aug	162.0	139.1	22.9	1,224.5
Sep	135.9	140.3	-4.4	1,220.1
Oct	150.2	140.2	10.0	1,230.1
Nov	130.4	141.6	-11.2	1,218.9
Dec	152.1	143.0	9.1	1,228.0

[1]Includes dealers in new and used (passenger) automobiles, department stores, furniture stores, household appliance stores and jewelry stores.

[2]Minus sign indicates decrease in net credit; otherwise an increase to be understood.

[3]End of month.

Source: "The Volume of Consumer Instalment Credit, 1929-38," NBER, Feb 1940, Appendix A, p. 2.

the descent into the Great Depression. Things grew rapidly worse. In the second quarter of 1930 only a paltry $8.6 million in credit was granted in the five retailing groups compared with $343.8 million in the second quarter of 1929.

Table 12.5				
Net Credit Change and Monthly Total Installment Credit Outstanding ($ million)				
Month	Five Retailing Groups (Table A-2)		Automobile Dealers (Table A-8)	
1929	Net	Total	Net	Total
Sept	-$1.8	$2,503.1	-$6.4	$1,449.8
Oct	7.7	2,510.8	-3.3	1,446.5
Nov	-51.6	2,459.2	-53.8	1,392.7
Dec	-17.4	2,441.8	-75.2	1,317.5
1930				
Jan	-136.5	2,305.3	-93.3	1,224.2
Feb	-111.0	2,194.3	-76.2	1,148.0
Mar	-41.3	2,153.0	-20.3	1,127.7
Apr	19.3	2,172.3	14.5	1,142.2
May	-19.1	2,153.2	-25.1	1,117.1
Jun	8.4	2,161.6	12.8	1,129.9

[1]End of Month.

Source: "The Volume of Consumer Instalment Credit, 1929-1938," NBER, Feb 1940, pp. 2 & 9, Appendix A.

Both the net credit change from Tables 12.4A and 12.4B of -$19.1 million in May 1930 for retail establishments alone and the data in Table 12.5 (above) for automobile dealers plus the five retailing groups reinforce our pick of May 1930 as the month when the Great Depression was fully operative. *It took the nation no more than seven months from the beginning of the descent into the Great*

Depression in November 1929 to reach the point where the Great Depression was fully operative.

Historians' Views of the 1929 Crash and the Great Depression

Most historians have treated the 1929 Crash as a set of events that began on October 24 and ended on October, 29, though not all agree. William K. Klingaman, for example, has taken the position that the 1929 Crash really began in September and ended in November:

> A close examination of the historical evidence reveals that the collapse of the fabled bull market of the 1920s actually began in earnest during the first week of September, when the stock market embarked upon a long, agonizing slide that accelerated with breathtaking speed in the second half of October, plunging thousands of Americans into the depths of despair before it finally ground to a halt in the middle of November, leaving the richest country in the world exhausted, vulnerable, and very frightened, on the brink of the Great Depression. [16]

In his capacity as Chairman of the International Acceptance Bank, Paul M. Warburg, described by Noyes as making "the most accurate prediction made in that strange era," wrote from the viewpoint of an historian in the institution's 1928 annual report: [17]

> History, which has a painful way of repeating itself, has taught mankind that speculative over-expansion invariably ends in over-contraction and distress.... If orgies of

16 Klingaman (1989), p. 229.

17 Noyes (1938), p. 324.

> unrestrained speculation are permitted to spread too far, however, the ultimate collapse is certain not only to affect the speculators themselves, but also to bring about a general depression involving the entire country.[18]

Considering past events, Warburg also described the inflationary impact of speculation:

> From the economic lessons taught by the aftermath of the Great War, we learned that the excessive creation of money or bank credit without an equivalent production of assets spells inflation. Yet the public mind does not appear to realize that the creation of an inflated purchasing power is not a government monopoly.[19]

Clearly, Warburg considered that stock portfolios held by speculators constituted "an inflated purchasing power." We concur, as we believe Charles Persons would, and we are confident speculators would have agreed, perhaps even jubilantly. Not only did speculators have an inflated purchasing power, they were inflating it further by driving stock prices up. Certainly, the speculators thought they were getting rich. To us, this says that Warburg considered speculation to be *a monetary phenomenon.* If so, we agree.

Instead of predicting a crash, Warburg doubtless hoped his warnings would galvanize the Fed, President Hoover and Congress to take appropriate actions to rein in speculation. The "ultimate collapse" that he predicted was indeed of "speculative over-expansion." Unfortunately, as his publicly expressed warning fell on unresponsive ears, speculative over-expansion, having resumed late in 1929, only collapsed utterly in June 1930 as the "Little Bull Market" ended. Based on this logic, our nation was certainly firmly into the Great Depression by June or July of 1930.

---

18 *Commercial & Financial Chronicle,* March 9, 1929, p. 1444.

19 Ibid.

"Sudden and Violent Change"

As to the business investment side of the equation, as we read in Chapter 3, Keynes spoke these words in his Chicago lectures in 1931:

> I shall concentrate on the variability of the rate of investment. For that is, in fact, the element in the economic situation which is capable of sudden and violent change. [I]t is out of the disequilibriums of savings and investment, and of nothing else, that the fluctuations of profits, of output, and of employment are generated.[20]

Keynes was quite entitled to a focus on investment in his lectures since a drop in business investment likely began slowly, perhaps as early as the spring of 1929, as we suggested in our examination of the inverted yield curve in Chapter 8 (Table 8.1). We certainly consider the Crash to have greatly accelerated this drop in business investment. However, as to the "sudden and violent change" Keynes spoke of and attributed to the business sector, there is more to say.

What came about almost immediately was the rapid and dramatic reversal in the willingness of Americans to keep accepting and bearing the risks of debt. This reluctance to take on more debt, as we have said, sharply impacted consumption and, inevitably, business.

An observation made by Nobel laureate Lawrence Klein in his book, *The Keynesian Revolution,* provides useful commentary regarding this sea change:

> I want to comment on the more general Keynesian philosophical outlook on consumption. It is an implicit supposition in Keynesian economics, especially the business-cycle aspects, that capital formation is volatile (impulsive, dynamic, variable), while consumption is passive (regular, stable, steady). Consumption is seen as adjusting to the macro-environment that is created by investment. This is not to say that consump-

20 *CW of JMK, Vol. XII,* 1973, pp. 354-5.

> tion remains constant, but that the consumption function does. Consumption moves along the stable function.... The volatility of consumer durables and spending on luxuries... have been large enough to make consumption as a whole volatile. The history of the postwar economy, first in United States, then in western Europe, and then in Japan, is grossly misunderstood if one fails to appreciate the autonomous role of consumption.... The Keynesian role of consumption is, however, outmoded.[21]

We include these comments by Keynes and Klein in order to make it clear not just that consumption can shift independently of business investment, but also, contrary to Klein's assertion, that, in fact, the consumption function does *not* "remain constant." As Tables 12.3A and 12.3B shows, *consumer demand indeed shifted suddenly and truly dramatically in November and December 1929.* The growing consumption as evidenced by the positive net credit change in the period of 1928 through August 1929 shifted, no less aggressively, to the making of debt repayments by foregoing consumption, as reflected, once again, in the negative net credit change in the immediate aftermath of the Crash all the way through March 1933.

Describing the Mood of the Times

In *The Deflation of 1930*, we will devote much attention to the business sector. However, our attention in this chapter remains on the sudden change in sentiment or mood which affected all corners of society almost immediately in and following the week of the Crash. We turn to several other valued voices to help us do that before introducing our Cast of Characters, our forthcoming breakdown of Americans into categories that highlight their states of mind. Several respected writers whom we quote amply throughout *How the Crash Caused* have memorably described the moods and motivations of Americans overall during this period.

---

21 Klein (1966), pp. 202-3.

We start—out of chronological order—with John Kenneth Galbraith, who in his classic 1954 *The Great Crash 1929* offered the following observations about the tenor of the times and especially about segments of society at large, including those who went from indifference to Wall Street happenings before the epidemic of speculation to becoming obsessed with what was going on. We revisit Galbraith's description from Chapter 8:

> By the summer of 1929 the market not only dominated the news. It also dominated the culture. That *recherché* minority which at other times has acknowledged its interest in St. Thomas Aquinas, Proust, psychoanalysis, and psychosomatic medicine then spoke of United Corporation, United Founders, and Steel. Only the most aggressive of the eccentrics maintained their detachment from the market and their interest in auto suggestion or communism. Main Street had always had one citizen who could speak knowingly about buying or selling stocks. Now he became an oracle.[22]

We interpret Galbraith's comments about this enthusiastic, one might say giddy mood, as applying to just about anyone paying attention to what was going on and then freely offered opinions, regardless of expertise or profession. By late 1929, Wall Street had been the hot topic for some time. About that excessively zealous mood, Galbraith continued:

> We do not know why a great speculative orgy occurred in 1928 and 1929. The long accepted explanation that credit was easy and so people were impelled to borrow money to buy common stocks on margin is obviously nonsense. On numerous occasions before and since credit has been easy, and there has been no speculation whatever. Furthermore, much of 1928 and 1929 speculation occurred on money borrowed at interest rates which for years before, and in any periods since, would have been considered exceptionally astringent.

22 Galbraith (1954), p. 74.

> Money, by the ordinary tests, was tight in the late twenties. Far more important than rate of interest and the supply of credit is the *mood.* Speculation on a large scale requires a pervasive sense of confidence and optimism that ordinary people were meant to be rich. People must also have faith in the good intentions and even in the benevolence of others, for it is by the agency of others that they will get rich....[A] feeling of trust is essential for a boom. When people are cautious, questioning, misanthropic, suspicious, or mean, they are immune to speculative enthusiasm. Speculation... is most likely to break out after a substantial period of prosperity.... Finally, a speculative outbreak has a greater or less immunizing effect. The ensuing collapse automatically destroys the very *mood* speculation requires.[23] (Galbraith's emphasis)

Stepping backwards in time, Noyes, in nearly contemporary comments from earlier in this chapter, spoke of "ill-fated Stock Exchange illusions," how talk ended of the New Economic Era as tremors of doubt hit Wall Street. From the perspective of this top contemporary financial editor, a lot of people, especially many supposedly in the know about Wall Street, were experiencing a dramatic and rapidly changing attitude.

Another economist who spoke of mood was Irving Fisher. In his book, *Booms and Depressions,* published in 1932, he referred to the psychological factor affecting financial market prices and the market behavior of individuals given their "optimism and pessimism" or "loss of confidence."[24] For example:

> Hoarding is a slowing of the currency turnover of the extremist kind. It is the supreme manifestation of popular

---

23 Galbraith (1954), pp. 169-71.

24 Fisher (1932), pp. 13, 32, 34, 179.

moods in a depression.[25]

> The first touch liquidation has a depressing effect on moods; and this first approach of the pessimistic mood retards circulation.... Anything which causes a slight revulsion of mood may be the last straw.[26]

While Galbraith and Fisher wrote of people in general and Noyes referred to those in the know financially, Peter Temin zeroed in on one of our Cast of Characters, as we shall see shortly—businessmen. According to Temin, business executives facing post-Crash realities lost confidence and made decisions:

> The large fall in consumption in 1930, deriving from a variety of diverse and as yet still incompletely delineated sources, prevented recovery in that year. Goods that could not be sold were not produced. The fall in aggregate demand spread throughout the economy. And as the fall of 1930 wore on and business did not recover, as might have been expected from observation of previous reductions in business activity in the twentieth century, *businessmen lost the confidence that underlies private investment.* The economy continued to decline.[27] (emphasis ours)

In addition, Temin considered the views of media, government officials and "prominent people" who, from late 1929 and for awhile onwards, remained staunchly, even stubbornly, optimistic and, to rephrase Temin, appeared to deny the obvious. About this united public front that must have seemed disingenuous, even at the time, Temin wrote:

> Newspapers in late 1929 were full of reassuring statements by prominent people. The Federal Reserve board, Alfred P

25 Ibid., p. 35.

26 Ibid., p. 40.

27 Temin (1976), p. 172.

Sloan, Jr., and many others, saw no connection between the stock-market crash and business conditions in November 1929....

But this evidence is suspect. For while all the economic news in late 1929 appears to be positive, there was an enormous increase in these reassuring statements.... Is this not evidence that what was once assured was now in question? Should positive statements be taken at face value or as attempts to deny the obvious?

The business press did not report business as usual, but it did not foresee disaster either. The picture that businessmen shared among themselves in late 1929 was one of a mild decline in business activity....By the middle of December the editors [of *Business Week*] could announce, "We feel that, so far as industrial activity is concerned, the worse will be over in the next six weeks."

The industry forecasts that appeared through the last quarter of 1929 were in the same vein as these comments about the aggregate volume of business. Business in various lines was expected to be worse than 1929, which was a very good year, but not worse than 1928, which was hardly a bad one. The explicit forecasts that appeared at the start of 1930 compared the expected business conditions in this year favorably with 1927 and about evenly with 1928.

But these forecasts were accompanied by expressions of doubt. There were uncertainties in the situation that exceeded the uncertainty implicit in any prediction of the future.[28]

---

28 Temin (1976), pp. 76-7.

Oh Yeah?

In 1931 Viking published a slim, red cloth-covered volume of sixty-four pages called, evocatively, *Oh Yeah?*. Compiled by a journalist named Edward J. Angly, *Oh Yeah?* was a compendium of carefully selected, publicly available quotes made between 1927 and 1931 by contemporary leaders, including President Hoover, Wall Street movers and shakers, businessmen, economists, academicians and journalists that served to lay bare the woeful incongruousness of the public pronouncements at the time.

Angly's book, widely cited though now out of print, laid it all out for everyone to read — the delusions, outright lies, mistakes, misdirection, manipulation. It's not hard to imagine how updated versions of *Oh Yeah?* covering more recent financial crises might have been as startling as this now difficult-to-find book.

Angly, a New Yorker born in 1890, was a graduate of the University of Texas and a World War II war correspondent. While *Oh Yeah!* seems to be his main legacy, Angly must have had a wicked sense of humor because the book's selections were intended to amuse, shock and infuriate in that measured tongue-in-cheek way often used by journalists.

Our interest in this book grew over time because many who wrote about the Crash and Great Depression, whether contemporaneous or later, used quotes from the book to illustrate how the pundits of the day came out with a steady stream of optimistic calmatives intending to allay public fears about the state of the economy and the stock market. Unable to find a used copy to purchase, we tracked it down in a library. What follows are some sample quotes from *Oh Yeah?*:

Herbert Hoover: "The fundamental business of the country, that is production and distribution of commodities, is on a sound and prosperous basis."—October 25, 1929.

John D. Rockefeller, Sr.: "Believing that fundamental conditions of the country are sound and that there is nothing in the business situation to warrant the destruction of values that has taken place on the exchanges during the past week, my son and I have for some days been purchasing sound common stocks. We are continuing and will continue our purchases in substantial amounts at levels which we believe represent sound investment values."—October 30, 1929

Stuart Chase, Economist: "We probably have three more years of prosperity ahead of us before we enter the cyclic tailspin which has occurred in the eleventh year of each of the four great previous periods of commercial prosperity."—November 1, 1929

Monthly Review, National City Bank: "There are no great failures nor are there likely to be."—December 2, 1929

E. G. Biechler, Frigidaire: "Following my visits to a number of cities in the last sixty days I have reached the conclusion that this is going to be a good business year."—January 1, 1930

Dr. Julius Klein, Assistant Secretary of Commerce: The stock market crash affected approximately only 1,000,000 persons, the speculative element."—January 10, 1930

Herbert Hoover: "While the crash only took place six months ago, I am convinced we have now passed the worst and with continued unity of effort we shall rapidly recover. There is one certainty of the future of a people of the resources, intelligence and character of the people of the United States—that is, prosperity." (address at annual dinner of the U.S. Chamber of Commerce)—May 1, 1930

Alfred P. Sloan, Jr., General Motors Co.: "I see no reason why 1931 should not be an extremely good year."—November 1930

Robert P. Lamont, Secretary of Commerce: "We have already weathered the worst of the storm and signs of stability and recovery are already appearing."—December 6, 1930

How Does our Estimate of "Beginning in May 1930" Compare with The Forecasts?

In contrast to the persistent cheer-leading of national leaders, the statistics reveal public reticence. We saw in Tables 12.3A and 12.3B (pages 314-15) that automobile installment sales statistics showed a barely positive $2.2 million in the total net credit change in the second quarter of 1930, comparing most unfavorably with the enthusiastically positive $270.5 million in the second quarter of 1929. Comparison with the second quarter of 1928, when the net credit change was $235.6 million, is almost equally unfavorable. The NBER study also included positive net credit change statistics for 1926 and 1927. In the second quarter of 1926, net credit change was $185.4 million, and despite the 1927 recession, the second quarter statistics were still a positive $70.0 million.

Up to March 1933, potential automobile buyers may have entered dealers' showrooms, but they didn't drive out of the lot with shiny new cars or installment sales contracts anywhere near the scale of the 1920s. Installment sales fell consistently as potential buyers chose to buy a steadily diminishing number of automobiles — new or used — and instead used available cash to pay back their debts. About the factor of consumer demand, the statistics in Tables 12.3A and 12.3B and tell a sorrowful story.

Professor Temin, who likely chuckled his way through *Oh, Yeah?*, brought in Frederick ("Fred" to those, like Temin, who knew him) Lewis Allen to reinforce Temin's point about the shift in people's expectations or mood in the wake of the Crash:

> The problem of hindsight is apparent even by 1931. Fred Allen, writing *Only Yesterday* in the year, betrayed by his title how profoundly he thought the world had changed since late October 1929. The stock-market crash was for him the dividing point between unbounded optimism and equally uncontainable pessimism, and he took it as a matter of course everyone in 1929 saw the significance of these events that he could see in 1931.[29]

As Temin implied, what was actually happening as the weeks and months dragged on was a far more complicated phenomenon than even intelligent and thoughtful commentators could grasp, regardless of their chronological vantage points.[30] Since this Temin quote mentions Allen's classic *Only Yesterday: An Informal History of the 1920's*, we add in what Allen himself called the "state of mind" (to us, synonymous with "mood") of the culture immediately after the Crash, offering as a backdrop and, for perspective, the blunt realities:

> The *New York Times* averages for fifty leading stocks had been almost cut in half, falling from a high of 311.90 in

29 Ibid., pp. 74-5.

30 We regret not being able to share our work with Messrs. Noyes and Galbraith to help with the questions, and we wholeheartedly acknowledge and thank Professor Temin for his efforts and share this work with him with great respect and humility.

> September to a low of 164.43 on November 13th; and the *Times* averages for twenty-five leading industrials had fared still worse, diving from 469.49 to 220.95.
>
> The Big Bull Market was dead. Billions of dollars' worth of profits—and paper profits—had disappeared. The grocer, the window-cleaner, and the seamstress had lost their capital. In every town there were families which had suddenly dropped from showy affluence into debt. Investors who had dreamed of retiring to live on their fortunes now found themselves back once more at the very beginning of the long road to riches. Day by day the newspapers printed the grim reports of suicides...
>
> Prosperity is more than an economic condition; it is a state of mind. The Big Bull Market had been more than the climax of a business cycle; it had been the climax of a cycle in American mass thinking and mass emotion.[31]

Allen's book was an immediate best-seller when it came out in 1931, and we believe he completed his highly readable and informative work in June 1931, a mere twenty months after the Crash ended.[32] His words show that his almost contemporaneous conclusions comported with those of Noyes as to how quickly expectations changed in late 1929. We add that Allen was writing as an historian and cultural commentator rather than as an industry forecaster or market influencer, such as those whom Temin quoted earlier and Angly gathered in *Oh Yeah*?

---

31 Frederick Lewis Allen, *Only Yesterday*, John Wiley & Sons, Inc., 1931, pp. 255-6.

32 Ibid., pp. 311-5. In his four-page "Source and Obligations" section, Allen thanked a great many people and institutions. He must have compared notes very widely. He dated his thanks June 1931, likely as he turned his manuscript over to John Wiley & Sons for publication.

Our Cast of Characters Helps Provide Answers

Going beyond these generalized comments from respected writers, we bring *How the Crash Caused* to a close and simultaneously set the stage for the second volume by introducing our Cast of Characters. This Cast of Characters helped us discern the distinct perspectives of the different participants in these dramatic events. It is in the nuances that we came to see how drastic changes in mood altered behavior in each group of individuals as they contended—from their perspectives—with the effects of the Crash and its aftermath in their lives. As they witnessed what was happening at work and with family members, friends, neighbors and others in their community whom they knew and cared about, their perspective quickly changed. Their views—and moods—also depended on how they dealt with rumors, the national and local news they read and what they heard politicians and influential people say on the radio as they translated such macro views into the microeconomic language pertinent to their individual circumstances.

It was with the deep desire to understand better what Allen called "American mass thinking and mass emotion" that we sought to develop a helpful framework for finding answers to longstanding questions of the sort on which economists have frequently reflected. Professor Temin in *Did Monetary Forces*, for example, asked, "Did the stock of money fall because of a fall in the supply or a fall in the demand?"[33] In economists' terms, was there a shift *along* the supply curve or *in* the supply curve? Was there a shift *along* the demand curve or *in* the demand curve? In layman's terms, did factories stop making or did people stop buying? In attempting to answer these long-pondered questions, we made use of Temin's examination of what he called expectations, states of mind (like Allen) and motivations to create our Cast of Characters. Surveying American society, we identified twelve categories of individuals, each with particular

33 Temin (1976), p. 96; discussed in Chapter 4.

concerns. This breakdown enabled us to get a handle on these impacted constituents and helped us gain more understanding about the breadth of the Crash's impact.

We describe our Cast of Characters and their behavior in two consecutive time periods: 1) as the Crash hit home and 2) in late 1929 into early 1930. What follows is an overview of where they likely found themselves during the first time period. We have ranked them generally in a declining order based on our sense of the intensity of their response to the Crash and the degree to which they and their circumstances impelled them to change course in November 1929

• **Repentant Ex-Speculators (post-Crash).** This was by far the unhappiest group of people. Just weeks before November 1929, many considered themselves well-to-do, even comfortably rich. Those unable to meet margin calls during Crash week, however, faced the possibility of financial ruin. As discussed in Chapter 9, this most unfortunate subset of speculators met with what we call "unexpected residual losses." These speculators could owe their brokers sums far in excess of their margin requirements, which many had naively thought was the limit of possible losses. Their motivation — and it was truly compelling — was to get out of debt, by whatever means it took, as fast as they could. (Some never could, requiring brokerage houses to write off the debts. Among this category were doubtless some who chose to take their own lives.)

• **Wall Street Professionals.** This group, which included brokers, dealers and bankers, was beset by great concerns and regrets. Many were utterly exhausted from the intensity and demands of market events and perhaps had personally lost significant sums in the Crash and then faced increased debts having responded to margin calls themselves. In addition, these professionals had their firms and colleagues to worry about and manage, including the branch managers of the roughly 1400 branch offices of Wall Street brokerage firms around the country. Undoubtedly these circumstances would occupy this group well through November.

• **Debtors (in general).** There are two main types of debtors: businesses and consumers.[34] Until now corporations and individuals have been our focus because IRS tax filer data, as we shall see in *The Deflation of 1930*, shows they were heavily in debt. However, we recognize that just as all businesses are not corporations, all individuals are not only consumers. Some individual debt is taken on by sole proprietors of businesses such as shop owners who borrow money to renovate stores or purchase seasonal inventory. Individuals—as consumers—on the other hand, take on debt for purchasing houses and consumer goods such as cars, radios, washing machines, etc. In addition, in our years of focus, many individuals—as speculators—went into debt to their brokers to purchase stocks on, say, a 50% (or higher) margin. Common to all debtors is that they owe principal and interest payments (together called "debt service") to their various creditors. Following the Crash, this category—whether proprietors or consumers—found themselves very apprehensive. Many remembered the severe deflation of 1920-21—only eight years earlier—and the special pain of having to pay debt service in a deflationary period on loans taken out at high rates of interest prevalent in earlier times of credit stringency. For consumer debtors in particular, they well understood the losses they would suffer if they could not pay, particularly repossession of items purchased on installments on top of all prior payments. This fear ranked high and led to rapid changes in consumption behavior.

• **Businessmen.** Businessmen (as was the going term in 1929) manage businesses and the specific functions of businesses such as sales, production and employment of workers.[35] Their objectives are to maximize profits and minimize losses. In depressions, businessmen in profitable businesses may tend to take longer term outlooks, while those in unprofitable businesses become more focused on short-term

---

34 We discuss indebtedness by governmental entities in Chapter 5 and 5 Appendix in *The Deflation of 1930*.

35 We prefer "business executives" in recognition that they are far less overwhelmingly male today than in 1929.

objectives like obtaining loans to tide their businesses over or laying workers off. Post-Crash, businessmen likely spent many sleepless nights wondering what lay ahead for them and their firm.

• **Corporate Financial Executives.** These executives handle the financing strategies of their corporations, though they themselves, as employees, have limited liabilities.[36] Corporate financial executives' objectives are those of businessmen in general; however, they focus especially on minimizing financial risk. In challenging times of great uncertainty, corporate financial executives are especially alert and focused on minimizing the risks of insolvency for the company (which means running out of cash) and at worst, bankruptcy.

• **Public Officials.** Public officials manage the "public good"—all the government functions at federal, state and local levels. Many public officials who took their responsibilities seriously and performed them conscientiously were now apprehensive about tax revenue losses, budget cuts, layoffs or even, as ultimately occurred, the inability to pay essential salaries, such as for teachers. In addition, even in crises, elected public officials are also motivated by an overall desire to be reelected, and appointed officials want to be reappointed. The Crash caused general anxiety among this group. (At a macro level, it was during the Depression that an awareness of something called "the economy" emerged, but public officials, especially at the state and local level, played no official role in shaping its definition and simply dealt with crises as best they could as problems presented themselves.)

• **Consumers.** In "boom times" such as the 1920s, consumers had become motivated by aggressively marketed "easy" credit that enabled them to improve their comfort, happiness, not to mention their status. With increasingly widespread electrification consumers had been busy buying the many appealing newly invented and manufactured household goods as well as services such as insurance all

36 Unlike in the financing of partnerships and other unincorporated businesses where creditworthiness relies on that of their proprietors.

sold by businesses. [37] The Crash led many to rethink their priorities. (Few Americans in the 1920s thought of themselves as "consumers" or realized their importance to "the economy," a term not coined or understood until after the Great Depression.)

• **Successful Speculators (post-Crash).** By November 1929, successful speculators had realized wealth and were at least materially out of the stock market. The really successful speculators among them had divested by early September 1929 and were proud of their good judgment and prowess, although some still had hopes of repeating their earlier investing success. Given that they had realized gains and gotten out of the market before the Crash, those funds may—or may not—have been "burning holes in their pockets" in late 1929.

• **Workers.** This important, large and diverse group of Americans held jobs and earned wages and salaries. Their motivations were to feel financially secure by earning enough to provide comfortable lifestyles for themselves and their families. Many aspired to climb out of the working class, send their children to college and achieve the fabled American Dream. Among this category were also many people classified as self-employed, including professionals—doctors, lawyers, architects, etc.—and sole proprietors of small businesses. With the Crash, many awoke from their dreams and faced uncertainty.

• **Insider Speculator Instigators**. This small group of Wall Street insiders—"ringleaders," as Noyes called them—had been stoking the fires of speculation by promoting a particular stock they themselves had already purchased. Their behavior stimulated demand in that stock by non-insider speculators who responded to the rumors, bought in and bid up the per share prices. The Insider Speculator Instigators rode the stock prices up to pre-determined levels, then sold their holdings and pocketed the gains before outsiders learned of their sales and began selling as the stock prices fell. As a rule, Insider Speculator Instigators had made fortunes in the late 1920s and wanted to keep those fortunes. In November 1929, this group was nervously "lying low."

---

37 By the late 1920s, 85% of the non-farm population had electrical power.

• **The Unemployed.** In November 1929, no statistics tracked the number of persons unemployed, because up to the Crash, it was generally thought that everyone who wanted employment could find a job. Only as the Depression set in and progressed did involuntary unemployment become apparent and, in fact, a serious and growing problem. Counted or not, the involuntarily unemployed or those laid off, many of whom had families to support, were motivated by the increasingly desperate need for income to buy the basics—and to meet their debt obligations.

• **Voters.** As to the mood of American voters, Alexander Dana Noyes commented, "A public which had been brought from a state of frantic exhilaration to the depths of despair, of whom a very great part had been plunged from seeming prosperity into poverty, could in any case have been depended on to find a scapegoat, and that scapegoat is usually the government."[38] Elections became an important means for voters to express their anger or despair, but in November 1929, elections were still a year away. Voters at all levels of the economic ladder were in assessment mode, depending on their circumstances.

What Were Our Characters' Motivations in Late 1929 into Early 1930?

Having described our Cast of Characters right after the Crash, we now attempt to convey their states of mind and their actions in those critical post-Crash weeks and months.

• **Repentant Ex-Speculators (post-Crash).** This group had been, in Noyes's words, "brought from a state of frantic exhilaration to the depths of despair," and "plunged from seeming prosperity into poverty." Many lived their post-Crash days, like Groucho Marks, unable to sleep, humiliated and with a desperate need to get out of debt. In November 1929, those who still had money or at least had

---

38 Noyes (1938), p. 357.

jobs were "licking their wounds" and trying to figure out what to do next.

• **Wall Street Professionals.** The members of this group lived through everything the former group had, either first hand as remorseful speculators themselves or as financial professionals dealing with repentant ex-speculator clients. As stock prices continued to decline in November, these professionals were compelled to continue sending margin calls to long-time customers, friends among them. November cannot have been a happy time for these cast members. Nonetheless, Table 10.1 (p. 239) shows that the NYSE market value was slightly higher on January 1, 1930, than it had been on December 1, 1929. The first quarter of 1930 opened with Wall Street Professionals feeling hopeful, which we'll discuss in Chapter 5 in *The Deflation of 1930*, but first, everyone had to get through November and holidays that may have been hard to celebrate.

• **Insider Speculator Instigators**. This small group of Wall Street insiders was attentive to signs of opportunity, such as those that appeared in early 1930, though they kept a low profile, generally not wanting to call attention to themselves. (Some were, no doubt, among the Repentant Ex-Speculators (post-Crash).)

• **Debtors (in general).** As we have seen, carrying debt was commonplace in the 1920s. Following the Crash, many indebted individuals, certainly those feeling insecure about their employment going forward, became worried about how much debt they owed. Those who remembered the pain of having to pay debt service during the severe deflation early in the decade found themselves highly motivated to meet their debt obligations as quickly as possible and ultimately get out of debt by focusing their resources on repaying their loans.

• **Businessmen.** This group was in a vigilant "wait and see" posture, although as Temin wrote in a quote earlier in this chapter about the mood in the business world, collapse was not widely predicted in their forecasts. Businessmen paid careful attention to news and advice from respected sources. If they themselves had not had in-depth exposure to finance, they looked to whoever served as their corporate financial executive or "chief financial officer"—a term not yet in use—for reliable advice. It is highly unlikely that capital expenditures such as for plant expansion were still being planned for, much less budgeted. Meanwhile, many Businessmen also endeavored to respond to Hoover's urgings to issue encouraging statements about conditions in their industry and firm.

• **Corporate Financial Executives.** The Crash caused this group to become cautious and, in their work capacities, particularly anxious to preserve corporate cash and liquidity. As Irving Fisher noted in terms of debt management practices, the objective was to minimize the volume of debts payable anytime soon—"soon" being Fisher's key debt factor in measuring over-indebtedness. A strong objective for this group was to lengthen the term of corporate debt liabilities by borrowing "long" to pay off short-term debts. If the corporation had participated in the call money market, a savvy corporate financial executive would have exited that market, received cash back and likely kept it on deposit so as to have safe (and versatile) possession of the cash.

• **Public Officials.** Most government policy-makers at all levels had taken their lead from President Hoover, who had a strong reputation for competence and managerial efficiency. Hoover, as we know, did not believe it was the proper task of government to compete with business initiative and enterprise. Thus, his actions were limited to morale building, getting decision-makers together and acts of what we might call jawboning. As Temin pointed out, "a blue-ribbon group of business executives formed at the suggestion of President Hoover in December 1929 merely publicized favorable reports of the business conditions in its pronouncements in the spring of 1930."[39] State and local public officials, meanwhile, were beginning to see the fear and distress around them, while being well aware they had few financial resources or specific programs to offer assistance. At this time, help remained the responsibility of private charitable

39 Temin (1976), p. 78.

organizations, not governments. Public officials would have their day in the sun several years later once FDR became President and the federal government started spending revenue (thereby creating deficits) on all manner of programs and projects that would help at the local level. As Bernard Baruch pointed out in *The Public Years*:

> Those who argued that relief was not a responsibility of the federal government were not callous men. They were captives of economic theories. They had been brought up to think of government as having no role in economics, and not even the great emergency seemed to them sufficient reason to amend their views. In their concern with economic abstractions, they were largely unconscious of the "human equation," of the fundamental fact that all theories of economics and government come back at last to the individual and his fate.[40]

• **Consumers.** Consumers examined purchasing decisions much more carefully. Indebted consumers, now anxious about the debt they owed, diverted their income from making even normal purchases of goods and services to repaying debts, as we saw confirmed in the statistics for credit sales of radios, automobiles and other retail goods.

• **Successful Speculators (post-Crash).** Suddenly in an environment where stock prices were often half or less than half of what they had been only weeks or months earlier, a few who had successfully navigated the Crash period couldn't pass up the temptation to reenter the market with expectations of a quick recovery and the hope of solid gains that would surely follow.

• **Workers.** Though most workers were still employed at the end of 1929 and in early 1930, they nonetheless worried about their future prospects and, in response, they quickly lowered consumption. Indebted workers cut back in order to get out of debt faster, and the

---

40 Bernard Baruch, *The Public Years*, Holt, Rinehart and Winston, 1960, pp. 231-2.

few who weren't in debt experienced a strong incentive to increase the portion of their incomes that they saved for the day the pink slip might arrive.

• **The Unemployed.** Those who had suffered cutbacks in hours or actually lost jobs felt fearful and adrift, uncertain how long they would be out of work. They were well aware that there was no such thing as a governmental safety net, and they saw firsthand, as lines grew longer, that charities were becoming overwhelmed. A mere two weeks following the Crash, financier and political advisor Bernard Baruch wired a U.S. senator, saying, "Think it would be good idea for you to suggest that the United States government get a [public] program ready for…[public] improvements to be put into effect as soon as unemployment commences to show itself…."[41] Government construction projects were fast-tracked, but no real federal funding for public works programs came until the Emergency Relief Construction Act in June 1932. Following the Crash, since there were no established programs to deal with the jobless, many sought assistance from family, private charity organizations or the limited local social services. This was indeed the beginning of distressing times for the unemployed. (See Voters)

• **Voters.** Our period of focus in this chapter—following the Crash, up to the end of the Little Bull Market in the Spring of 1930—was too early for government inaction to rile up voters. The Crash took place barely a year after this group soundly elected Hoover, Coolidge's pro-business, conservative Commerce Secretary, and most voters had naively anticipated ongoing prosperity. Hoover's supporters had not yet lost faith in their president and his administration's policies, and there was still optimism that the downturn would be brief. We must keep in mind that American voters at this time had no expectations that the federal government existed to regulate private sector matters other than to fund wars, to enact tariffs that would protect American business, to collect taxes and to

41 Baruch (1960), p. 229.

provide protection from illegal activities, such as bootlegging. Even then, regulation was with a light hand. Such issues as the economy, a concept only vaguely formed then, and unemployment were deemed private sector matters. However, by the time of the midterm Congressional elections in November 1930, voters' concerns with economic conditions caused the loss of many Hoover-supporter seats and, in fact, gave Democrats a new one-seat majority in the House of Representatives.

The Stories Data Tell

We originally created a Cast of Characters to come up with, in essence, archetypes for how different Americans were experiencing the Crash and its aftermath. We endeavored to describe who they were — their expectations, states of mind and motivations — and to imagine their reactions and responses in their various spheres. Through this exercise we were able to identify what kinds of statistical measurements we would need to test and verify our observations. In short, we asked ourselves what kinds of data would show us exactly how people were behaving. The more research we did, the more important data became. The more data we scoured, the more obvious certain behaviors became.

One theme quickly emerging from the data and among many of our Cast of Characters had to do with indebtedness. It was clear that, for the indebted, debt repayment following the Crash became top priority over consumption, especially consumption that depended on more borrowing. With this observation about debtor behavior, we discovered data that confirmed our observation substantially.

We will begin *The Deflation of 1930* by discussing Yale economist Irving Fisher, who had personal experience in what he called over-indebtedness. With resilience, Fisher turned his misfortune into scholarship, critically exploring the topic of debt. Unfortunately, when Fisher wrote his influential *Booms and Depressions: Some First Principles* in 1932, the implications of his ideas were incomplete regarding empirical data. What Fisher lacked were measures of "due and payable now," which we have found in the IRS balance sheet information. In our second volume, along with presenting much additional statistical evidence, we honor Irving Fisher's contribution to the debt conversation by presenting extensive corroborating insights from the IRS archives and elsewhere.

If we project ourselves into the various roles our characters played, we get a sense of how each autonomous individual in each role reached decisions about his or her actions. It is difficult not to arrive at the conclusion that the actions of individuals in each role, when aggregated, were sufficient not just to bring the economy to a halt but to put it into reverse.

Another, highly important thematic factor that we explore in our next volume is deflation. We consider what caused deflation in 1929-1933 and how it had an abhorrent impact on the length and severity of the Great Depression. Understanding the Great Depression requires understanding deflation. Gaining this understanding awaits us in *The Deflation of 1930*.

Table 12.6

Statistics of U.S. Economic Activity
($ billion)

	Jul. '29	Aug. '29	Sep. '29	Oct. '29	Nov. '29	Dec. '29
Annualized personal income	$86.3	$86.9	$86.4	$86.3	$83.6	$82.8
Index of factory employment	108.1	108.4	107.3	106.6	104.4	101.9
Index of industrial production	114	114	112	110	105	100
Index of wholesale prices	96.5	96.3	96.1	95.1	93.5	93.3
Friedman & Schwartz demand deposits	$22.8	$22.6	$22.6	$24.4	$21.7	$22.6
Fed member bank loans			$26.2			$26.2

*Oct 4, 1929

Sources: *HSUS* 1789-1945, pp. 328-330, 344; *Monetary History*, p.712; *BMS*, p.72.

Coda: Incipient Conclusions and Looking Ahead

THE DICTIONARY DEFINES "incipient" as "beginning to exist or appear."[1] We regard this first volume of *The Great Deleverage Series* as having accomplished its immediate objective of using empirical evidence to explain how the Crash of 1929 caused the Great Depression to commence at full force in the second quarter of 1930. We have done this using installment credit statistics that show how the shock and magnitude of the Crash caused would-be buyers of automobiles and four other categories of costly goods to use less and less of the widely available financing vehicle of installment credit. But this is not the whole story. Other factors contributed to the severity and painful duration of the Great Depression, including an underlying phenomenon that became increasingly clear to us and deserved further study and analysis. This we have done in our second volume in *The Great Deleverage Series.*

As we hope readers are well aware, in our view, installment credit statistics constitute a valid and valuable lens through which we can then perceive a factor that commenced at the peak of the late 1920s expansion in August 1929 (as determined by NBER) and continued at least until the trough of the Great Depression's contraction in March 1933—repayment of that accumulated debt.

---

1 *Random House Webster's College Dictionary;* Random House, Inc.; 1997; p. 659.

From early 1922 onwards (See Chart 4.1 on page 118), borrowers eagerly took on more and more debt as lenders just as eagerly offered credit. Then, the October 1929 Crash brought about a major pivot, revealed through our installment credit lens, as borrowers immediately began repaying loans. As we observed in Chapter 10, Friedman and Schwartz calculated that, at what they called the "downside of the wiggle," $2,781 million was repaid in November 1929 by holders of demand deposits. From there, as the rate of repayment accelerated, the depression conditions that grew out of the Crash then lasted from the second quarter of 1930 until the first quarter of 1933 with no discernable counterforce that might have ended the contraction earlier.[2]

Because the IRS statistics—which we have relied on heavily to conduct our research and analysis for *The Great Deleverage Series*—demonstrate repayment of significant quantities of debt year by year from 1930 into 1933 and because historical analysis strongly suggests to us that significant repayment of debt—again, with no counterforce—leads to deflation, it became increasingly obvious for us to look into deflation as an overarching phenomenon of great significance. To our surprise and concern, we found little prior analysis of deflation's effects on post-Crash economic conditions.

Interestingly, as Peter Temin has written, "Neither Freedman and Schwartz nor the postwar econometric investigations of the depression paid much attention to the deflation."[3] In fact, a search of the subject index of *Monetary History* revealed just three, single-page entries, "Deflation, 41, 111, 167."[4] None of the comments made on page 41 or 111 referred to deflation in the United States in 1929-1933. The third citation, in Chapter 4, makes only a general reference to deflation during the period. That reference reads:

2 As one example, the Little Bull Market of early 1930 did not constitute an effective counterforce.

3 Temin (1976), p. 167.

4 Friedman and Schwartz (1963a), p. 825.

> In the 1929–33 episode, the climax occurred after more than three years of dragging deflation, after bank failures had cut the number of banks by more than a quarter and after the stock of money had fallen by nearly a third, and served only to close the stable door after the horse had been stolen.[5]

We examined Chapter 7 of *Monetary History* devoted to "The Great Contraction, 1929-33" for any further discussion of deflation without success.

By contrast, John Kenneth Galbraith made several comments on deflation in his *The Great Crash of 1929*. About deflationary pressures post-Crash, he wrote:

> The most important corporate weakness was inherent in the vast new structure of holding companies and investment trusts. The holding companies controlled large segments of the utility, railroad, and entertainment business. Here, as with investment trusts, was the constant danger of devastation by reverse leverage. In particular, dividends from the operating companies paid the interest on the bonds of the upstream holding companies. The interruption of the dividends meant default on the bonds, bankruptcy, and the collapse of the structure. Under these circumstances, the temptation to curtail investment in operating plant in order to continue dividends was obviously strong. This added to deflationary pressures. The latter, in turn, curtailed the earnings and helped bring down the corporate pyramids. When this happened, even more retrenchment was inevitable. Income was earmarked for debt repayment. Borrowing for new investment became impossible. It would be hard to imagine a corporate system better designed to continue and

5 Ibid., pp. 119-20. Presumably the horse referred to was the one discussed above on page 117.

accentuate a deflationary spiral.[6]

> [I]nstead of inflation the country was experiencing the most violent deflation in the nation's history.[7]

> The rejection of both fiscal (tax and expenditure) and monetary policy amounted precisely to a rejection of all affirmative government economic policy. The economic advisers of the day had both the unanimity and the authority to force the leaders of both parties to disavow all the available steps to check deflation and depression. In its own way this was a marked achievement—a triumph of dogma over thought. The consequences were profound.[8]

In our second volume of *The Great Deleverage Series* entitled *The Deflation of 1930: Its Causes and Pernicious Effects,* we go in-depth into the largely unexplored but powerful influence of deflation on the beginnings of the Great Depression. We continue our close look at the Crash period and beyond to show how deflation began in the period from the start of the Great Crash on October 24, 1929, through November of 1929, immediately after the Great Crash, and grew into a pervading force, unaddressed and unmitigated, making 1930 a highly significant year. As we demonstrate, by the middle of October 1930 deflation had become inescapable leading America inexorably onwards into the Great Depression. With clear and illustrative data, our second volume describes the onset and development of deflation and the serious problems it caused.

6 Galbraith (1954), p. 178-9.

7 Ibid., p. 18.

8 Ibid., p. 185-6.

About Appendices

For interested readers, Appendices to Chapters 5, 9 and 14 are available at www.TideMillgroup.com/Publishing

References

Volumes I and II of *The Great Deleverage Series*

Allen, Frederick Lewis. *Only Yesterday: An Informal History of the 1920's.* Harper & Brothers Publishing, 1931.

Angly, Roger. *Oh Yeah?.* Viking Press, 1931.

Appelbaum, Binyamin. *The Economists' Hour.* Little, Brown and Company, 2019.

Aronson, Alex. "Here's What Things Cost 100 Years Ago." *Country Living*, July 30, 2020.

Asch, Besta and A R Mangus, *Farmers on Relief and Rehabilitation.* Research Monograph VIII. Works Progress Administration, Division of Social Research, 1937.

Automobile Trade Journal and Motor Age, February 1930.

Barber, William. *From New Era to New Deal: Herbert Hoover, the Economists, and American Economic Policy, 1921-1933.* Cambridge University Press, 1985.

Baruch, Bernard. *The Public Years.* Holt, Rinehart, and Winston, 1960.

——. *My Own Story.* Holt, Rinehart and Winston, 1957.

Bernanke, Ben S. "Bankruptcy, Liquidity, and Recession." *American Economic Review*, Vol. 71, No. 2, Papers and Proceedings of the Ninety-Third Annual Meeting of the American Economic Association, May, 1981, pp. 155-159.

Bernays, Edward L. *Public Relations.* Forgottenbooks.com, 1945.

Bordo, Michael and Hugh Rockoff. "The Influence of Irving Fisher on Milton Friedman's Monetary Economics." NBER Working Paper Series, Working Paper 17267, August 2011.

Brooks, John. *Once in Golconda: A True Drama of Wall Street 1920-1938.* Allworth Press, 1969.

Brunner, Karl, ed. *The Great Depression Revisited.* Martinus Nijhoff Publishing, 1981.

Calder, Lendol. *Financing the American Dream.* Princeton University Press, 1999.

Clark, Evans. *Financing the Consumer.* Harper & Brothers, 1930.

Clarke, Sally. "New Deal Regulation and the Revolution in American Farm Productivity: A Case Study of the Diffusion of the Tractor in the Corn Belt, 1920-1940." *The Journal of Economic History,* March 1991, Vol. 51, No. 1, pp. 101-123.

The Commercial & Financial Chronicle, Vols. 128-130, 1929-1930.

Committee on Recent Economic Changes of the President's Conference on Unemployment. *Recent Economic Changes in the United States, Volumes 1 and 2.* NBER, 1929.

Craig, Steve. ""The More They Listen, the More They Buy': Radio and the Modernizing of Rural America, 1930-1939." *Agricultural History,* Vol. 80, No. 1, Winter, 2006, p 2.

Davis, L. Ronnie. *The New Economics and the Old Economists.* The Iowa State Press, 1971.

Fabricant, Solomon. "Profits, Losses and Business Assets, 1929-1934." *Bulletin 55.* NBER, 1935.

Federico, Giovanni. *Feeding the World: An Economic History of Agriculture 1800-2000.* Princeton University Press, 2005.

———. "Not Guilty? Agriculture in the 1920s and the Great Depression." *The Journal of Economic History, Vol. 65, No. 4, December 2005, pp. 949-976.*

Felix, Edgar. *Electrical Merchandising, Vol. 43, January 1930.*

Fellner, W J, et al. *Ten Economic Studies in the Tradition of Irving Fisher.* John Wiley & Sons, Inc., 1967.

Ferderer, J. Peter. "Institutional Innovation and the Creation of Liquid Financial Markets: The Case of Bankers' Acceptances, 1914-1934." *The Journal of Economic History,* Vol. 63, No. 3, *September* 2003, pp. 666-694.

Fisher, Irving. "The Debt-Deflation Theory of Great Depressions." *Econometrica,* Vol. 1, No. 4, October 1933.

Booms and Depressions: Some First Principles. Adelphi Company, 1932.

Fisher, Irving and James P. Warburg. "Reply to Senator Elmer Thomas and Professor Irving Fisher." *The Annals of the American Academy of Political and Social Science,* Vol. 171, January 1934, pp. 337-357.

Fisher, Irving Norton. *My Father Irving Fisher.* Comet Press Books, 1956.

Friedman, Milton. "A Theoretical Framework for Monetary Analysis." *The Journal of Political Economy*, Vol. 78, No. 2, March-April 1970, pp. 193-238.

Friedman, Milton and Anna J. Schwartz. *Monetary Statistics of the United States: Estimates, Sources, Methods.* Columbia University Press, 1970.

——. *Dollars and Deficits: Inflation, Monetary Policy and the Balance of Payments.* Prentice-Hall, 1968.

——. *A Monetary History of the United States 1867-1960.* Princeton University Press, 1963.

——. "Money and Business Cycles." *The Review of Economics and Statistics*, Vol. 45, No. 1, Part 2, Supplement, February 1963, pp. 32-64.

Galbraith, John. *The Great Crash 1929.* Mariner Books, 2009.

Ganzel, Bill. "One Farmer's 1930s Balance Sheet." http://lhf.org

Garraty, John. *The Great Depression.* Anchor Book Doubleday, 1987.

Goldsmith, Raymond, Dorothy Brady and Horst Mendershausen. *A Study of Saving in The United States Vol.3.* Princeton University Press, 1956.

Goldsmith, Raymond and Robert E. Lipsey. *Studies in the National Balance Sheet of the United States, Volumes 1 and 2.* NBER and Princeton University Press, 1963.

Grant, James. *Bernard Baruch: The Adventures of a Wall Street Legend.* Axios Press, 2012.

Grebler, Leo, David M. Blank and Louis Winnick. *Capital Formation in Residential Real Estate: Trends and Prospects.* Princeton University Press, 1956.

Haberler, Gottfried. *Prosperity and Depression: A Theoretical Analysis of Cyclical Movements.* League of Nations, 1937.

Hansen, Mary Eschelbach and Bradley A. Hansen. *Bankrupt in America.* The University of Chicago Press, 2020.

——. "Crisis and Bankruptcy: The Mediating Role of State Law, 1920-1932." *The Journal of Economic History*, Vol. 72, No. 2, June 2012, pp. 448-468.

Hart, Albert Gailord and The Committee on Debt Adjustment. *Debts and Recovery: A Study of Changes in the Internal Debt Structure from 1929 to 1937 and A Program for the Future.* The Twentieth Century Fund, 1938.

Hetzel, Robert L. "The Contributions of Milton Friedman to Economics." *The Economic Quarterly*, Federal Reserve Bank of Richmond, Vol. 93, Winter 2007, pp. 1-30.

Hickock, Lorena. *One Third of a Nation: Lorena Hickok Reports on The Great Depression*. University of Chicago Press, 1981.

Holthausen, Duncan M, Malcolm L. Merriam and Rolf Nugent. *The Volume of Consumer Installment Credit, 1929-38*. NBER, 1940.

Hoover, Herbert. *The Annals of America*, Vol. 15. *Encyclopedia Brittanica*, 1968, pp. 79-82.

——. *The Memoirs of Herbert Hoover 1920-1933: The Cabinet and the Presidency, Volume 2*. The Macmillan Company, 1952.

——. "Address on the 150th Anniversary of the Battle of Kings Mountain." Public Papers of the Presidents, October 7, 1930.

Hopkins, Harry. *The Realities of Unemployment*. BiblioGov, 1937.

Huertas, Thomas and Joan Silverman. "Charles E. Mitchell: Scapegoat of the Crash." *The Business History Review*, Vol. 60, No. 1, Spring 1986, pp. 81-103.

Hyman, Louis. *Borrow: The American Way of Debt*. Vintage Books, 2012.

Irwin, Douglas. *Peddling Protectionism: Smoot-Hawley and the Great Depression*. Princeton University Press, 2011.

Johnson, Paul. *A History of the American People*. Harper Perennial. 1997

Karabell, Zachary. *The Leading Indicators: A Short History of the Numbers That Rule Our World*. Simon & Schuster, Inc., 2014.

Keynes, John Maynard. *The Collected Writings of John Maynard Keynes*, Volume XIII. The Macmillan Company, 1973.

——. *The General Theroy of Employment, Interest and Money*. Palgrave Macmillan, 1936.

——. *The Treatise on Money*, Vol. 2. The Royal Economic Society, 1930.

Kindleberger, Charles. *The World in Depression 1929-1939*. University of California Press, 1986.

Klein, Lawrence R. *The Keynesian Revolution*. The Macmillan Company, 1966.

Klein, Maury. *Rainbow's End: The Crash of 1929*. Oxford University Press, Inc, 2001.

Klingaman, William. *1929: The Year of the Great Crash*. Harper & Row, 1989.

Lawrence, Josephine. *If I Have Four Apples*. Grosset & Dunlap, 1935.

Lippmann, Walter, "The Peculiar Weakness of Mr. Hoover," *Harpers*

Magazine, Volume 161, (June, 1930)

MacKay, Charles. *Extraordinary Popular Delusions and the Madness of Crowds.* L. C. Page & Company, 1932.

Marsh, John. *The Emotional Life of the Great Depression.* Oxford University Press, 2019.

Marx, Arthur. *Life with Groucho.* Simon & Schuster, 1954.

Mazur, Paul M. *American Prosperity: Its Causes and Consequences.* Viking Press, 1928.

Meltzer, Allan H. *A History of the Federal Reserve, Volume 1: 1913-1951.* University of Chicago Press, 2003.

Mitchell, Broadus. *Depression Decade: From New Era through New Deal 1929-1941.* Holt, Rinehart, and Winston, 1947.

Mitchell, Wesley C. *Business Cycles and Their Causes.* University of California Press, 1941.

New York Stock Exchange. *New York Stock Exchange Year Book 1929-1930,* 1930.

The New York Times. January 4, 1932; October 22, 1929, et al.

Noyes, Alexander. *The Market Place: Reminiscences of a Financial Editor.* Little, Brown and Company, 1938.

———. "Financial Markets: New Year Prophesies, New Year Uncertainties, and Underlying Economic Facts." *The New York Times,* January 4, 1932, p. 28.

Olney, Martha. *Buy Now Pay Later: Advertising, Credit, and Consumer Durables in the 1920s.* The University of North Carolina Press, 1991.

———. "Avoiding Default: The Role of Credit in the Consumption Collapse of 1930." *The Quarterly Journal of Economics,* Vol. 114, No. 1, February 1999, pp. 319-335.

Ott, Julia C. "When Wall Street Met Main Street: The Quest for an Investors' Democracy and the Emergence of the Retail Investor in the United States, 1890-1930." *Enterprise & Society,* Vol. 9, No. 4, Cambridge University Press, December 2008, pp. 619-630.

———. "The Free and Open People's Market: Political Ideology and Retail Brokerage at the New York Stock Exchange, 1913-1933." *The Journal of American History,* Vol. 93, No 1, June 2009, pp. 44-71.

———. "The Free and Open People's Market: Public Relations at the New York Stock Exchange, 1913-1929." *Business and Economic History,* thebhc.org, Vol. 2, 2004.

Persons, Charles E. "Credit Expansion, 1920 to 1929, and its Lessons." *The Quarterly Journal of Economics*, Vol. 45, No. 1, November 1930, pp. 91-130.

Phillips, Chester A., Thomas F. McManus and R. W. Nelson. *Banking and the Business Cycle A Study of the Great Depression in the United States.* The Macmillan Company, 1937.

Pierce, Phyllis S., ed. *The Dow Jones Averages 1885-1995.* 4th Edition. Irwin Professional Publishing, 1996.

Roth, Benjamin. *The Great Depression: A Diary.* Public Affairs. Perseus Books Group, 2009.

Rubenzer, Steven and Thomas Faschingbauer. *Personality, Character, and Leadership in the White House: Psychologists Assess the Presidents.* Potomac Books Inc, 2004.

Samuelson, Paul. *Economics* (Seventh Edition). McGraw Hill, 1967.

———. *The Collected Scientific Papers of Paul Samuelson.* The MIT Press, 1966.

Schumpeter, Joseph. "Irving Fisher's Econometrics." *Econometrica*, Vol. 16, No. 3, July, 1948, pp. 219-231.

———. *Business Cycles: A Theoretical and Statistical Analysis of the Capitalist Process. Volumes I & II.* McGraw-Hill Book Company, 1939.

Schwartz, Anna. "Understanding 1929-1933," in Karl Brunner's *The Great Depression Revisited.* Martinus Nijhoff Publishing, 1981.

Seldes, Gilbert. *The Years of the Locust (America, 1929-1932).* Little, Brown & Company, 1933.

Shlaes, Amity. "Calvin Coolidge Revisited: New Find on 1929 Crash." *Forbes*, Vol. 193, No. 7, July 14, 2013.

———. *The Forgotten Man: A New History of The Great Depression.* Harper Collins, 2007.

Smith, Richard Norton. *An Uncommon Man: The Triumph of Herbert Hoover.* Simon & Schuster, Inc. 1984.

Stam, Jerome and Bruce Dixon. "Farmer Bankruptcies and Farm Exits in the United States, 1899-2002." U.S. Department of Agriculture, Economic Research Service. Agriculture Information Bulletin Number 788, 2004.

Steel, Ronald, *Walter Lippmann and the American Century*, Little Brown and Company, 1980.

Temin, Peter. *Did Monetary Forces Cause the Great Depression?.* W. W. Norton & Company, 1976.

Tobin, James. "Neoclassical Theory in America: J. B. Clark and Fisher." *The American Economic Review*, Vol. 75, No. 6, December

1985, pp. 28-38.

Warburg, James P. and Irving Fisher. "Reply to Senator Elmer Thomas and Professor Irving Fisher." *The Annals of the American Academy of Political and Social Science,* Vol. 171, January 1934, pp. 337-357.

Watkins, T. H. *The Hungry Years.* Henry Holt & Co, 1999.

Westerfield, Ray B. "The Balance Required by Borrowers." *The Journal of Political Economy,* Vol 33, No. 3, June 1925.

White, Eugene N. et al. *The Housing and Mortgage Markets in Historical Perspective.* University of Chicago Press, 2014.

Wickens, David L. *Residential Real Estate, Its Economic Position as shown by Values, Rents Family Incomes Financing and Construction, together with Estimates for all Real Estate.* NBER, 1941.

Wicker, Elmus R. *The Banking Panics of the Great Depression.* Cambridge University Press, 1996.

——. *Federal Reserve Monetary Policy 1917-1933.* Random House, 1966.

Wigmore, Barrie. *The Crash and Its Aftermath.* Greenwood Press, 1985.

Willis, H. Parker. "Who Caused the Panic of 1929?" *The North American Review,* Vol. 229, No. 2, February 1930, pp. 174-183.

The authors also acknowledge the importance of http://www.jstor.org to our ongoing research efforts.

Governmental Sources and References

Asch, Besta and A. R. Mangus, *Farmers on Relief and Rehabilitation.* Research Monograph VIII. Works Progress Administration, Division of Social Research, 1937.

Board of Governors of the Federal Reserve System, *Banking and Monetary Statistics 1914-1941,* 1943.

Board of Governors of the Federal Reserve System, *Annual Report of the Board of Governors of the Federal Reserve System, 1929, 1930, 1931.*

U. S. Commerce Department, Bureau of Economic Analysis. *The National Income & Product Accounts of the United States, 1929-76 Statistical Tables,* 1981.

——. U. S. Census Bureau.

Historical Review of State and Local Government Finances, 1948.

Historical Statistics of the United States, 1789-1945.

Fifteenth Census of the United States: 1930, Agriculture, Vol. 1.

Committee on Recent Economic Changes of the President's Conference on Unemployment. *Recent Economic Changes in the United States, Volumes 1 and 2.* NBER, 1929.

Hetzel, Robert L. "The Contributions of Milton Friedman to Economics." *The Economic Quarterly*, Federal Reserve Bank of Richmond, Vol. 93, Winter 2007, pp. 1-30.

Hoover, Herbert. "Address on the 150th Anniversary of the Battle of Kings Mountain." Public Papers of the Presidents, October 7, 1930.

Stam, Jerome and Bruce Dixon. "Farmer Bankruptcies and Farm Exits in the United States, 1899-2002." U.S. Department of Agriculture, Economic Research Service. Agriculture Information Bulletin Number 788, 2004.

U.S. Treasury Department. Internal Revenue Service. *Statistics of Income for 1929, 1930, 1931.*

Internal Revenue Service. *IRS Historical Fact Book: A Chronology, 1646-1992.* Forgotten Books, 2018.

In addition, the authors express their gratitude to the Federal Reserve Bank of St. Louis, FRED and FRASER in particular. Their comprehensive libraries made our research possible.

National Bureau of Economic Research (NBER) References

Bordo, Michael and Hugh Rockoff. "The Influence of Irving Fisher on Milton Friedman's Monetary Economics." NBER Working Paper Series, Working Paper 17267, August 2011.

Committee on Recent Economic Changes of the President's Conference on Unemployment. *Recent Economic Changes in the United States, Volumes 1 and 2.* NBER, 1929.

Fabricant, Solomon. "Profits, Losses and Business Assets, 1929-1934." *Bulletin 55.* NBER, 1935.

Goldsmith, Raymond and Robert E. Lipsey. *Studies in the National Balance Sheet of the United States, Volumes 1 and 2.* NBER and Princeton University Press, 1963.

Holthausen, Duncan M, Malcolm L. Merriam and Rolf Nugent. *The Volume of Consumer Installment Credit, 1929-38.* NBER, 1940.

Wickens, David L. *Residential Real Estate, Its Economic Position as Shown by Values, Rents, Family Incomes, Financing, and Construction, Together with Estimates for all Real Estate.* NBER, 1941.

Index

A

Active speculators, 299, 300
Aggregate demand, 77, 111, 127, 335
Aggregate U.S. Corporate Balance Sheet, 1, 139, 189, 302
Allen, Frederick Lewis, 19, 231
    America's Mood, 15
    Impact of the Crash on Americans. 323, 340-42
Appelbaum, Binyamin. 112, 113
Aronson, Alex. 33
Assembly line. 23, 26, 32, 33

B

Balanced federal budget. 94
Bank crises. 9, 12, 105
Banking and Monetary Statistics. 3, 47, 106, 116, 122, 137, 173
Bankruptcy. 5
Barber, William J., 96n
    About candidate Hoover's credentials, 59, 60n
    Hoover's grasp of Economics 70, 72
    Hoover's technique for proper government, 62-64
Baruch, Bernard,
    About the 1920s, 22
    Government in economics, 350-51
BEA (Bureau of Economic Analysis) 47, 312
Bernays, Edward, 31, 32, 39, 41
Beyond their means, 285
Black Monday, 259
Black Thursday, 221-25, 227, 231, 236, 259
    Beginning of The Crash, 322
Boom, 79, 86, 220, 275, 345
    Baruch, Bernard, his viewpoint, 22
    Beginning of the stock market boom, 194
    Call Money high, 201
    Florida real estate 42, 170
    Galbraith, John Kenneth, on the booms end, 218, 228

Keynes, John Maynard, (1928-29, excess of investmentn), 79
How a boom is generated, 88
Mitchell, Charles; his impact, 202
Peak in August 1929, 220, 318-20
Seldes, Gilbert, viewpoint, 214
Booms and Depressions; Some First Principles, 114
Bordo, Michael, 115, 116
Bottom up analysis, 17, 315, 320
Brokers' bulletins, 209
Brokers' loans, 180, 182-87
Fed/NYSE definitions, 244-45
Growth of, 171-73, 177, 195, 215-16, 274
Nomenclature, 244
Origin of Stock Exchange Practices (SEP), 175
Bulletin 55, 47, 56, 151, 152, 153, 154, 155, 156, 157, 158, 160, 161,, , 162, 163
Bureau of Labor Statistics, 49
Burns, Arthur, 151
Business confidence, 90

C

Caldor, Lendol 43, 44
Call loan rates, 178, 198, 206, 207, 275
Call loan renewal rate, 275, 276
Call loans; see also call market and call money loans
Brokerage industry, 197-98
Loan decline, 247, 251-56, 273-74
Loan expansion, 215
Margin accounts, 177-78; see also Call market
New York City member banks, 260-61
Nomenclature, 244
NYSE, 171-74
Tables and data, 181-84
Call market, 203; see also call loans and call money market
Brokers' spreads, 199
Non-bank others, 261
Rates, 258, 265
Renewal rates, 276
Repayment, 13-15, 246

Short-term borrowing, 249, 256
Speculation, 3
Call money market, 187, 200, 203, 249, 349; see also call loans and call market
Black Thursday, 236
Brokers' credit considerations, 238
Increase of loans, 213
Lending, 14, 175-180, 181n, 183-84, 198
Non-bank lenders, 215
NYSE; the Fed, 173
Capone, Al, 58
Cash management, 244
Cause-and-effect linkage, 3, 308
Changes in consumption behavior, 344
Chaplin, Charlie, 58
Character of the contraction, 108
Clark, Evans, 26, 27, 29, 31, 58, 69
Collapse of investment, 87
Commercial paper, 251, 258, 276, 277
Compensating balances, 263, 272
Component of consumption, 125, 127
Consumer credit:, 34
Contagion of fear, 108
Contraction, The Great 101
Corporate financial officers, 12
Corporate Financial Officers, 12
Corporate Financial Statistics, 188
The Crash, 4, 6, 12-20, 22, 179, 202, 243-44, 259, 320
1929; Great Depression; cause, 1-3, 7, 23, 134, 149, 321-22
Automotive industry, 16-17, 311-14
Autonomous spending, 23
Beginning of the Crash, 322-23, 329
Borrowing; debt, 13, 43
Brokers' loans, 179, 180, 181n, 182
Call loan money market impact, 170
Call market loans, 245, 250-52
Call loans; speculation, 170
Cast of characters, 342-52
Conclusions; the future, 315, 354-57

Contraction, 134
Credit; debt; repayment, 315-21, 324
Galbraith's account, 221-22, 225-36
Great Depression begins, 321- 324
Indebtedness, 285-86, 293, 301-03
Industry views, 211-12
IRS data; statistics, 139-59, 298, 301-02
Fisher, Irving, his viewpoint, 114
Installment credit, 325-28
Last days before the crash, 214, 216
Margin accounts; residual losses, 236-39, 247
Margin calls, 17-18
Mood of the times, 332-35, 340-52
Over-indebtedness, 287-88, 294
Panic before the crash, 214, 216
Pecora hearings, 198, 237
Pivot in behavior, 306-13,
Pre-crash data, 188-90, 254-56
Pre-crash lenders, 254-55,
Reversal of consumer behavior, 1-2, 99, 331-32
Role of non-bank others, 261
Short-term rates, 256-58
Stock market losses, 237-39
Credit granted, 3, 16, 17, 318, 320, 323
Cure of unemployment, 91
Cyclical fluctuations, 81, 85, 99, 154, 280

D

Dates of maturity, 295, 301
Davis, J. Ronnie, 77, 94, 95, 96
Day traders, 301
Debt-Deflation Theory of Great Depressions, 114
Debt obligations, 7, 11, 15, 147, 236, 290, 296, 311, 318, 347-48, 296
Created depression conditions, 303
Growth in years before the Crash, 18
Repaying reduces consumption, 127-28, 294Debtors, 12, 189, 301, 344, 348
Debt repayment, 308, 316
Becomes a top priority over consumption, 352

Cause of The Great Depression, 12, 17, 325
Consumers spending less, 18, 128, 301
Debt service, 344, 348
Demand for money
Friedman, Milton and Anna J. Schwartz on wealth elasticity, 280
Temin's conclusion, 131-32
Temin relates to spending, 283
Department stores, 144, 325
Dots, The, 7, 299
Downside of the wiggle, 271
Drop in demand deposits, 268
Downward readjustment, 15, 307, 308, 317
Downward spiral, 12, 18
Drastic liquidation, 243, 247, 257
Durant, William, 34, 36
Dust Bowl, 58

E

Easing of credit, 243, 310
Economic realities, 15
Efficiency experts, 31
Efficiency of markets, 104
Electrification, 33
Ellington, Duke 58
Endogenous, 6, 7, 23, 134
Equation (1), 131, 132
Erie railway receivership, 5
Evidentiary-Grade Data, 137
Exogenous, 6, 22
Expressions of doubt, 336

F

Fabricant, Salomon, 151, 152, 154, 160
Faschingbauer, T. R., 71
Federal Reserve, 14n, 25, 46-48, 107, 109-10, 119, 122, 137, 176, 220-21, 315n
Attempt to curb speculation, 276
Blaming the Federal Reserve for The Great Depression, 115-17
Efforts to inspire restraint, 6, 196-97, 199-205, 209

Flawed Federal Reserve policy, 9, 101, 121
Fueled stock speculation, 3
Involvement with call loans, 181-84
Its creation expanded availability of credit and statistics, 171-73
Lender of last resort, 75
No connection between stock market crash and business conditions, 336
Feeling of trust, 334
Find a scapegoat, 347
Fisher, Irving
Dramatic change of mood in America, 15
Fisher's legacy, 286-88
Impact of debt payment from a deposit balance, 250n, 284
On monetarism, 114-16
On over-indebtedness, 294-95, 302
Fitzgerald, F. Scott, 58
Florida real estate boom, 42, 170
Ford, Henry 33, 34
Freud, Sigmund, 31
Friedman, Milton, 95n, 105, 136
In praise of, 110, 111n
Fisher, Irving, his influence on, 115, 116
Fall in quantity of money, 116-17
Friedman, Milton and Anna J. Schwartz, 355
Bank loan repayments, 104-17, 250-51, 258-59
Flawed Federal Reserve policy led to monetary collapse, 9
The Great Contraction, 101-02
Praise for the Fed's handling of loans called to brokers, 181n
Sharp wiggle from bank loan repayments, 105, 266-75
Sub-optimized economic results, 279, 282-84
Temin, Peter, criticizes Friedman and Schwartz, 122, 129-32
Furniture stores, 325

G

Galbraith, John Kenneth, 194, 197, 340n
Comments on deflation, 356-57
The Crash punctures stock market illusions, 323
The Crash and The Great Depression, 6-7
End of the speculative boom, 218
Federal Reserve inaction, 201-03, 205

Narrative of The Crash, 221-22, 225, 227-28, 230, 232-36
Speculative orgy, 194
Speculators, 208-10, 218
Witnesses a change in American's mood, 15, 333-35
Gross Domestic Product (GDP), 10, 20, 50, 51
General Motors, 34, 169, 209, 258, 260, 339
General Motors Acceptance Corporation, 34, 169, 258
Gross National Product (GNP), 20, 124-25, 146-48, 161, 297
In 1929, 10, 20
In 1931, 128
Fall in autonomous aggregate spending, 123
Fall in GNP, 10, 55-56
Fall in value of stocks related to GNP in 1929, 322
Origin of, 50-51
Personal consumption expenditures and fixed investment, 10-11
Rates of change, 190
Tax returns related to GNP in 1929, 298
Goldsmith, Raymond W., 56, 122, 148, 149, 150, 295, 296
Gold Standard, 20
Great Depression, 7-10, 12
Major causes, 1-2
The beginning of, 16-18
The 1920's legacy of, 22-23
Understanding through data, 45-46
Hoover, Herbert on 56-57, 73, 75
Keynes, John Maynard, his perspective, 76, 78-79,
Consumers' impact, 127-28, 308-09, 318
Failures of the Federal Reserve, (Friedman and Schwartz, Fisher), 101-15
Fall in personal consumption, 121-23
IRS archives tell the story, 137, 139, 149, 158
Impact of the Crash, 315-21, 323-25
Gross income, 158, 160, 297, 298
Gross National Product, (GNP), 20, 124-25, 297

H

Haberler, Gottfried, 80, 81, 99
Harrison, George, 203
Heavily in debt, 344
Heller, Walter, 113

Hetzel, Robert L. 110, 111
Hickok, Lorena, 23
Highly credit-worthy company, 258
Holding company, 290
Hoover, Herbert
- Flawed protagonist, 57
- Mississippi flood, 58
- Barber, William on leadership, 59
- Commerce Secretary, 60
- Advisory Committee; on Statistics, 63
- Conference on Unemployment, 65
- As President; role of the federal government, 73
- Statistics of U.S. Economic Activity, 219

Hopkins, Harry, 23
Household appliance stores, 325
Huertas, Thomas, 203, 204, 205
Hyman, Louis, 37, 38
Idle cash, 180, 258
- Five investment options for, 149-151
- Friedman and Schwartz assumed investment opportunities, not repayment, 282-84
- Used to repay bank loans, 259, 261-62, 265, 272-73

Income-based tests, 296
Income-Expenditure Approach, 18, 76, 77, 96, 99, 123, 126, 136
Independent factor, 103, 107
Inflated purchasing power, 330
Installment buying, 24, 25
Installment credit, 3
- Peaks for purchases of automobiles, 16
- Demand for radios, 34
- Expansion of, 165
- NBER study, 315-18
- Olney, Martha, her research, 294n
- Origins of, 24
- Reduction of, 224-25

Invisible hand, 48

J

Jay Cooke's suspension, 5
Jewelry stores, 325

K

Kahn, Otto Hermann, 193, 210
Kennedy, David M. 2, 3, 113
Keynes, John Maynard, 44, 76-80; see also Income -Expenditure Approach
    Evolution of the Income-Expenditure Approach, 96-99
    Chicago lectures, 85-94, 331-32
    Treatise on Money, 138-39
Keynesian school, 9
Klein, Julia, 300, 308
Klein, Lawrence
    On Keynes' thinking, 78-79, 80n, 96-98
    On consumption, 331-32
Klein, Maury, 200, 203, 204n, 205
Klingaman, William K., 202, 329
    Days before the Crash, 216-17
Knickerbocker Trust Company's bankruptcy, 5
Kuhn, Loeb and Company, 193

L

Lawrence, Josephine
    Attitudes about home ownership, 40
    Cultural attitudes, 30-37
Lehman Brothers, 38
Liberty or Victory Bonds, 24
Life magazine, 32
Lindberg, Charles, 58
Loan repayment, 246
    Beginning of in 1929, 13, 17
    Impact on the money supply, 128-29

M

M-1, 106, 119
M-2, 102, 106, 119
Margin calls, 6, 18, 178, 218, 285, 348
    On Black Thursday, October 24, 222-23, 244-47
    Collateral impact, 322-23
    Days after the Crash, 236

Impact on Wall Street professionals, 343
speculators, 290-91
Margin loans, 177, 244
Margin requirements, 177, 178, 343
Mazur, Paul, 38, 39
McCracken, Paul, 113
Meeker, Edward, 150
Member banks, 165, 176, 266
Changes in the banking position, 269-70
Expanding availability of credit, 171-74
Loan statistics, 183-85
Mitchell, Charles E., lending to support the money market, 203-04
Statistics on changes in call money loan volume, 253-55
Supporting the call loan market, 260-61
Mitchell, Charles E.
Supporting the stock market, 201-205, 204n
Mitchell, Wesley Clair, 67-68, 99, 114, 151
Causes of depression, 81-85
A founder of NBER, 63-64
Model T, 33, 34, 35
Monetarism, 100, 105
Monetary collapse, 9, 103, 107
Monetary History, 76, 102, 109, 113, 119, 121, 270
Failures of the Federal Reserve System led to The Great Depression, 9
Fisher, Irving, his influence, 115
Friedman and Schwartz limited mention of deflation, 356
sub-optimized economic results, 279
Non-monetary forces started The Great Depression, 9
Temin, Peter, his viewpoint, 129-31
Monetary policy, 100
Failure of the Fed (Friedman and Schwartz), 107, 111-13
Money matters (Friedman and Schwartz), 102
Temin, Peter, his theory on the causes of the Depression, 123
Theory (Friedman and Schwartz), 279
Money markets, 175, 193, 251
Money matters, 102, 104, 113
Money squeeze, 4, 195
Money stock, 105, 109, 130, 132, 280, 282; see also stock of money and money supply

Defined by Friedman and Schwartz, 102-03
Growth of, 184-85
November's precipitous plunge, 272
Money supply, 18, 105, 283-84; see also money stock and stock of money
Decline in, 283-84
Money Supply Series, 266
Shrinkage of, 128-30, 244, 250, 271
At year-end 1929, 119
Of the times, 232-35
Voters and businessmen, 347-48
Mortgages, 141, 147, 186, 207
Indebtedness, 165-66
Making home ownership possible, 24, 40
Over-indebtedness, 285-86, 303
Much deeper in debt than was prudent, 1
Muscle Shoals, 74

N

National banks, 172, 293
National Bureau of Economic Research (NBER), 56, 66-67, 81, 160, 162-63, 168; see also *Bulletin 55*
Bulletin 55, 151-58
Borrowing by Americans, 291-92
Inception of, 64
Installment credit and sales, 16, 315, 318-19, 325, 339, 354-55
Linking the Crash to The Great Depression, 308
The peak of 1920s' expansion, 220
National Income and Products Accounts (NIPA), 47, 55-56, 76, 125, 136, 191
Confirms fall in autonomous aggregate spending, 123
GNP in 1929, 20, 297, 322
Regarding GNP, 10, 50-55, 123
Net credit change, 16, 318, 319, 321, 323, 324, 325, 328, 332, 339
Net income on taxable returns, 297
New construction, 92, 93
New York City banks, 184, 185, 253, 254, 259, 266, 268
New York Stock Exchange Yearbook, 180
Non-bank lenders, 182, 256
Non-bank others, 173, 174, 181, 254, 255, 259, 260, 261, 268

Nonmember banks, 117, 253, 255
Noyes, Alexander Dana, 6, 182, 199, 308, 323, 329, 334-35, 340-42, 347
  About speculation and speculators, 192-96, 205, 208-11, 213-14, 218, 306-07
  Downward readjustment, 15, 321
  Economic realities, 15, 321
  On Paul Walburg's prediction, 2-4
Noyes, C. Reinhold, 37

O

Olney, Martha, 27
  Families maintain installment payments, 294n
Organized buying support, 217
Ott, Julia C., 25, 26, 40, 41
Out-of-town banks, 181, 253, 254, 259, 260, 267, 269
Over-indebtedness, 288, 295
Over-production, 310, 311
Own a home, 293

P

Pay off the loan, 285
Pecora Hearings, 193, 299
Personal indebtedness, 295
Persons, Charles, 172, 292n, 330
  Crash impact on the auto industry, 311
    radio sales, 309-11
  Credit inflation, 30
  Debt expansion, 30
  Depression due to credit expansion, 165
Pivot
  From borrowing to repayment, 13, 308
  In Behavior, 306
Plunge in credit use, 316
Precipitous drop in fixed investment, 1, 9-10
President's Conference on Unemployment, 62, 65, 66, 67
Prices of financial assets, 281
Prime Rate, 263
Prolonged liquidation, 87
Public works projects, 64, 94

Q

Quick liabilities, 294

R

Rate of interest, 68, 79, 80, 90, 92, 93, 94, 176, 274, 334
Rate of investment, 79, 88, 90, 94, 98, 99, 331
Reading Railway, 4, 210
Receivership, 4, 5
Recent Economic Changes, 67, 168, 291
Reconstruction Finance Corporation, 75
Reluctance to borrow, 318
Reluctance to lend, 318
Renewal rates, 178, 206
Repaid their lenders, 1, 2
Repaying bank loans, 128, 129, 261, 263, 273
Repayments of debt, 1, 318
Repentant Ex-Speculators, 12, 343, 347, 348
Resources in cash and credit, 213, 311
Restoration of confidence, 90, 91, 92
Revolving credit, 272
Rockoff, Hugh, 115, 116
Roosevelt, Eleanor, 23
Roosevelt, Franklin D. (FDR), 23
Roth, Bnjamin, 58
Rubenzer, S. J., 71

S

Schumpeter, Joseph, 79, 150, 151, 287
Schwartz, Anna J., 105
Segmented markets theory, 207
Seldes, Gilbert, 150, 214, 354
Sharp wiggle, 105, 266, 273, 277
Shock and magnitude, 17, 315, 321, 323, 325, 355
Silverman, Joan, 203, 204, 205
Slow liabilities, 295
Slump
    Keynes, John Maynard, (1928-29, deficiency of investment), 79
    How a slump is generated, 88
Smith, Adam, 48, 61, 70, 112

Solow, Robert, 113
Sources and uses analysis, 9, 18, 277
Speculation, 159, 167, 176, 214, 218, 225, 236, 286, 298, 306-07
Background, 42
Fisher, Irving, his losses, 114
Furious speculation, 192-94
Impact of leverage, 178-79
Loans' contribution, 182-85, 202
Losses from speculation, 238
Manipulation, 208-11, 346
Numbers of, 300
Restraint, 197, 199, 201, 346
Speculative over-expansion, 329-30
Stock Exchange Practices (SEP), 174
In stocks, 170-72
Speculative element, 200, 240, 300, 338
Speculative over-expansion, 329, 330
Stagflation, 283
Statistics of Income, 10, 137, 138, 139, 150, 152, 156, 160, 161, 162
Stock Exchange Practices, 174, 175, 237, 289, 299
Stock of money, 280, 346; see also money stock and money supply
Decline of, 108-09, 271
Is a function of, 130-32
Non-monetary forces, 103-04
Stock tips, 299
Strauss, Samuel, 30
Sudden and violent change, 88, 99, 331
Supply function for money, 131
Survey of Current Business, 47, 168, 312, 313
Suspended banks, 5

T

Temin, Peter, 96n, 116-16, 117n, 136, 145, 283-84, 336, 340-42, 348-49
Crediting Keynes for the spending approach (deficiency of investment), 78-79, 98-99
on Friedman and Schwartz only touching on deflation, 355-56
Friedman and Schwartz's view about money stock, 129-32
About Inadequate data, 133-35
Regarding drop in personal spending and consumption, 121-27, 335

Tightening their belts, 2, 7
Top down, 9, 17, 309
Total credit outstanding, 318, 319, 321, 323, 324
Total deduction, 298
Twain, Mark, 36
Twentieth Century Fund, 26

U

Ultimate collapse, 2, 3
Unbounded optimism, 340
Uncontainable pessimism, 340
Unwilling to take on more debt obligations, 311
Upside of the wiggle, 267, 268, 270
U.S. Department of Labor,, 49
U.S. Treasury Bills, 176
U.S. Treasury Department, 1, 137

V

Viner, Jacob
    Deficit financing proposal, 94-96
Violent downward readjustment, 307, 317
Visible signs of danger, 196

W

Wall Street Professionals, 12, 343, 348
War bond campaign, 24
Warburg, Paul, 286
    Warnings of a crash, 2-3, 15, 199, 329-30
Western Electric, 4
Wigmore, Barrie, 207, 274
    On brokerage call loans, 197-98
    Declining financial valuations, 289-90
    Non-bank call loan issuers, 260-61
Willingness to borrow, 86
Working Capital, 142, 143

Y

Yield curves, 206, 207, 275, 276

Regarding Permissions

The formation and very rapid growth of Amazon in recent decades have changed the publishing business radically. From our vantage as authors, who have agreed with our publisher to take responsibility for seeking and securing the necessary permissions from the copyright owners whose works we quote, the impact of these changes has been significant.

Considering our extensive use of statistical information, we count ourselves very fortunate that the federal government does not seek copyright protection on the works it produces. This includes all manner of official undertakings from congressional investigations to publications of the Federal Reserve System, the Treasury Department, the Commerce Department, the Department of Agriculture, the Bureau of the Census, etc. We made ample use of this free information requiring no permission, while also footnoting sources for readers' reference. We, as historians attempting to tell an important story with data as evidence, are grateful to all the entities we have been able to access that have fulfilled their responsibilities over the decades to make information available to the public.

Early on we consulted with copyright lawyers, literary agents and experienced industry professionals. Uniformly they responded that our work, because of its transformational nature regarding what is already known of 1929-1933, should be enough to justify fair use.

Certainly the consolidations, attrition and other changes in the publishing world over the course of many decades have made it more difficult to identify who owns what as it relates to works published in the distant past. Examples include several of our historically most insightful sources, including Alexander Dana Noyes who published *The Market Place* in 1938 and Gilbert Seldes who published *The Years of the Locust* in 1933, as to the chain of ownership of their particular publisher and their copyrights.

We hope our sincere and great respect for authors and publishers of for-profit works of economic theory and history is apparent throughout *The Great Deleverage Series*. For queries, please contact us at permissions@tidemillgroup.com.

About the Authors

John C. Harvey is an inventor/entrepreneur, videogame developer, and economic historian. With his co-inventor, Jim Cuddihy, he has received 103 U.S. patents, and licensees of their technologies have included Cisco Systems, Direct TV, and Dish Network. The videogame he and colleagues have developed is targeted to educational applications in the fields of macroeconomics, finance and investments and is called "Beat the Fed." He has degrees from Yale University in history and the University of London in economics, and an MBA in finance from the Wharton School. He served as an officer in the U.S. Navy. He and co-author Mary Keil met through Wharton and have worked together on many ventures since then.

Mary Keil worked in commercial banking at Citibank before she and John Harvey co-founded the partnership that became Personalized Media Communications. She co-authored *Enterprise in the Nonprofit Sector* and *Come Rain or Come Shine: Friendships Between Women.* Keil received a Tony nomination for producing the musical *Starmites* and executive-produced with John Harvey the independent feature film *Swing,* which she also wrote. Now living in Humboldt County, CA, she graduated with a B.A. in economics from Connecticut College and received an MBA from the Wharton School.

www.ingramcontent.com/pod-product-compliance
Lightning Source LLC
LaVergne TN
LVHW100250210926
848480LV00003B/884
9798991073486